Praise for Scott W. Berg's

Grand Avenues

"A definitive biography about a significant, but forgotten, figure in American history." —*Tucson Citizen*

"Elegantly written. . . . Vividly reconstructs L'Enfant's life."
—*Bloomberg News*

"Compelling. . . . A well-deserved portrait of an enigmatic historical figure who has long been overlooked."
—*Winston-Salem Journal*

"Berg presents this mixture of biography and urban history with a gusto equal to its subject." —*St. Louis Post-Dispatch*

"Poignant. . . . Particularly useful in linking L'Enfant's personal struggles to the larger political and constitutional issues to which they were related." —*The American Interest*

"The reader never will be able to walk the streets of Washington again without envisioning the haughty genius of Major L'Enfant . . . looking down from Jenkins Hill . . . [and] in his mind's eye, seeing one of the world's great capital cities spread out before him."
—*The Buffalo News*

"A fascinating story of narrative history." —*The Roanoke Times*

SCOTT W. BERG

Grand Avenues

Scott W. Berg holds a B.A. in architecture from the University of Minnesota, an M.A. from Miami University, and an M.F.A. in creative writing from George Mason University, where he now teaches nonfiction writing and literature. He publishes frequently in *The Washington Post* and lives in Reston, Virginia.

www.scottwberg.com

www.grandavenues.com

The Story of Pierre Charles L'Enfant,
the French Visionary Who Designed Washington, D.C.

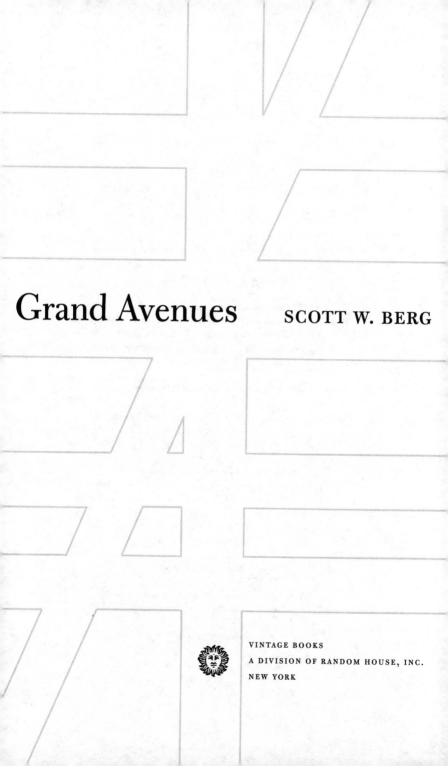

Grand Avenues

SCOTT W. BERG

VINTAGE BOOKS

A DIVISION OF RANDOM HOUSE, INC.

NEW YORK

FIRST VINTAGE BOOKS EDITION, FEBRUARY 2008

Copyright © 2007 by Scott W. Berg

All rights reserved. Published in the United States by Vintage Books, a division of Random House, Inc., New York, and in Canada by Random House of Canada Limited, Toronto. Originally published in hardcover in the United States as *Grand Avenues: The Story of the French Visionary Who Designed Washington, D.C.* by Pantheon Books, a division of Random House, Inc., New York, in 2007.

Vintage and colophon are registered trademarks of Random House, Inc.

The Library of Congress has cataloged the Pantheon edition as follows:
Berg, Scott W.
Grand avenues / Scott W. Berg.
p. cm.
Includes bibliographical references and index.
1. L'Enfant, Pierre Charles, 1754–1825. 2. City Planners—France—Biography.
3. City Planning—Washington (D.C.)—History—18th century. I. Title.
NA9085.L47B47 2006
711'.4092—dc22
[B] 2006021764

Vintage ISBN: 978-1-4000-7622-2

Author photograph © Mark Finkenstaedt
Book design by Soonyoung Kwon

www.vintagebooks.com

Printed in the United States of America
10 9 8 7 6 5 4 3 2 1

for Carter, who got me started,
and Elliot, who helped me finish

I ventured the chance and gave imagination its full scope.

—Peter Charles L'Enfant to Alexander Hamilton,
APRIL 8, 1791

Contents

Contents

A Note on L'Enfant's English

Whether the young Pierre Charles L'Enfant imagined that America would become his adopted land as he sailed the Atlantic from France during the winter of 1777 is unknown. But soon after his arrival in the New World he did anglicize his name to "Peter," and when nearly all of his contemporaries among the French engineer corps returned home, L'Enfant stayed. Later, when offered ten acres of property and the freedom of New York City in return for his services as the architect of Federal Hall, the first home of the new American government under the Constitution, L'Enfant refused the real estate but accepted the honorary citizenship. When his work on the federal city of Washington came to its abrupt end in February 1792 and when, in the early years of the nineteenth century, his professional and financial prospects failed him completely, still L'Enfant stayed.

Despite nearly half a century as an American, L'Enfant never mastered the English language. His surviving letters and other writings, the largest portion of them found in the Digges-L'Enfant-Morgan Papers at the Library of Congress, are serious challenges to accurate transcription. But somehow in nearly every document L'Enfant's meanings and intentions remain clear. His language is full of pride, sensitivity, and determination, which shine through despite his linguistic limitations. The story of Peter Charles L'Enfant is one of genius and failure, of magnificent gestures and miscalculations of all dimensions, and his writings reflect this contradictory nature. When quoting L'Enfant, I have left his prose alone as much as possible, making only small fixes of spelling and mechanics, so that the reader might share in its unvarnished intensity.

Lat. Congreſs Houſe, 38.53. N,
Long. 0. 0.

EASTERN BRANCH.

References

N.I.

Washington, by George Isham Parkyns, 1795

Grand Avenues

CHAPTER 1

A Pedestal Waiting for a Superstructure

WEDNESDAY, MARCH 9, 1791

Major L'Enfant entered Georgetown well after dark, nearing the end of one exhausting journey and anxious to begin another. He arrived on foot, blanketed by a steady rain, his breath visible and his overcoat wet, his boots caked with mud, and his belongings packed onto his horse. The stagecoach that had been L'Enfant's southward conveyance had broken down many miles back, but the architect had not waited for another, eager to get to the banks of the Potomac River and begin what promised to be the culminating work of a lifetime.

The major was alone. He was unmarried, without family in the United States, and if there had been any romantic ties in New York City, where he'd lived for most of the past seven years, they had been cut. His father, once an accomplished painter of battle scenes for the court of Louis XV, had died four years earlier. His mother was at home in Paris leading a widow's life in her apartment at the royal tapestry manufacture, sheltered by the king's soldiers from the strikes, protests, and bread riots proliferating elsewhere in the city. The French Revolution was gaining steam, but L'Enfant was not dwelling on the troubles in his homeland. He had already helped to bring about one revolution in America, and that was where his sights and thoughts remained.

The name and talents of Peter Charles L'Enfant were well known to many of America's most influential citizens, and his Federal Hall in New York was the most famous building in the nation. Now he had embarked upon a task that he knew would eventually require the labor of many thousands of men and the outlay of vast sums of money, a task that would also require that he maintain the approbation of the young nation's most eminent leader. Still the major thought of himself as the man who would single-handedly bring forth an entire city through the force of his own will. For other men it would have been a waking dream, but L'Enfant saw it as his destiny and his due.

He carried a letter dated the first of March from Secretary of State Thomas Jefferson. Jefferson's instructions, approved by the president, gave L'Enfant the task of surveying the area along the Potomac River between Rock Creek, bordering Georgetown, and the mouth of the Eastern Branch, more than three miles to the southeast, in order that some section of that ground might be transformed into the new and permanent seat of government for the United States. The project was not just ambitious, it was unprecedented: the capital of a new world empire was to be set down in a quiet, sparsely inhabited territory of hills, forests, farms, and wetlands.

This city would not take shape through the slow accretion of time. It would not *happen;* it would be *made.* If it were to succeed, L'Enfant believed, it had to be planned by only one man. Though Jefferson's letter did not ask him to create a plan for the capital, L'Enfant had every expectation that his would be the hand holding the pencil, his the mind shaping the streets, squares, and monumental spaces, and his the name most closely associated with its realization. It was a deed in need of a fertile and tireless imagination, and he knew of only two individuals who possessed the necessary breadth of vision and reservoirs of commitment for its accomplishment: himself and the president. He had never failed George Washington in fifteen years of service to the American cause, and he would not do so now.

The spring was shaping up to be dour and difficult, and as L'Enfant moved downslope in the direction of the Potomac, past modest, well-kept structures of wood and brick, the streets were quieter than usual thanks to the chill and rain. The long journey surely would have awakened the old twinges in his leg. He had taken the wound twelve years earlier during the siege of Savannah, when, as a Continental Army captain desperate for distinction, he had rushed forward with a squad of men in a doomed attempt to set fire to a British infantry barrier. A musket volley at close range had ended his brief career in battle, and the resulting injury would eventually, in his old age, require the use of a cane. The wound would also become a badge of honor, an irrefutable soldierly credential he would invoke again and again when he felt his adopted country had turned its back on him.

Accustomed to the patient rhythms of agriculture and dominated by the wealth of a very few intertwined families, Georgetown in 1791 was a prosperous port town finishing the fourth decade of a growth spurt fueled mainly by the proceeds of tobacco exportation. Situated on a sedate stretch of water just below the Potomac's final set of falls, peopled by roughly twenty-five hundred whites and five hundred African slaves, the town was a convivial stopover for travelers taking overland trips along the eastern seaboard. Provincial and unassuming as it could seem, Georgetown was also familiar with the dialects of all fourteen states and the accents of many countries; its leading ladies dressed in European fashions, and its harbor was often host to foreign ships.

L'Enfant passed homes, attorneys' offices, and dry goods emporiums, watchmakers and barbershops and furniture stores, until he reached his destination just a few storefronts from the lapping waters of the Potomac. The Fountain Inn was a simple two-story wooden tavern and hotel with a stable on the premises. The entire operation was better known as Suter's, thanks to the popularity of its proprietor, John Suter, friend and host to politicians, businessmen, ambassadors, and other varieties of wandering gentlemen. L'Enfant was a distinguished arrival, sent to Georgetown by the president himself, but he made little time for conversation. Rather than settle into his rooms for the evening, he asked for directions and went back out into the damp toward the home of Mayor Thomas Beall. According to Jefferson's instructions, that was where L'Enfant was to make arrangements for the assistants and materials necessary for his surveying work.

L'Enfant was thirty-six years old in March 1791 and, aside from any lingering ache in his leg, in good physical health. It is one of the many blunt ironies of the major's life story that no authenticated image of him exists, outside of a single small silhouette made around 1785. Contemporary observers never quite agreed on a physical description, supplying only a vague outline of a man on the tall side with a prominent nose who, at least in the period before his work on the capital, usually presented an elegant appearance and carried himself as a gentleman. But those who crossed professional paths with L'Enfant were unanimous in describing him as a passionate talker, an unquenchable egoist who was monomaniacal about his work and convinced that he was the only person who could do that work so well. He certainly wasn't the kind of man to wonder if others might prefer that he wait until morning to begin.

Mayor Beall might have been taken aback by the late hour, but he had no reason to be anything but affable and offered the major a greeting and an apology, for it turned out that he knew nothing of the architect's needs and had no help at hand. L'Enfant was quickly able to establish his bona fides and receive the necessary assurances, but the mix-up was vexing. How had Jefferson, Washington's second on matters regarding the federal city, failed to prepare the mayor of Georgetown for this moment? L'Enfant knew that the surveyor Andrew Ellicott had also taken a room at Suter's and was already four weeks into the arduous work of setting off the ten-by-ten-mile square, tilted on its point, that was to contain the new seat of government. Had Ellicott's arrival met with a similarly unaccountable lack of advance notice? Workers had to be hired and paid, tools procured; there were myriad moving parts to put in motion.

An artist in possession of the most advanced professional training available in Europe, L'Enfant had left Paris at the age of twenty-two, arriving in America early in 1777 as a temporarily commissioned lieutenant in the Continental Army. Over the next six years he'd risen to the rank of captain and finally to major as he experienced firsthand the physical deprivation, precarious progress, and principled sacrifice of the War for Independence. The list of men he'd befriended and impressed along the way included many of the most famous soldiers and politicians of his time. Still, all that adventure was only a prelude: this inchoate seat of federal government along the Potomac was now of paramount importance, and here the greatest of L'Enfant's ambitions would be fulfilled.

The next day he rose to an unfortunate sight: the rain through which he'd slogged the night before had not lessened in vigor. The survey he was to perform for Washington and Jefferson required visibility, the ability to find high ground and grasp the rise and fall of hundreds and even thousands of acres of land. Given the conditions, he might have been forgiven for staying inside to rest and catch up on some long-overdue correspondence. But he had waited years for this opportunity and was past ready to begin. Without bothering to wait on the supplies and assistants that Mayor Beall was hastily arranging, L'Enfant donned his hat and coat, retrieved his horse, and rode off into the rain.

The largest stone in the political foundation of L'Enfant's journey had been laid eight months earlier, in July 1790, with the passage of the Residence Act. These six paragraphs of federal legislation authorized President Washington to place a district of one hundred square miles somewhere along the Potomac between the Eastern Branch and the Conococheague Creek, eighty miles upriver, for the establishment of a national capital. No state would have jurisdiction in this territory following the transfer of the federal government from Philadelphia, a move set for December 1800. It was a deadline so close—less than ten years away—as to seem fanciful, even laughable, to many Americans.

The establishment of the federal city spoke of the preeminence of George Washington, who had been given control over nearly every aspect of its creation, from the choice of its location to the appointment of surveyors and commissioners. But it spoke just as loudly of angry divisions between North and South, both of which had schemed and argued since the end of the War for Independence to claim the national capital. Not only was the presumed political, economic, and social bounty of the seat of government at stake; so too was something more ineffable: the chance to become the locus of the world's next great empire. Washington's proclamation placing the district just upriver from his home at Mount Vernon, halfway between northernmost Maine and southernmost Georgia, had finally quieted nearly a decade of backroom deal making, congressional oration, and fiery newspaper editorializing over more than thirty potential locations, including undeveloped sites along the Delaware and Susquehanna rivers as well as the existing locales of New York, Baltimore, and Philadelphia. From this point forward, the arguments would circle around what the city should be, not where to put it or whether it should be built at all.

For the residents of the region where the Potomac and the Eastern

Branch met, the choice of ground was not a matter of ideological symbolism or sectional disputes. It was, rather, a matter of sizable personal gain. L'Enfant's arrival was important to the propertied men of Georgetown and other landholders within the limits of the new federal district, who were ready to watch his every move—what he viewed and measured—because these movements would presumably offer their best clues to the president's intentions. It was something of a lottery: once Washington pointed to a surveyor's map of the district and said the capital would rise *here,* the landowners in and around that spot might find their financial dreams come true. As L'Enfant headed out of Georgetown on the morning of March 10, there were eyes on his back and talk behind it.

In a set of notes on the implementation of the Residence Act written for Washington in November 1790, Thomas Jefferson had proposed making a direct appeal to avarice.

> When the President shall have made up his mind as to the spot for the town, would there be any impropriety in his saying to the neighboring landowners, "I will fix the town here if you will join and purchase and give the lands." They may well afford it from the increase of value it will give to their own circumjacent lands.

Washington agreed and wanted any announcements or visible preparations to strongly suggest that the city's exact location was open to negotiation should one group of landholders be willing to offer more advantageous terms than another.

The president and the secretary of state had reasons to prefer either one of two sites: the ground just across Rock Creek from Georgetown or the unrealized "paper town" of Carrollsburg on the prong of land where the Potomac met the Eastern Branch, 160 acres laid out on speculation into 268 building lots but still absent of streets and new structures. The Rock Creek choice meant immediate proximity to a preexisting social and commercial infrastructure, while the other boasted excellent undeveloped terrain and shoreline on two navigable rivers. Though today these spots both rest comfortably within the capital, in 1791 Washington and Jefferson viewed them as entirely separate contenders for the location of the seat of government. They knew that the asking price of lots circling the area they designated for the Congress House and the President's House would climb steeply the moment their decision was made public, and so they were looking to obtain as much land as possible before such an announcement was made.

Washington had begun this quest by supplying William Deakins and Benjamin Stoddert, two of the district's property owners, with survey maps and telling them to acquire as much land as possible in their own names. Provided these were clean buys, free of legal baggage or disputed boundary lines, the lots would be transferred to the federal government and paid for "so as to excite no suspicion that they are on behalf of the public." Even a few hundred acres in hand as L'Enfant began his work would give the government some leverage going into what threatened to become bare-knuckle negotiations. It needed that leverage soon: Deakins, Stoddert, Jefferson, and Washington were all racing against the creation of eminent domain laws in Maryland that would require the payment of more than fifty dollars per acre, a price the president thought well out of the reach of the federal treasury.

These undercover preparations help to explain why L'Enfant was told to begin his work on the Eastern Branch. In theory, his presence along that river with surveyor's tools in tow would create the impression that the president was about to make his choice. Should the ruse succeed, went the logic, those with property near Georgetown—a much larger and more vocal group of men than the wealthy few with an interest in and around Carrollsburg—would sell more quickly and cheaply rather than watch the center of American government, and the profit, head to their neighbors' ground.

In a letter to Deakins and Stoddert written a week before L'Enfant's arrival, Washington had explained that "nothing further is communicated" to the architect beyond the instructions to begin the survey away from Georgetown on the Carrollsburg terrain. The major may well have known that he was being made into a human feint at the very start of things, but he clearly didn't put much energy into the role. As L'Enfant would so often demonstrate, his genius was neither political nor financial. In his own mind, he was not here to pay attention to intramural maneuverings and small-town jealousies. He was here to design a capital to equal the greatest capitals in the world. It would take him only one day of riding and thinking to render all of Washington and Jefferson's manipulations virtually meaningless.

As L'Enfant headed out to tour the landscape, Andrew Ellicott was camped in the field miles to the north of Georgetown with a cobbled-together collection of assistants and workers. For nearly a month he'd been clearing foliage and taking the methodical measurements that would allow him to lay out forty stone markers, one every mile around the diamond of land that would become the federal district. Ellicott was a native Pennsylvanian born the same year as L'Enfant, and like L'Enfant he'd risen to the rank of major during the War for Independence. In peacetime Ellicott had become America's premier surveyor, and in that capacity he'd already finished off the Mason-Dixon Line between Pennsylvania and Maryland, fixed the western and Canadian borders of New York State, and measured the height of Niagara Falls.

Most of Major Ellicott's usual crew, including his younger brothers Benjamin and Joseph, were still finishing the work in New York, so he'd had to hire chain men, axmen, and other menial workers locally to begin the federal district boundary. The one expert assistant he'd been able to bring along at the start was a most unique player in the tale: Benjamin Banneker, a free African American tobacco planter and self-taught astronomer whose primary tasks were to maintain Ellicott's delicate stargazing equipment and to take the daily readings that established the site's cardinal directions relative to the heavens. A Marylander nearly sixty years old, Banneker had provided himself with an impressive education by perusing astronomy and mathematics textbooks supplied by one of Ellicott's cousins, and his particular expertise gave him a schedule like that of no one else involved in the project: on his back most of the night taking meridian measurements, heading for bed after his noon readings, and waking at dusk to repeat the cycle.

L'Enfant understood the importance of the tasks Ellicott had given his team of surveyors. But he also knew that he was no Ellicott: no patient, nose-to-the-wheel engineer. Jefferson's instructions asked that L'Enfant provide "aid" in the form of "drawings of the particular grounds most likely to be approved for the site of the federal town and buildings." "Drawings of the particular grounds," taken one way—Jefferson's way, certainly—might have meant nothing more than a basic topographical survey. But Jefferson was not the person L'Enfant was aiming to please. He'd gone into battle at George Washington's command, had joined in an elite fraternal order of Continental Army officers with him, and had already designed a building as a setting for his greatest honor. L'Enfant knew the president as a man with a preternatural eye for talent, a man who did not discourage all-encompassing expressions of vision, and it was through Washington that he would grasp

the title of planner of the federal city. Jefferson expected routine progress reports twice a week and an orderly process, one task leading neatly to the next, while L'Enfant's strongest desire was to wrap his mind around the entire project immediately, to picture the future city rising from the tidewater landscape in one torrent of inspiration.

L'Enfant would later report that in order "to obtain a knowledge of the whole I put from the Eastern Branch towards Georgetown up the heights and down along side of the bank of the main river and along side of Goose

11

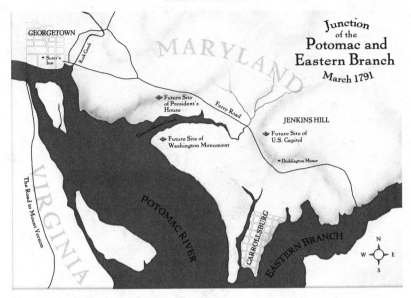

Junction
of the
Potomac and
Eastern Branch
March 1791

GEORGETOWN
Suter's Inn
Rock Creek

MARYLAND

Future Site of President's House
Ferry Road

JENKINS HILL

Future Site of Washington Monument
Tiber or Goose Creek

Future Site of U.S. Capitol

Duddington Manor

VIRGINIA
The Road to Mount Vernon

POTOMAC RIVER

CARROLLSBURG

EASTERN BRANCH

N
W · E
S

and Rock creeks as far up as their springs." This convoluted description reveals little about the sequence of his ride but leaves no doubt that he set out to cover every inch of ground he could in one day's tireless exploration. Every so often he might have huddled against the rain to hastily record his impressions in a small field notebook, but the opportunity to sketch or survey at length would have to be reserved for another, clearer day. He concentrated instead on observing and remembering.

The territory that would eventually form L'Enfant's canvas was made of six thousand acres at the center of the new federal district. Wedged in the elbow of two rivers, the undulating landscape offered considerable variety: fields of tobacco and corn, small forests of maple and black cherry and tulip poplar, waterside bluffs and patches of tidal marsh, all of it spotted with great Georgian homes made of brick and the smaller wooden structures of tenant farmers and slaves. Capping this area to the north was a five-mile-wide arc of higher, more broken ground, out of which flowed dozens of small springs that joined and widened into creeks before spilling into their larger cousins, the Potomac and the Eastern Branch, en route to the Chesapeake Bay a hundred miles to the southeast.

These waterways shaped and dominated the geography. Rock Creek wound southward out of a series of stream valleys lined with tall grasses and cattails and thick with white oak and sassafras trees, while Goose Creek, also known as the Tiber, bisected the site and formed a wide, shallow inlet where it met the Potomac. The unassuming Tiber was the feature most important to L'Enfant's work; nearly every major topographical element he would eventually exploit in his plan related directly to this shallow and languid tributary. The triangle of lower, more level ground to the south would become a frame for one of the world's most famous public green spaces, the National Mall, while the series of gently ascending bluffs and terraces to the north would provide a hilltop home for the individual occupying the country's most powerful office. But nothing would turn out to be more important to L'Enfant's thinking and the city's future than the spot one and a half miles east of the Potomac where the Tiber narrowed to become a series of springs falling from a wide, prominent rise in the land.

This rise was the eminence L'Enfant would soon christen Jenkins Hill— after a nearby farmer who did not, in fact, own most of the land—and that would eventually be known as Capitol Hill. Moving as far as he could up its thickly wooded slopes, L'Enfant began to get his first sense of the entire space between Rock Creek, more than two miles to his northwest, and the Eastern Branch, still a mile to the south. The rounded crest of Jenkins Hill ran gently down to the Eastern Branch, while at its westernmost edge, where the Tiber began to widen on the way to the Potomac, the change in elevation was more dramatic. Jenkins Hill was something simple and obvious, "a pedestal waiting for a superstructure," as the major would soon write to Washington. It was the essential discovery of the day: a high and central place to provide a visual anchor and hub for the city, a place from which the wide, commodious streets and avenues already beginning to emerge in his mind could run from the center of the city to the banks of its two sustaining and sheltering rivers.

L'Enfant had come to Georgetown from New York City by way of Philadelphia. A small city by European standards but cosmopolitan to American sensibilities, Philadelphia had been wedged between the Delaware and Schuylkill rivers during the seventeenth century in what would become the new nation's standard rectilinear grid. With the decision made to place the capital in an undeveloped location, L'Enfant determined to avoid yet another procession of indistinguishable street corners. The former Parisian had seen his native city opening new and dramatic corridors during his childhood and knew firsthand the value of monumental views in juxta-position with intimate spaces, of streets running straight to create vistas or subtly shifting to corral one's line of sight, of experiencing both awe and small delights in the same casual walk across town.

The best overland route between the site's two enclosing rivers was the ferry road running along the ridge of Jenkins Hill and down to the Eastern Branch, where L'Enfant had been told by Washington and Jefferson to spend a conspicuous portion of his time. The far shorter, less lauded Eastern Branch was actually much better suited to waterborne traffic than the shallower and constantly silting Potomac, something the fishermen and ferry operators working its banks and the Anacostan Indians before them knew well. The huts and landings L'Enfant found spread along the edge of the water would soon help to set him on the path to even broader thinking. Here, in infant form, was the city's umbilical connection to the rest of the world. America was a kinetic country, one dominated by hoof and wheel and keel, and its capital would respect this fact. It would have thoroughfares for carriages and wide greenswards for walking, yes, but waterways as well. L'Enfant would create a city to which all roads, rivers, and oceans would lead.

As he rode across the land, the major entertained two views of the terri-tory: the rain-veiled one in front of his eyes, and another in his imagination. The architect's eye lingered on each building just long enough to perform the mental trick of erasing it from the landscape. L'Enfant would use every possible square inch to give the president a city worthy of its founder. The city itself would be the American Paris, but better than Paris—a Paris reborn as a republican Rome, a seat of wisdom and power on display for the rest of the world.

Whatever the city became, L'Enfant would say to Washington, it must not become another Philadelphia. It must not be so simple and uninspiring.

Newly incorporated as the town's only newspaper, the *George-Town Weekly Ledger* was an unrelenting booster for the region's future as a federal city, and not a single one of its readers was immune to the prestige or financial possibilities present in the coming transformation. L'Enfant's arrival was announced with obsequious regard, even if the information seems to have been suspiciously secondhand.

Wednesday evening arrived in this town Major Longfont, a French gentleman employed by the President of the United States to survey the lands contiguous to Georgetown, where the Federal City is to be put. His skill in matters of this kind is justly extolled by all disposed to give merit its proper tribute of praise. He is earnest in the business and hopes to be able to lay a plan of that parcel of land before the President on his arrival in this town.

George Washington was in Philadelphia, finishing business left over from the recently adjourned First Federal Congress, a session dominated by Alexander Hamilton's proposal for a central bank of the United States, the imposition of an equally controversial liquor tax, and continuing military skirmishes with Indians in the upper Ohio River valley. The closing gavel had sounded on the third of March, and the president was taking a breather to gather his wits and his belongings for the trip to Georgetown and then Mount Vernon. He'd also planned an extensive tour of the southern states, to begin shortly after his return. Washington had never ridden south of Virginia in peacetime or in war, and this would be his chance to cement some sectional goodwill while sounding out reactions to the Constitution.

All that Washington had communicated, through Jefferson, was that he expected to pass through Georgetown by the end of the month. L'Enfant had three weeks to prepare for the president's arrival, three weeks to conceive a city so magnificent and thorough in its design that Washington could not help but bestow his unrestrained approval. This was the job in front of L'Enfant, and he began his work aware that time was absurdly short for stakes so extraordinarily high.

CHAPTER 2

An Infinity of Small Moments

Paris, the city of Pierre Charles L'Enfant's birth, was in 1754 a gray and over-crowded place, a hive of more than half a million people suspended between two ruinous wars. New inhabitants poured in from the provinces, thousands each year, stuffing themselves into the nooks and niches of a medieval city plan that strained to take them in. Thick with noise and covered with soot and grime, much of Paris also stank. Its crowned and cobbled streets were lined with gutters carrying all manner of refuse: rotting garbage, human and animal waste, great pasty mounds of soaking ashes, spoiled food, industrial residue, dead vermin. It was an urban setting as densely populated, as formidable, as any in the world.

Neither the Rive Droite, the portion of Paris north of the Seine, nor the Rive Gauche, to the south, featured an east-west thoroughfare. Two carriages rarely met in the twisting *rues* without risking a collision, while pedestrians were in constant danger of losing limb or life. Any route through the city might end abruptly in a bottleneck of streets far too narrow to accommodate wave after wave of walkers, wooden carts, and horse-drawn carriages. The effect for most denizens of the city was hardly romantic: they found the physical reality of Paris disquieting in its randomness and oppressive in its complexity.

The daily burden of confronting this labyrinth belonged to everyone who could not claim nobility and to many who could. The closer one moved to the literal and symbolic center of Paris—the Île de la Cité with its famous mismatched churches, the immense Nôtre-Dame and the diminutive Sainte-Chapelle—the closer and taller the apartments grew, to five and six stories, while builders and landlords let their imaginations wander as high as seven and eight rentable floors. The well-off lived luxuriously on the lower levels, while two or three flights up, the standard of living was strictly petit bourgeois, leaving the poor haphazardly stuffed into subdivided attic stories. Indoors, these divisions were conscientiously maintained. Out on the streets, while commoners may still have doffed their hats to their social betters, *egalité* was the practical rule.

Ringing this bulging urban belly in a thick belt were the large suburbs known as "faubourgs," a word signifying something akin to "places beyond the city gates." The crumbling ruins of two ancient rings of fortifications, one north of the Seine and one south, served to informally divide the official municipality and citizenship of Paris from these attached communities. Along the southeastern rim of the city was one of the most notorious faubourgs, the Saint-Marcel, a district of roughly five hundred acres and tens of thousands of residents sliced in two by the mud-choked Bièvre River canal snaking malodorously northward toward the Seine.

The Saint-Marcel had a hundred years earlier taken in the poor who had been displaced by the construction to the northwest of Marie de Médicis's Luxembourg Palace and its spacious gardens. Wedged against the suburb's eastern side was the faubourg Saint-Victor, dominated by the austere hulk of the Salpêtrière, one of a trio of state hospitals built in the seventeenth century by Louis XIV for the "correction" of vagabonds. The Salpêtrière was home to thousands of indigent women of all ages, including beggars, waifs, and especially prostitutes. Not a few of the institution's wards came from the turbulent Saint-Marcel next door, where the city's horse market, its army barracks, and a chain of factories helped to provide an ample supply of clients.

The air of unwholesomeness in the streets of L'Enfant's childhood was given a physical cast by the smoke and pungent smells issuing from the industrial plants lining the Bièvre River canal. Thousands of workers streamed each day into a long line of tanneries, taweries, breweries, glue works, and laundries. At the heart of the Saint-Marcel, larger and more imposing than any of the neighboring establishments, was the venerable tapestry workshop called the Gobelins Manufacture, a collection of buildings that had been constructed piecemeal over the past two centuries and named after the famed fifteenth-century Flemish painter Jehan Gobelin, one of the first to make camp by the waters of the Bièvre for the purpose of creating art.

By 1754 the Gobelins had grown into a mélange of tightly spaced courtyards, workshops, classrooms, and apartments built in support of three separate studios, in which lived and worked a large and insular community of painters, weavers, administrators, teachers, doctors, clergymen, and laborers. Bordered on the north and east by poverty and tumult, the workers of the Gobelins were also neighbors to a strangely rural repose. Weavers peering out of the westward-facing windows along the curve of the Bièvre saw a patchwork of small hunting chalets and private gardens belonging to churchmen and manufacturing barons; to the south, the clustered streets and buildings of Paris ended as the land rose suddenly to grain fields, vineyards, and mushroom farms dotting the horizon with patiently turning windmills.

At the Gobelins the tapestries destined for the châteaus of the nobility and the halls of court and king were made. Weavers laboriously and meticulously duplicated *cartons,* fully realized oil or watercolor paintings made by artists in the royal employ. Months or even years were devoted to producing a woven panorama, each the product of an enterprise established during the previous century by the ministers of the Roi Soleil and now devoted to the royal apparatus of Louis XV, his great-grandson. A master weaver, completing a few inches each day, might devote much of a lifetime's work to the decoration of a single residence or suite of rooms. Most of the inhabitants of the Gobelins held no illusions about their place in the social order. They understood that as artists and workers they were essentially servants, but they also understood that theirs was the most powerful set of masters in the world.

Pierre Charles L'Enfant was born at the Gobelins on August 2, 1754, into a world blanketed by the long shadow of the Bourbon kings. He was the third

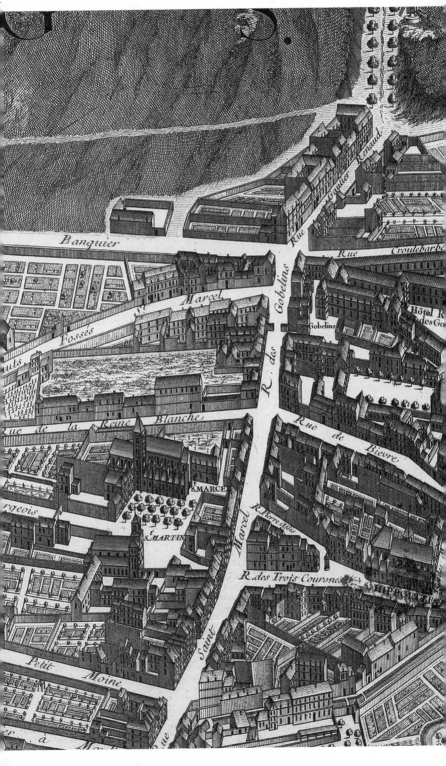

Detail from the
Plan of Paris,
by Louis Bretez,
created under
the direction of
Michel-Etienne Turgot,
1735–39

child and second son of Marie Charlotte L'Enfant, twenty-five years old, and Pierre L'Enfant, a painter in the service of the king who was exactly twice the age of his wife. Marie was the daughter of a minor marine official at court, while Pierre was an artist of good reputation whose attachment to the Gobelins had been preceded by a Noël L'Enfant and a Guillaume L'Enfant. Though we have no proof of a blood tie, these namesakes were likely relations, as residence at the Gobelins was often a family affair and nearly as often an inheritance.

The Gobelins housed royal artists who worked all over the city, without employing them directly, and while Pierre L'Enfant may have painted the occasional *carton,* his place in this larger community of officially sanctioned artists had been consecrated nearly a decade before, in 1745, with his admission as an *académicien* at the Royal Academy of Painting and Sculpture, the most select, rigid, and prestigious school of art in the Western world. His elevation to the position, a type of junior faculty post, had coincided with his time on the siege plains of the Austrian Netherlands as a battlefront artist during the War of Austrian Succession, one of France's most complicated and least memorable military conflicts. The elder L'Enfant's lasting artistic legacy was a series of panoramas in watercolor tracing the course of conflict across the Low Countries between 1744 and 1748, from Dunkirk on the English Channel to Tournai four hundred miles to the southeast. Pierre L'Enfant spent more than three years traveling with the French and Saxon forces in the employ of the war minister Count Marc-Pierre d'Argenson, his days spent studying and sketching cities and landscapes that he then filled with *grenadiers, mousquetaires, généraux,* and on at least three occasions King Louis XV himself.

The work of drawing siege scenes required special attention to the formal arrangement of cities and the particulars of fortifications, as well as the ability to organize and animate views that spread across many square miles and usually included a long stripe of horizon. The genre had been brought to its apex a century earlier by the Flemish master Antony Francis van der Meulen, during Louis XIV's own forays onto the field of battle, and was eventually passed to the elder L'Enfant through his mentor and fellow Gobelins resident Charles Parrocel. Such an artist had to take his tools many hundreds of miles from Paris to sketch in pencil and watercolor scenes that were often handed over to others to set in oils or weave into great hangings.

Pierre L'Enfant's art was designed to make heroes of contemporary soldiers and their king, regardless of the place of such art in the increasingly neoclassical French vanguard. Indeed, the vanguard was not impressed. Denis Diderot, the hugely influential philosopher and cultural critic, used a critique of Pierre L'Enfant's contributions to the Salon of 1761—a pair of unheralded drawings depicting the battles of Laffeld and Fontenoy—to deliver a backhanded au revoir to the entire genre.

> It is, after all, necessary to be a master colorist, a master draftsman, a master of the art of landscape, and a skillful and delicate imitator of nature; to have a prodigious variety of imaginative resources; to recreate an infinity of small moments, to excel in the details, to possess all the qualities of a great painter and at that in the highest degree, in order to offset the coldness, the monotony and the ugliness of so many long parallel lines of soldiers, of the square or oblong arrangement of battalions and the symmetry of their tactics. The time of melees, of maneuvering and military might, of the giant battle-scene, is past.

Diderot was also the guiding force behind the *Encyclopédie*, the effort to pour all the empirical knowledge of the world into one literary catch basin that would become the most famous icon of the French Enlightenment. This cultural and philosophical awakening was in full swing by the middle of the eighteenth century. Centuries-old conceptions of God and nature were evolving in leaps and bounds as a mania spread for more tangible and utilitarian ways of understanding the world. Amateur science—botany, astronomy, metallurgy, geology, electrical physics—was all the rage. Medicine based in academic rather than theological training began to lose its stigma. And it was no longer blasphemous—in certain quarters, at least—to suggest that one's relationship to God might be mediated by individual conscience and not through the ministrations of clergy. Heaven and hell, according to the new philosophies, might well be spiritual metaphors as much as extraterrestrial addresses. At the far end of this path lurked the most exciting and heretical notion of all, that kings might owe their eminence not to an ancient and God-granted charter but to the reasoned acquiescence of the people themselves.

Such a conclusion would require another thirty years to fully emerge. In 1754 the most visible civic upheaval in Paris involved the city's Parlement—

a powerful secular council, nothing like the British institution of the same name—which was in a state of royal suspension thanks in part to its insistence that last rites be administered not only to those possessing certificates of loyalty to the Church of Rome but to all who professed themselves believers. For the family of Pierre L'Enfant, in service to His Most Christian Majesty, eligibility for last rites was probably not in doubt. The day after his birth, Pierre Charles was baptized around the corner at Saint-Hippolyte, whose apse topped the surrounding streetscape.

In the Gobelins, Pierre Charles L'Enfant's childhood unfolded as a series of paradoxes. His was a Third Estate life lived in modest apartments but devoted to the production of the most luxurious works of art for some of the wealthiest men, and the most sumptuous rooms, in the world. It was a life of relative anonymity, lived to generate and sustain the immortal fame of king and country. It was a life young Pierre Charles would eventually leave behind, but not until he had taken from it the experiences and training necessary for his later work as a planner of cities. Growing up at the Gobelins, he also developed a thirst for individual recognition from highly placed patrons that would fuel all the triumphs and bitter disappointments of his career.

Whatever worldly destinations Pierre L'Enfant might have imagined for his second son, they are not likely to have included the American continent. Those with military connections, such as the elder L'Enfant, had heard of a line of French forts set amid a great wilderness extending southward from Canada to Louisiana and standing as a tenuous block to the prospect of a westward English expansion. Some might also have been aware of the *voyageurs,* the intrepid French fur traders who had already spent at least six decades living and working deep inside the continent among Jean-Jacques Rousseau's "noble savages." And news might also have circulated in the streets of the Saint-Marcel of the prostitutes and incorrigibles shipped from the Salpêtrière and other overcrowded hospitals to mysterious outposts such as Biloxi and New Orleans. But no one in Paris, king or commoner, soldier or painter, yet suspected how soon or how dramatically the situation in America would bully its way to the front of everyone's attention.

The trouble began in May 1754, three months before the birth of Pierre Charles L'Enfant. In a small, wooded hollow in southwestern Pennsylvania, a young and inexperienced colonel named George Washington ordered a detachment of 140 green Virginia colonials to return the fire of a small platoon of French soldiers. That, at least, was the tale according to Washington; in the competing version, he had opened fire on the traveling party of a French ambassador. The scene, however interpreted, descended into chaos, after which ten of the Frenchmen lay dead, scalped by Washington's Indian allies. The ranking Frenchman, Joseph Coulon, Sieur de Jumonville, wounded and attempting to offer an explanation of his presence in the wilderness, was tomahawked into oblivion before he could finish. The bloody skirmish became known as the Jumonville Affair. No one thought to christen it a battle, much less imagine it as part of a nascent global war, but without question the situation had shifted and the tension increased.

This news of French casualties at the hands of British soldiers in America would not finish its eastward voyage across the Atlantic until September. In the meantime, Louis XV was still le Bien-Aimé, the Well-Beloved. The Bastille still stood fat and glum at the eastern edge of Paris; the accused heretics, seditious writers, and delinquent nobles who were imprisoned there consumed wine and cheese in rooms that many members of the lower orders would have envied. To most residents of the city, life was messy and sometimes contentious, noisome and pungent and congested with souls, but it was also suffused with rhythm, routine, and deference—hardly an obvious breeding ground for revolution. The will of the king was still officially indistinguishable from the will of the nation and the labor of its people, and if Parisians were learning to separate the man sitting in the seat of power from the seat of power itself—a giant step in every way—they were content to question His Most Christian Majesty's uses of power but not his basic right to hold it.

Pierre Joseph L'Enfant, the family's firstborn son, died in 1758 at the age of six of an unrecorded ailment, leaving four-year-old Pierre Charles to deal with the confusion of an older brother's sudden absence and a new role as the oldest male child. It was an important year for the L'Enfants in another, equally momentous way. One year earlier Pierre L'Enfant's military patron, War Minister d'Argenson, had been dismissed from the service of the king, and now the elder L'Enfant was transferred to assist with the decoration of the Hôtel de la Guerre, the offices of the French War Ministry newly under construction in the town of Versailles, just a few blocks away from the legendary royal residence of the same name.

Louis XIV had removed his court from Paris in 1682 with great pomp, after making the château and gardens of Versailles supreme above all other places. More than fifty million livres and two hundred lives were expended on construction during its first two decades, with the aim of physically consolidating the magnificence of the French court under the eye and thumb of the Roi Soleil. By the late 1750s, under the reign of Louis XV, the town and château had matured into a small city complete with ornate social protocols, intricate administrative hierarchies, and a reputation unmatched in European history for wealth and opulence. Versailles was a royal stage on which the magisterial actors of the French court played their parts: whenever and however young Pierre Charles first viewed the expanse of André Le Nôtre's formal gardens and the grandeur of Louis Le Vau's facades, he would have been acutely aware that he was present only as a member of the audience.

Class divisions aside, Versailles was a lesson in the uses of space that no architect or planner could possibly ignore or, for that matter, fully assimilate. Just a few miles outside of an urban fabric made of impossibly tight spaces and layer upon layer of accumulated history was a city's worth of ground devoted to one man's limitless westward view. How Versailles first imprinted itself on the eyes and mind of the future designer of Washington, D.C., can never be known. It's enough to imagine Pierre Charles walking with his father through one of the château's massive entrance archways and onto its great western plaza. Here he would have seen for the first time in his life a true *man-made* vista, a place where the eye could run all the way to the horizon without interruption, a world seemingly without end.

No doubt it seemed a fantasy of sheer power and cosmic size. It might even have seemed heavenly, the sudden introduction of so much space to his impressionable eyes. But the sight of Versailles might also have been unaccountably disconcerting: the sudden removal of comfortable limits to the world, the will of one man claiming and remaking the landscape for his own public glorification and private satisfaction.

The medieval face of Paris coexisted with a beauty and stateliness that had been superimposed by several generations of French kings in their efforts to create fitting settings for the exercise of royal prerogative and civic pride. Beginning with Henri IV's accession to the throne in 1594, the Bourbons had been nothing if not enthusiastic urban planners. Much of this energy and wealth was devoted to opening up spaces in the cramped streets of medieval Paris to let in air and light, a grandeur all the greater because it lay in such stark relief to the old tangled intersections and grime-covered building fronts everywhere.

For two centuries, a smattering of sophisticated and graceful urban squares had been appearing in Paris. By the 1750s each zone of the northern half of the city seemed to have its own: the triangular Place Dauphine at the western tip of the Île de la Cité; the circular Place des Victoires just north of the Louvre; the eight-sided Place Vendôme farther to the west; the Place de Grève fronting the Hôtel de Ville along the Seine; and in the far eastern end of the city, the Place Royale, which Victor Hugo, the city's great literary memorialist, would one day call home. Parisians used these major public spaces to identify their neighborhoods, and each became home to its own regular schedule of pageants, festivals, and celebrations.

Only one of the city's squares was under construction during Pierre Charles's childhood, but it was soon to become the largest and most public of them all. An hour's walk from the Gobelins lay the emerging Place Louis XV—today the Place de la Concorde—a monumental square connecting the Louvre and Tuileries Gardens to the Champs-Élysées and designed as a palace forecourt to commemorate the same wartime exploits of Louis XV that his father had recorded in watercolor a decade earlier. Between 1755 and 1762 the Place Louis XV took shape, an open octagon, five hundred feet on each side, built to frame an equestrian statue of the king; its southern side was open to the Seine, and its northern border was dominated by a pair of massive and symmetrical facades designed by Ange-Jacques Gabriel and named the Garde-Meubles after the royal furniture repository housed there. Modeled on Claude Perrault's even more gargantuan eastern front of the Louvre, the Garde-Meubles were the apex of neoclassical architecture in the city and an important inspiration for Thomas Jefferson, who would years later make his residence nearby and subsequently propose Gabriel's work to L'Enfant as a template for the most significant pair of buildings in the United States.

Given the particular set of talents Pierre Charles L'Enfant would display as an architect and a planner, he was clearly paying attention during his boyhood years, and the lessons he absorbed were primarily visual and spatial ones. It was most likely at the Gobelins, in classes for the children of its workers, that he first learned to draw; in any event, in September 1771, at the age of sixty-seven, Pierre L'Enfant signed his son's *billet de protection,* the letter of initiation from a faculty member admitting a student to the Royal Academy of Painting and Sculpture.

With this matriculation under his father's tutelage, Pierre Charles L'Enfant was immersed in a highly codified and advanced system of artistic education. The program had been drawn up a century earlier by Charles Le Brun, *premier peintre du roi* to Louis XIV, and modeled with great fidelity on the ancient academies of Rome and Florence. The goal was simple and unyielding: to train students in a single heroic style sanctioned by king and court. The world of the Royal Academy was one of absolute authority and hierarchy, prizing public art that proclaimed noble and elevated ideals over every other form of expression.

An ironclad timetable ruled each day and also the year-by-year progress of each student. The curriculum began with copied drawings and progressed to plaster casts and eventually to life drawing from nude models. When students weren't drawing, they were attending lectures on architecture, arithmetic, astronomy, history, perspective, geometry, optics, and anatomy. Twice each week students attended their *discours,* at which an academy instructor would demonstrate the virtues of a particular work from the royal collections according to the categories of invention, proportion, color, expression, and composition.

Most of a student's hands-on work, his repetitions and experimentations, happened in the private studio of his master, a mentor with whom he lived and learned. The attachment of Pierre Charles L'Enfant to his father meant long hours in close study with an expert in the creation of panoramas of battle. It was an education that included, to various degrees, the study of city design, fortification engineering, and natural landscape, as well as an appreciation of the power of the horizon line to render the human figure more or less noble in proportion. To these topics would have been added informal lessons in politics, military history, the tactics of siege craft, and, not least, the potential for professional honor or disgrace inherent in the act of depicting the royal person.

Entry to the Royal Academy also brought the younger L'Enfant to his new schoolhouse, the Louvre. In the eighteenth century the old medieval palace of kings and conquerors was more a brooding relic than a place of bright splendor. Ever since the departure of Louis XIV for Versailles, the Louvre had, in fact, become a kind of ruin. A large portion of the complex lacked roofs. The surrounding precincts were overgrown and pressed ever more tightly against its outer walls, while a shantytown sheltering squatters occupied the center of the Cour Carrée, the courtyard at the Louvre's far eastern end.

But within these aging walls, the scientific and artistic academies of France still met in fertile exchange, an array of splendid but indifferently organized resources at their call. Stuffed beasts from exotic lands and preserved human organs shared gallery space with an enormous collection of scale models of French towns, while down interminable hallways students could hear distant whinnies from the building's ducal stables. On the ground floor were the simply appointed, high-ceilinged rooms for artists and masters. No academy student paid much attention to the symbolism of learning his craft in the world's greatest museum of art because the Louvre had as yet no intimation of that future. These students and professors were simply propping their easels in rooms that no one else was using, though the fact that they were practicing their crafts in a crumbling shell of majestic origin had a certain undeniable cachet.

Enrolling at the Royal Academy drew Pierre Charles L'Enfant into the heart of Paris as never before. As he exited his lectures at the Louvre, he would have had the opportunity to view the Tuileries Gardens, a masterpiece of public space designed by André Le Nôtre, the same man responsible for the gardens at Versailles. Just beyond the Tuileries lay the Place Louis XV, now complete, which neatly organized the nearby streets while seamlessly attaching itself to the fabric of medieval Paris. During his years as an academy student, L'Enfant watched the Champs-Élysées punch its way westward from this royal square, ruler straight and 160 feet broad—a figure that L'Enfant would later duplicate down to the foot in the grandest of his avenues in America's capital. The Champs-Élysées was a first in the Western world: a public road disappearing over the horizon and leading to an unknown, seemingly infinite place. It was a piece of the private, absolutist pleasure of Versailles brought within reach of every French subject. It was the glorious city of kings and nobles made theirs.

As Pierre Charles L'Enfant absorbed the aesthetic lessons taught by his father, by the other professors at the Royal Academy, by life in the city, and by visits to Versailles, Parisians of every station heard more and more about America. George Washington's Jumonville Affair had turned out to be the earliest spark of the transcontinental conflagration called the Seven Years'

War, a conflict that ended in 1763—just as the equestrian statue of the king was going up to finish the Place Louis XV—with the disgrace of France in the face of a superior British navy and the loss of its possessions in Canada, the Mississippi Territory, and India.

The war's cost to France in prestige and in livres created a flood of national resentment, which in turn created the perfect setting for an appreciation of the efforts of the American colonists to resist George III's increasingly repressive measures. One potential harbinger of war after another—the opposition to the Stamp Act in 1765, the Boston Massacre in 1770, the Boston Tea Party in 1773—was reported breathlessly in the ever more numerous and influential Parisian papers. When Louis XV died in May 1774, largely detested thanks to his military mismanagement and the accusation that his court had manipulated the price of grain—damning in a city that so depended on bread—the nation treated the crowning of the aimless young Louis XVI as the arrival of a savior. His reign was to be a washing away of the old and a consecration of the new. And nothing in the imagination of Old Europe was newer than the New World.

One year later, in June 1775, reports raced through much of Paris of shots fired and British soldiers repulsed at Lexington and Concord, with loss of life on both sides. With the blood of American militia staining the ground, the French imagination was fully lit. Here was a battle with a name and with its own martyrs, and now the very language of the discussion changed. *La guerre!* cried Parisians, who also bestowed a new title on the colonists: *les insurgés,* the insurgents. *Liberté,* formerly the ethereal jewel of Enlightenment philosophy, became an object of concrete aspiration, the very real crux of an improbable political experiment across the ocean. Talk about America became barely disguised talk about the home country. Romantic images of the citizen-soldier, the militiaman, and the yeoman farmer dropping his plow and raising his rifle to resist British imperialism stood out with special clarity.

Pierre Charles L'Enfant, meanwhile, was now twenty-one and rapidly approaching the day when he would have to choose a path in life. His studies at the Royal Academy had gone about as far as they could. Other, more decorated students, including young Jacques-Louis David, had gone off to study in Italy as winners of the Prix de Rome that all but ensured that a student would become an academy professor on his return. Just at the moment when Pierre Charles must have fully understood that he was not destined for a similar measure of artistic renown, and that the literal and figurative prizes of the academy would not be his, news spread that certain people in Paris were recruiting soldiers to join in the cause of American independence. All a man had to do was put himself forward and establish his usefulness, and he might suddenly have a chance for honor, adventure, and—not least of all— career advancement in a hierarchy that seemed from afar a whole lot less crowded near the top than the one at home.

It was an opportunity for *gloire,* that ineffable ideal that still meant more to many a young Frenchman of good connections and patriotic ego than money, property, or position. Born out of Louis XIV's commitment to French military superiority and his desire to been seen as a great war hero— "In my heart I prefer fame above all else, even life itself," he'd written in his memoirs—the love of glory had since passed straight into the cultural consciousness to the point that it was epidemic. No young Frenchman during the mid-eighteenth century would have had a moment's trouble recognizing it: stronger than family, friendship, or sexual desire, *gloire* was the grail of a wholehearted quest for personal and national distinction, ideally realized through an achievement on the battlefield that would leave one's name written permanently into the books of history.

Neither Pierre Charles nor his father was a noble or a military officer, but the L'Enfants were closely acquainted with both, and in July 1776 they took advantage of those connections. At the beginning of the month, as Thomas Jefferson was in Philadelphia delivering the final draft of the Declaration of Independence to the Continental Congress and as the people of Paris were encountering the first translation of Thomas Paine's incendiary *Common Sense,* a Connecticut businessman named Silas Deane arrived at the offices of the War Ministry for the express purpose of encouraging a transatlantic alliance between France and the newly united American colonies. Deane found the ally he needed in the person of Pierre-Augustin Caron de Beaumarchais, the larger-than-life and fantastically wealthy playwright fresh off a string of trans-Channel theatrical successes, most recently *The Barber of Seville.* Camped out in his town house on the rue de Condé, a stone's throw from the western wing of the Luxembourg Palace, Beaumarchais broadcast an open secret: he was ready and willing to spend his name and his fortune on the cause of American freedom.

In late August the translated text of the Declaration of Independence finally reached Paris and electrified the political discourse in the city. The document galvanized the thinking class in a country that had never known a written charter. On the eleventh of the following month Deane and Beaumarchais met to draw up their first list of French volunteers in the service of the American cause. By a request from George Washington as conveyed through the Continental Congress, one of their first priorities had been the recruitment of sorely needed artillerists and engineers. They had snared one of the best in Philippe Charles Tronson Du Coudray, a difficult but brilliant French lieutenant colonel who asked for and received the untenable promise of a major general's commission in the American army. Deane and Beaumarchais met that day in the rue de Condé to finalize an agreement creating Du Coudray's train of officers. When they were finished, near the bottom of the list was Pierre Charles L'Enfant, temporarily commissioned as a volunteer lieutenant.

L'Enfant now became a soldier, an unexpected and dramatic turn in the course of his life no matter what his rank or assignment. He'd been placed under Du Coudray's command as an "engineer," a designation that might have made some sense given his father's experience with the portrayal of cities and fortifications, but many of his fellow recruits were the sons of nobility trained at L'École Royale du Génie de Mézières, the elite school charged with producing the officers of the engineers corps. Du Coudray would soon make it clear that he didn't appreciate L'Enfant's talents or his presence, which he attributed to an irregular favor from Beaumarchais.

It seems that Du Coudray was correct in his way, that L'Enfant was indeed something of an odd man out, an extra who had gained his position by means of some informal family connection to the playwright. His father's work, unlike that of most Royal Academy professors, often put him in the town of Versailles and the halls of the War Ministry, where it wouldn't have taken him long to learn of Deane's offer. Pierre Charles wouldn't have been the first to receive such a helping hand; Beaumarchais took steps to get other young people with no military training, including his own nephew, on board his ships. L'Enfant's age was listed as twenty-seven instead of twenty-two, an alteration that if not a typographical error does suggest that someone may have tried to make him appear more experienced than he was.

And there is something else to consider: in October 1776, just weeks before his son was to leave to fight in the American War for Independence, seventy-two-year-old Pierre L'Enfant finally retired from public work and began receiving his royal pension. So Pierre Charles, who previously had walked directly in his father's steps, appeared to be renouncing the life of the artist at the very moment the baton was ready for him. Or, in an alternate reading, he had completed his apprenticeship and was simply emulating his father, ready to paint great military deeds that seemed much more likely to unfold in America than at home.

There's no way of knowing which version to prefer, as no statement of L'Enfant's reasons for leaving France has come to light. In any case, he made his way north along the Seine to the raucous port town of Le Havre, where a four-hundred-ton, twenty-six-gun frigate named the *Amphitrite* was waiting to take him and the rest of Du Coudray's men across the ocean. On December 14, 1776, after a series of maddening delays, the *Amphitrite* finally glided into the English Channel, laden with three dozen military officers and a store of supplies that included twelve thousand pounds of gunpowder, a quarter-million gun flints, six thousand rifles, five hundred rock picks, three hundred hatchets, and twenty thousand cannonballs.

Many of those leaving on the *Amphitrite* would soon return to France with nothing good to say about the Americans and little regard for the cause of American independence. No matter: other French sailors and soldiers would soon head for war in the colonies, and some of these men would make an enormous difference. But no one from France would leave an American legacy more sizable than Pierre Charles L'Enfant's. By all outward appearances the runt of this litter, L'Enfant would eventually seize the chance to leave his permanent imprint on one of the most important patches of earth in the United States.

CHAPTER 3

A Powerful Friend Among the Princes of the Earth

By the end of April 1778 the Continental Army encampment at Valley Forge had become a very different place from the harsh and undersupplied purgatory of the deep winter months. The weather that spring was changeable, capricious: one morning would break calm and charming, the next chill and swept by rain, a third dark and heavy with fog. For months the possession of an entire uniform and a working rifle had marked an enlisted man either as a new arrival or as extraordinarily lucky. Now the camp was overflowing with firearms, shoes, coats, and food: grains, fruits, eggs, and more cattle than the army needed. All the men had known in abundance since their removal from Philadelphia in November was hardship and want. Now they had *goods*. And if the flow of supplies made their days and nights more tolerable, the future had brightened further thanks to a rumor from across the ocean: if the talk could be believed, King Louis XVI had finally resolved to join the War for Independence on the side of the American colonies.

Valley Forge was already full of Frenchmen—overfull, said some: generals, artillerists, aides-de-camp, translators, and, among the contingent of engineers, one young man of particular artistic skill whose name everyone seemed to interpret as "Longfont." The highest-ranking French officer, Major General Lafayette, was only twenty years old, but he was wealthier than any other man in the camp or in the country, including General George Washington. For more than a year now these foreigners had woven themselves into the fabric of the army, but they were present only as advisers, secret volunteers, and de facto mercenaries, while the Continental Congress waited on an open declaration of alliance from the king of France.

"France": the word was evocative of large fighting ships, mammoth armament factories, and a long and storied history of involvement in other countries' wars. It meant a lasting, virulent hatred of Great Britain and royal coffers sufficient to exercise that hatred. Those coffers loomed large in the American imagination, set in relief against the threadbare Continental Congress seated in York, Pennsylvania, after abandoning Philadelphia to the British. The French were anything but cautious and parsimonious. They were extravagant in their attachments and their enmities, a people who fought wars as professionals in the service of an all-powerful king who was, in the imagination of the American troops, wise just so far as he vigorously opposed his counterpart across the English Channel.

Morale at Valley Forge had survived the worst of the winter, and now after months of mud and snow it was finally possible to chase away some of the maddening uncertainty. Rum and other spirits were rationed more liberally to the enlisted men, while the wives of the generals held a number of small soirees for the officer corps. Twenty-three-year-old Caty Greene, wife of General Nathanael Greene and niece of the governor of Rhode Island, used what French language and literature she'd absorbed from her tutors and her cultured aunt to create a sort of bare-bones salon for the younger Frenchmen, who sang and danced and gratefully gossiped in their native tongue, happy to spend time in the presence of a vivacious hostess so close to them in age.

Away from the gatherings of Caty Greene, the younger French officers engaged in their own less-genteel distractions. The host of one such party was Frederick William Augustus Henry Ferdinand, better known as Baron von Steuben, a forty-seven-year-old Prussian of great girth and energy whose appreciation of himself was even larger. The baron had brought with him to America a résumé full of exaggerations and outright lies—not least his noble title and his claim that he'd personally served Frederick the Great, the legendary warrior-king of Prussia, as a lieutenant general—but he also brought a deep well of genuine military talent. Steuben had come to Valley Forge for the singular purpose of bringing the entire army under one system of formation and maneuver. Only a few weeks into the job he was already succeeding beyond General Washington's most optimistic expectations. The baron was an ebullient and generous figure in private, while in the performance of his public duties he tried halfheartedly to project a stern and curmudgeonly air, swearing and muttering in German and French as he stalked the parade grounds, until finally he would throw up his hands and instruct Benjamin Walker, his translator and assistant, to turn his curses into English for the benefit of the American soldiers. The troops loved him for taking their training so personally, roaring at the Prussian's antics as they learned to watch their steps and bearing.

Young men of intelligence and talent were drawn to the baron, who liked to maintain a small and rowdy court of his own away from the sober quarters of Washington, Henry Knox, and the other American generals. In addition to several wagonloads of trunks, two homes' worth of furniture, and Azor, his Swiss greyhound, Steuben had brought along to the camp at Valley Forge three precocious French assistants newly made captains: Stephen Duponceau, Louis de Pontière, and, his most recent addition, Peter Charles L'Enfant. Steuben and his aides were a kind of movable feast, leaving behind empty cupboards and impromptu promissory notes wherever they traveled, and though Steuben tended to hold forth at any gathering, he was more than willing to give his aides a turn at center stage.

This night belonged to them. It was a party for young officers with a single cheeky and entirely ironic rule: anyone wearing an intact set of breeches would not be admitted. Duponceau, who would also remain in America and eventually become president of the American Philosophical Society and a trailblazing linguist, later reported that the baron's contribution to the festivities was to name the assembled guests his "sansculottes." "Thus this determination was first invented in America," wrote Duponceau, "and applied to the brave officers and soldiers of our revolutionary army." The fellow feeling was strong. The group was fervent, whip smart, and destined for fame.

Almost everything good and satisfying in L'Enfant's life, as well as some of his deepest and most enduring heartbreaks, was to grow out of his association with the men he first met at Valley Forge.

Here, telling ribald jokes in the fluent French he had absorbed during his West Indian childhood, was ruddy-cheeked Alexander Hamilton, the ambitious and supremely self-possessed aide to Washington who would one day become his first secretary of the treasury and the untiring helmsman of the American systems of finance and manufacturing. Hamilton's life would intertwine with that of L'Enfant, who was five months older, for many years and in many vital ways. They had much in common: both were immigrants—to their adversaries, "foreigners"—who became fierce patriots; both had impetuous temperaments, astonishing capacities for work, and great difficulties admitting themselves in the wrong; both were incapable of continuing any project unless they were permitted to think on an all-encompassing scale; and both had a way of ignoring their detractors, to their eventual detriment. Their association would begin to wither near the end of the century, but in the meantime Hamilton came to believe in L'Enfant's talents so completely that he would hire or recommend him for nearly every one of his most auspicious jobs.

Close by Hamilton was South Carolinian John Laurens, General Washington's personal secretary. Laurens's father, Henry, was president of the Continental Congress and one of the few members of that body to comprehend Washington's unconventional military talents and uncommon adaptability from the beginning of the war. The younger Laurens's bonds with Hamilton were romantic, though probably platonic, in their intensity. Both viewed themselves as military heroes in waiting, and both were biding their time for a chance at leadership on the battlefield. When Laurens got his opportunity two years later, during the revolution's southern campaign, he would become the first and only officer in the Continental Army to offer L'Enfant a field command.

The cohort also included the twenty-four-year-old Walker, Steuben's interpreter and future aide-de-camp to Washington, and John Marshall, twenty-two, who would eventually become secretary of state, chief justice of the Supreme Court, and Washington's first biographer. Younger still than all of these men was a determined and uncomplicated Virginian of twenty named James Monroe, whom no one in camp would have envisioned as a future president. Lieutenant Monroe would never forget about L'Enfant, and four decades later, as secretary of both state and war under James Madison, he would act as L'Enfant's benefactor when L'Enfant seemed to have run out of patrons entirely.

As the expectation of intercontinental alliance increased, so too did the regard among these Continental soldiers for the young French officers in their midst. In addition to Duponceau and de Pontière, L'Enfant's acquaintances included Beaumarchais's nephew, Augustin François Des Epiniers, and Jean Baptiste Ternant, an inspector recently attached to Steuben whose path would intersect L'Enfant's a half-dozen times before and after Ternant became French minister to the United States. The most visible French soldier, of course, was Lafayette, Washington's personal confidant. Surely no one believed more fervently in *liberté,* and the marquis's romantic image of himself, along with his astonishing wealth and his effusive love of the American cause, made him a celebrity at Valley Forge second only to General Washington. To watch Lafayette ride into battle shouting ecstatic slogans of encouragement or to listen to him fill a casual camp conversation with patriotic exhortations made it possible for homesick American soldiers to believe that the War for Independence was about an ideal the world might embrace and not only about sitting and waiting or retreating while popular sentiment wavered and supplies ran low.

No register of guests was kept on this night of the sansculottes, but it was intended to be a high-spirited gathering, and probably most or all of these figures were present. By May 1778 these young men, French and American, had come to think of themselves as charter members of the New World's military aristocracy. What defined them as such was not any great success in battle but each man's unshakable loyalty to George Washington and the cause he personified. Duponceau authored a typical tribute: "I could not keep my eyes from that imposing countenance; grave, yet not severe; affable, without familiarity. Its predominant expression was calm dignity, through which you could trace the strong feelings of the patriot, and discern the father, as well as the commander of his soldiers."

This is the image of Washington that L'Enfant and nearly all of the other officers at Valley Forge carried with them, with remarkably little deviation, for the rest of their lives. They had seen the general close at hand and found no separation between the archetype and the man.

L'Enfant owed his presence at Valley Forge to an accident so absurd as to suggest the hand of providence. The first summer of his American adventure had been spent as the juniormost member of a team inspecting and evaluating fortifications on the banks and small islands of the Delaware River, punctuated with frequent breaks so that the pompous and irritable Du Coudray could travel to face Congress and complain about his failure to receive the generalship Deane had promised. That he hadn't been made Washington's second in command was not Du Coudray's only complaint. He also had plenty to say, little of it good, about the abilities of the American soldiers and even about some of his own. He especially didn't care for L'Enfant, whom he called a "creature of B"—meaning an unwanted addition to his entourage by Beaumarchais—"good for drawing figures" and "embellishing plans with cartouches" but otherwise unskilled as an engineer.

This opinion might have caused L'Enfant more trouble had Du Coudray not drowned in the Schuylkill River on a rainy day in September 1777, when his horse took fright during a routine ferry crossing and plunged itself into the current. Du Coudray's passing was difficult to mourn. The death of a man who had been promised a place above all of Washington's American-born generals solved a large set of problems, including a few for L'Enfant, whose surviving correspondence never again mentioned his first commander. His death, however, also meant that L'Enfant and his fellow officers had been cut adrift. Along with the rest of Du Coudray's train, L'Enfant went first to Philadelphia, seeking back pay, then to Boston, on the Continental Congress's list of officers slated to return to France.

Once he was in Massachusetts, L'Enfant's fortunes took a critical turn. Instead of boarding the frigate *Boston* to join his fellow volunteers for the voyage home—on the ship bearing John Adams, who'd been named commissioner to France, replacing Silas Deane—he found his way into the employ of the portly, charismatic baron. However the assignment occurred—on this point the documentary record is silent—his attachment to Steuben completed a convivial scene that Duponceau described as "an old German baron, with a large brilliant star on his breast, three French aides-de-camp, and a large, spoiled Italian dog." There was little time to enjoy the easy company, though. Washington needed discipline and regularity in his army above all else, and so the baron and his entourage—his aides, including L'Enfant, assured the rank of captain—had traded in their scarlet coats for the blue ones of the Continental Army and headed for Valley Forge on February 19, 1778.

Valley Forge was no wilderness outpost. It was, rather, an expanse of carefully chosen farmland made into a fortified garrison, a rough triangle of twenty-two hundred acres protected on the north by the Schuylkill River, on the west by the Valley Creek and the high, craggy land beyond, and on the south, facing Philadelphia, by a ridgeline made into a firing platform for a four-mile-long line of artillery. The number of men occupying the site never dropped below ten thousand, making Valley Forge much less a "camp" than a city—the third largest in America at its most populated—with brigade posts for neighborhoods and a municipal hall in the form of Washington's headquarters. The sky L'Enfant first beheld as he rode with Steuben across the Schuylkill was full of smoke from the burning of green spring wood, while the ground beneath his feet was a morass of brown snow and frozen mud. The place was full of sound and motion, soldiers on patrol and picket duty, digging out redoubts or adding to the hundreds of log huts that would eventually become the camp's most recognizable emblem.

Captain L'Enfant, it seems, soon gained a reputation as a willing and skillful artist, endearing himself to Caty Greene and his fellow officers with his small pencil portraits. As the baron began training the Continental troops to hoist their rifles smartly, to close ranks with dispatch and wheel in unison, he kept L'Enfant and his talents near at hand. It may have been an important reason Steuben was happy to attach L'Enfant to his staff in the first place: organizing an army would mean creating a field manual, for which he would need a competent illustrator. L'Enfant's training at one of the world's most prestigious academies of art would have made him a particularly attractive candidate for the job.

Official news of the French alliance came ashore on the night of April 13, 1778, at the quays of Falmouth, Maine, in the person of Simeon Deane, older brother to Silas. Simeon set off at once on a four-hundred-mile gallop straight to York, Pennsylvania, and the Continental Congress without rest, exuberantly spreading news of the pact along the way.

An official bulletin from the Congress reached George Washington on May 4. The rumor his men had cultivated for weeks now had turned out to be true. This was news: real, war-changing news. On the morning of the fifth, Washington rode to the front of the assembled army as his general orders for the day were read out by one of his aides. It must have been a pleasure such as Washington rarely felt. He had asked his soldiers to endure a bitter and deadly winter for the revolutionary cause; most had responded with faith and perseverance, and now they could finally be rewarded.

The next day began with the assembly of all brigades and the reading of prayers, followed by a "grand review" on the central parade ground: a set of drills choreographed by Steuben and his assistants and involving the entire army. L'Enfant was attached to Baron Johann de Kalb, a German general, with orders to direct troops into position and mend any breaks in formation. The celebration's centerpiece was the firing of thirteen cannons high on Mount Joy and the execution of a *feu de joie,* a complicated cascade of running rifle fire by several different brigades, punctuated with three hearty cries of "Huzza!": one for the king of France, one for the "friendly European powers" (those that now would presumably fall neatly into line behind France), and one for the American states.

The event was as much a celebration of Steuben's successful efforts to curse the soldiers into proper order as it was an appreciation of the French alliance, and it neatly coincided with the ceremony elevating the baron to the rank of inspector general. The day ended gleefully, with the army gathering under and around a large pavilion prepared for the occasion. Even Washington, who usually avoided fraternizing with his officers, joined in.

It was a stirring tableau, the general raising a glass to each brigade as it marched past the reviewing platform, but it wasn't the crowning moment of L'Enfant's time under Washington's command. His most meaningful service was a portrait of the general he'd created as a favor for the Marquis de Lafayette. The work of art hasn't survived, its existence revealed only in a casual aside in a long and friendly letter that Washington sent to Lafayette in September of the same year.

"When you requested me to set for Monsr. Lanfang," he wrote, "I thought it was only to obtain the outlines and few shades of my features, to have some prints struck from." In Bourbon France only sanctioned court portraitists could perform such a service for the king, but here in America things were much more democratic. Here a soldier newly arrived in Washington's army—only a captain at that—could be granted a sitting with the most illustrious person on the continent based simply on his reputation as an artist of some talent. L'Enfant's father had painted Louis XV into his panoramas of the siege fields of the Austrian Netherlands, but the image was taken either at a distance or from other works of art, and it's unlikely that he ever exchanged a single word with the king. And even if the elder L'Enfant had somehow been granted such an audience, it would have been required of him that he participate in an elaborately choreographed minuet of deference.

The story of Peter Charles L'Enfant is, on one level, that of a search for a form of royal patronage in a place and time when the idea of royalty was being cut free of its moorings. Only one man, in L'Enfant's mind, bound together the two threads of that paradox. When, in November 1778, he left the Continental Army camp for Philadelphia to begin his work as the illustrator of Baron von Steuben's drill manual, his connection to George Washington was hardly at an end.

The Continental Congress paid L'Enfant a bonus of five hundred dollars for his contribution of eight illustrations to Steuben's *Regulations, Orders, and Discipline for the Army of the United States.* The "Blue Book," as it was better known, quickly standardized military drilling not only among Washington's own forces but up and down the seaboard as state militias adopted it for their own training. Ease of use was the highest priority. After perusing a draft in February 1779, Washington wrote Steuben to commend "the conciseness of the work founded on your general principle of rejecting every-

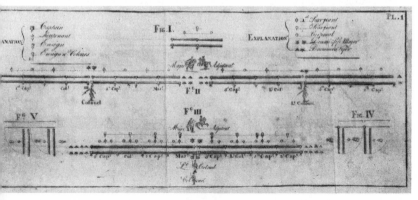

L'Enfant's first plate for *Regulations, Orders, and Discipline for the Army of the United States,* 1779

thing superfluous." And indeed the pocket-sized manual, 25 chapters in fewer than 170 pages, was squarely aimed at a mostly amateur army that had previously operated under several separate and incompatible systems of formation and maneuver.

L'Enfant's drawings, sparse and uncomplicated diagrams with the single goal of training men to deploy rapidly into battle lines and deliver maximum firepower, folded out to four times the book's width. Creating them was a laborious process, as each of his sketches had to be approved by Steuben more than once before the finished drawings were delivered to the engraver. Only on a few of the plates was L'Enfant allowed any artistic leeway—placing a set of officers on their rearing horses or sketching houses and a copse of trees into a diagram—but this was enough to show his considerable ease with a pencil.

What might seem like the logical moment of embarkation for the rest of L'Enfant's career as an artist, however, was merely an interlude between seasons of soldiering. As the baron went north to rejoin General Washington at White Plains, New York, Captain L'Enfant went south, into the new and ever bloodier maw of the war. It was a revealing decision. Surely Steuben or one of the other Continental generals would have found a place for L'Enfant on his staff; only a keen hunger for distinction in battle would have pulled him so far and so quickly in the opposite direction. Twenty-nine days of "marching," as L'Enfant called it, took him through Maryland, Virginia, and North Carolina, traversing wide swaths of political no-man's-land along the way. After abandoning Philadelphia, the British had decided to take the fight to the southernmost colonies, where, they rightly presumed, the white population was thick with Tories and large numbers of slaves—who were approaching half of the population in South Carolina—were willing to join their side in battle. The redcoats, it seemed, had chosen well. Savannah and Augusta had fallen without prolonged struggles, and now L'Enfant and the British forces were heading toward Charleston from opposite directions.

Much of importance for the major and for the war would happen in South Carolina, but not right away. L'Enfant arrived at Charleston in mid-May, just in time to watch the British raise their siege and march away for Savannah in order to consolidate forces for a heavier hammer blow. There now ensued a "period of inertia," as L'Enfant bitterly described it, an interlude he filled by frantically trying to exchange his rank of captain and his affiliation with the corps of engineers for an infantry majority. Nothing he'd ever done made him an obvious candidate to lead men into battle, but L'Enfant's hopes were not illusory, founded as they were on an offer made to him by John Laurens, one of his old Valley Forge companions.

Home again in Charleston and promoted to lieutenant colonel, Laurens was almost single-handedly championing a plan to enlist slaves on the American side in exchange for their freedom at the war's end. He was chasing rainbows; he and his father, Henry, still president of the Continental Congress, were about the only white South Carolinians of influence who seemed able to stomach the idea of black men holding guns. But Laurens had promised L'Enfant the rank of major at the head of one of these slave regiments, and so L'Enfant waited. All the while he sent regular updates northward to Steuben, bemoaning his lack of advancement, the poor leadership of the American generals, the disloyalty of the local citizenry, his ill health—just about everything.

> All I can tell you is that if I did a foolish thing in America it was to come to this province, where I stay rather by lack of means than by lack of will to go away. It is indeed the worst place on the continent since the war has begun, and the one in which Toryism is the most domineering; business is bad and people discontented.

L'Enfant finally got his wish for action six months later, when the French fleet suddenly appeared off the coast of Georgia near Savannah, intent on engaging the British forces. The French armada was known to start things without waiting for its Continental allies, and so American general Benjamin Lincoln, in charge of the troops at Charleston, mustered his men with all haste and left on September 8 for the march south. The plan was not complex: Lincoln's forces would join with the French ships to bring Savannah back into the revolutionary fold; the check on the British would be keenly felt, closing off their southern adventure before it could really begin and putting their American hegemony on the path to oblivion.

But if Savannah held such splendid promise, it delivered something else entirely. It was L'Enfant's misfortune that his one and only gallant moment in battle was associated with an action that did little except prove the fragility of the French and American alliance. The French fleet, twenty-two ships of the line and four thousand soldiers, was under the command of Count Jean Baptiste Charles d'Estaing, whose position was complicated by the fact that he was also the steward of French interests in the turbulent West Indies. The threat of British invasion there meant that he was able to engage in only limited operations on the American continent. He had arrived at Savannah with almost no advance notice and had promptly claimed the city in the name of Louis XVI. L'Enfant and the rest of Lincoln's troops arrived one day later, on October 1, and combined forces with the French auxiliaries to place the city under siege.

For eight days the French and American forces dug out trenches in slowly advancing parallels, only to have d'Estaing—one eye on his dwindling supplies and the other on the difficult autumn weather over the Atlantic—abruptly decide on October 8 that his return to the West Indies was overdue. Rather than retreat for another effort in the spring, he and Lincoln planned an all-out assault for the next day. It was not a formula for victory, as any advantage gained in a week of siege preparations was lost. Now the superior defensive position of the British would tell the tale.

In anticipation of the attack, L'Enfant volunteered to take a small squad of men forward in an attempt to set fire to the barriers of sharpened logs that were the last line of fortification before the ramparts themselves. Abatis, as they were called, were usually positioned on the face of a hill to make anyone attempting to breach them an easier target. It is unclear when L'Enfant made his dash forward—it may have occurred as a preliminary action or later in the battle, when clearing the abatis by other methods had failed. But whenever the effort was launched, it quickly came to no good. The wood of the barriers was too wet to light, leaving L'Enfant and his men mercilessly exposed. The shot he took in the leg did enough damage that he was reported dead by at least one observer, while another noted that he was the last man out of the depression where he had fallen.

"It is without partiality to say that never were greater proof of true valor exhibited than at the assault at Savannah," L'Enfant would later tell Washington, an accurate statement insofar as one's definition of "valor" included hopeless rushes against firmly entrenched positions. The delirious scene was best exemplified by John Laurens, who advanced far enough to stand on the ramparts and brandish his sword, accomplishing nothing other than to open himself to British rifle fire. Laurens somehow avoided death, but more than three hundred French and American soldiers did not. Such whooping, careless charges were not George Washington's preferred mode of operation, and had he been present and making the decisions instead of

Lincoln, the soldiers probably would not have been allowed to storm the British defenses. An unequivocal failure, the operation in many ways served to negate the triumph at Saratoga two years earlier and to recast the French alliance not as a panacea for American weaknesses but as a messy conjunction of inharmonious agendas.

The wounded were removed to military hospitals back in Charleston, where L'Enfant underwent a slow and painful recovery as that city watched the rested and rejuvenated British army approach northward from Savannah along the coastal islands. For several months his leg necessitated the use of a crutch for walking, but by January 1780 he had healed enough to join with the makeshift corps of engineers in fortifying the city, especially after the arrival of General Louis Duportail, who had taken control of the French engineers after the drowning of Du Coudray more than two years earlier. In Duportail L'Enfant found an appreciative and solicitous superior. "I attached myself wherever I could render the best service," L'Enfant wrote, and indeed there was work to do constructing and shoring up batteries and redoubts along the northern side of the city, where the British soldiers were sure to approach along the city's wide isthmus.

With the French fleet away, holding off the British siege of Charleston turned out to be as impossible as mounting a successful one at Savannah. As the redcoats finally emerged on the morning of March 30, 1780, L'Enfant took part in a brief flurry of activity, riding out to participate in yet another unnecessary charge and helping Laurens's disorganized pack of enlisted men to fall back behind the fortifications. The denouement was inevitable: the forces at Charleston were grossly outnumbered, undersupplied, and vulnerable, and the garrison surrendered in mid-May with only minimal resistance, making every one of the soldiers in the city, L'Enfant included, a prisoner of war.

Along with almost all of the other American combatants, L'Enfant was quickly paroled, bound by honor and under threat of execution to take no part in action or plotting against the British. His orders confined him to Christ Church Parish, a plantation district along the ocean just north of Charleston, and here L'Enfant's activities fade from view during a time he would later refer to simply and bitterly as "my hard captivity." Only in July 1781, fourteen months after his capture, was he finally granted his general parole, gaining the freedom to move wherever he liked under the condition that he would not "intentionally go within twelve miles of any military garrisons." Soon thereafter he headed for Philadelphia, where he waited to be included in an official exchange of officers that would release him from his parole restrictions and return him to active duty. While higher-ranking men such as Duportail and Laurens had been traded for British officers of equal rank and returned to fighting, the idling Captain L'Enfant could only read newspaper reports of General Nathanael Greene's brilliant southern campaign during the summer of 1781 and, in October, of the victory at Yorktown, the overdue fulfillment of the alliance first celebrated at Valley Forge.

On January 2, 1782, finally, L'Enfant was exchanged for a Hessian officer of no particular note, leaving him free to return to active duty after nearly two years of recuperation and parole. The tardy release was bittersweet, providing L'Enfant with an initiative he could no longer seize now that the war was winding down, with every expectation of a peace favorable to France and America. He had traversed many of the major sites of war, served in Washington's army, and was known to Washington himself. He'd been comrade to a constellation of personalities destined for international renown. But his involvement in actual fighting was now concluded and with only minor roles in two unfortunate campaigns.

Whatever military dreams L'Enfant had carried across the Atlantic would have to remain dreams. But seldom has the failure of one career been so advantageous for a second. Though there was no longer any demand for his services as a soldier, he found plenty for his talents with a pencil and his powers of imagination.

The first inkling of his future vocation came in the form of a note from the Chevalier Anne-César de la Luzerne, the first French minister to America, asking L'Enfant to create an extraordinary setting for an elaborate party.

The victory at Yorktown and a veneer of formal collegiality failed to fully obscure the growing resentment between the French and the Americans. Fault lines in the relationship included U.S. fears of French designs on western lands and a powerful, lingering prejudice against Catholicism, especially in its foreign forms. Many of the first newspaper reports and books written about Yorktown and the southern campaign barely mentioned French involvement, creating a myth of American self-reliance at the expense of the honor of many hundreds of French dead. And now tens of thousands of British loyalists were about to return to the fold, willing to make peace with their relatives and neighbors but never with their ancient European foes.

But some in power would do anything they could to reaffirm the health of the French-American alliance, as the first peace settlements recognizing American autonomy were being negotiated. This influential group—which included George Washington and most of his Continental Army officers—needed something on which to pin a public affirmation of unity. They found that something in May 1782, when Luzerne announced to the Confederation Congress the long-awaited birth of the dauphin, a son and heir to Louis XVI, earlier in the year. Washington himself signed the letter releasing L'Enfant from his dormant military obligations so that he could spend two months designing and erecting a setting worthy of an international fete.

It was an honor and a responsibility as national in scale as the illustrations for Steuben's Blue Book, and L'Enfant obliged in high style, turning the garden at Luzerne's rented Chestnut Street residence in Philadelphia into a lamp-lit arbor and building two temporary pavilions to create separate spaces for dancing and eating. These colonnaded additions were lauded in more than one local newspaper for their classical elegance and grace, while inside L'Enfant indulged himself as an illustrator according to the French minister's no-holds-barred instructions. One guest described a tableau high on one wall depicting "a rising sun surmounted by 13 stars (and the arms of America) with an Indian watching the sunrise and apparently dazzled by its rays—beside the Indian in the same picture was a woman, representing England, emptying a sack of gold into the hands of another Indian, who throws the gold at her feet with obvious contempt."

On the night of July 15, 1782, the air clear and warm, Pennsylvania militiamen kept order on the streets and helped to sort those with invitations from those without, while a crowd of thousands mingled outside L'Enfant's halls, pointing out famous men and women as they dismounted from their carriages for a party that lasted well into the morning. It was a politically inclusive and decidedly class-conscious event given in French style, with French guards in the garden, a French orchestra in the dancing pavilion, and thirty French chefs. Washington, Lafayette, and much of the Continental leadership attended, joining with prominent Whigs and former Tories to drink expensive spirits and consume ice cream and fruitcakes as they celebrated the rising fortunes of two countries that would never be on better terms.

Luzerne submitted a bill to the French War Ministry for more than five thousand dollars to defray the celebration's cost. Whatever monies, if any,

L'Enfant received out of this sum were negligible compared to the good the work did for his prospects of advancement. At the least the fete was another badly needed lever to bolster his claim that he was entitled to a promotion. The naked scramble for rank was a fact of life for every officer, and with the war fast coming to a close, L'Enfant's urgency was palpable. The majority that Laurens had hoped to extend, contingent on the formation of black regiments, had never materialized, and now Laurens was dead, having waltzed needlessly into a British ambush in August 1782, nearly a full year after the recapture of Yorktown.

"The affair at Savannah was I thought a glorious opportunity of distinguishing myself," L'Enfant wrote. His disappointment at the outcome "complete," he made his next appeal directly to George Washington, fixing on the elevation of a "much younger Captain of Engineers" named Bichet de Rochefontaine—actually only one year younger than L'Enfant—who had been promoted to major immediately after Yorktown. He held no animosity for Rochefontaine, but the corps of French engineers in America numbered fewer than twenty men in a clear hierarchy, and the promotion of any one was carefully scrutinized by the others. "I flatter myself Your Excellency will not oppose my promotion to a majority," L'Enfant wrote, adding that "what ever may be your sentiments on this subject, I shall pay the most implicit obedience to them."

During the course of his career, Washington had received an avalanche of letters like this one, and he had developed a simple, foolproof formula for his replies: acknowledge the rightness of the case and politely regret his inability to comply, with hopes that justice might be achieved through other, more appropriate channels. This was exactly what he did in his reply to L'Enfant, telling him that "your zeal and active services are such as reflect the highest honor on yourself and are extremely pleasing to me and I have no doubt they will have their due weight with Congress." It might have been a form letter of sorts, but it was no brush-off: Washington later expressed his satisfaction with L'Enfant to the Confederation Congress, and this nod, combined with support from Steuben and Duportail and the success of the fete for the dauphin, eventually did the trick. In May 1783 a congressional committee that included Alexander Hamilton finally provided him with the appellation—Major L'Enfant—to which he would cling tenaciously for the rest of his life.

As the official order to disband the Continental Army approached, its officers faced a set of profound and disorienting changes. Over eight long years of bloodshed and trial they had come to see themselves as a battle-tempered elite, a meritocracy intrinsically superior to the state and Continental politicians who, in their minds, deserved little credit for the war's outcome. Those closest to Washington, following their general's lead, were ready and willing to graciously step off the stage, but they wanted some way to hang on to the bonds they'd formed, a way to commemorate their glory and sacrifice. The idea for the Society of the Cincinnati had been conceived by Henry Knox early in the war but had since lain quiescent. Now Knox and Steuben hashed out the parameters of a hereditary order restricted to officers of the Continental Army who had served at least three years honorably or, in the case of wartime fatalities, the firstborn sons of same. Its aims were on the surface largely fraternal, but underneath lay a decidedly nationalist political philosophy.

For L'Enfant, a foreigner whose legitimacy in America came courtesy of the Continental Army, membership in the Cincinnati promised an official sense of belonging that he wouldn't otherwise possess in peacetime. He embraced the society, and it embraced him. Steuben, having already employed L'Enfant so successfully as an illustrator, sought him out again to design a badge, a medal, and certificates of membership. Working out of Philadelphia at his usual rapid clip, L'Enfant was able to produce the designs and have them sent to Steuben's temporary house at Fishkill-on-the-Hudson before the society's first formal meeting in June 1783. His sketch of the badge, a plainly ornamented golden eagle, was approved on the nineteenth, along with his drawings for the medal of Cincinnatus accepting and relinquishing his sword, and a suitably heroic border for the certificate, or "diploma," showing the same Cincinnatus cowing a bare-breasted Britannia as her warships meekly retreated.

If the creation of the Cincinnati buttressed the pride and camaraderie of the Continental officers, the idea of an exclusive hereditary order made up of the leaders of the American army horrified others, especially those who had not worn uniforms during the war. This opposition was wide and powerful, led by men no less adamant and influential than Thomas Jefferson, John Adams, and Benjamin Franklin, all of whom believed they were watching

L'Enfant's original sketch for the
Society of the Cincinnati eagle, 1783

the hoary hand of European-style aristocracy menace the very core of revolutionary
ideals. Jefferson told Washington that "I
have found but one who is not opposed to
the institution and that with an anguish of
mind, though covered over with a guarded
silence," and in the same letter he famously
described the Cincinnati as "against the
confederation—against the letter of some of
our constitutions—against the spirit of them
all." The less-strident Franklin, approaching his eighties, sarcastically suggested that
the hereditary requirement function backward in time rather than forward, bringing
every officer's ancestors posthumously into
the fold.

Washington took such suspicion and
ridicule seriously. He'd already been named
the first president general of the society, and
as such would necessarily bear the brunt of

any political opposition. He quickly proposed a compromise that would
scuttle the order's hereditary component, leaving the Cincinnati to die along
with its last surviving charter member. The entire proposition was very
much in doubt by September 1783, when L'Enfant insisted in a letter to
Henry Knox that he voyage to France in order to deliver letters of invitation
to Lafayette and other French officers as, in his words, the "charge des
affaires" for the society. L'Enfant argued that the badges should be cast in
solid gold rather than gilded, and only by craftsmen in Paris able to achieve
"perfection." Knox, Steuben, and Washington took to the idea immediately,
less out of respect for superior French handiwork than because of their
interest in firming up the amity between the leadership of the two nations in
the continually shifting sands of postwar international politics.

L'Enfant sailed from New York during the first week of November, carrying bank drafts from the financier Robert Morris and written greetings
from Washington to the Marquis de Lafayette and other French military
heroes of the War for Independence. In early December, as L'Enfant was setting foot on his native shores and greeting his family for the first time in

L'Enfant's design for the Society of the Cincinnati certificate of membership, 1783

seven years, Washington undertook a series of private and public goodbyes. They began on December 4 with an emotional farewell to Steuben and a handful of other Continental officers at Fraunces Tavern in New York and culminated two days before Christmas, when he stood before the assembled members of the Confederation Congress in Annapolis and tendered his resignation as commander in chief. The general bowed as Thomas Jefferson and the nineteen other congressmen raised their hats, following which he left his public employ behind in his usual quiet, stoic tone. "Having now finished the work assigned me, I retire from the great theater of action," he said. "I here offer my commission, and take my leave of all the employments of public life." He'd set aside his plow to lead the Americans to victory, and now he was voluntarily picking it up again.

As Washington, now fifty-one, rode back to Mount Vernon for what he hoped would be a long and uninterrupted sojourn as a gentleman farmer, L'Enfant continued his rounds in Paris to promote the society to all of the major French figures from the war, including Lafayette, d'Estaing, and General Rochambeau, the hero of Yorktown. He didn't stop there, visiting every officer he could find who'd served in Washington's Continental Army as well as all of the French provincials who had been part of the actions in the southern theater, assuring each man of a place in the Cincinnati. Rochambeau and Lafayette, in turn, courted the favor of Louis XVI, and a successful king's council in mid-December allowed L'Enfant to write to Washington on Christmas Day with welcome news: "The permission which this powerful monarch, the Most Christian King, has already given to his subjects to wear in his dominion the Order of the Society of Cincinnati, is not only a strong mark of his deference, but also an unmistakable proof of the sentiments of His Majesty towards America."

On January 16, 1784, unaware that back in America he and his fellow officers had finally received their official discharge from the Continental Army, L'Enfant spent a heady day as an honored guest in the homes of the most celebrated military men in France. His first visit was to d'Estaing and the naval officers to formally welcome them into the society as charter members, following which he wound his way to Lafayette's hotel in the rue de Bourbon for the first official meeting of the Cincinnati's contingent of French Continentals. Sixteen soldiers who had served under Washington, along with the son of the late Baron de Kalb, gathered there before marching en masse to the rue du Cherche-Midi and the residence of Rochambeau, where the officers of the French auxiliary army waited for their ceremonial induction. There, under the eye of the upper echelons of the French military, L'Enfant unveiled the first set of completed eagles, after which he and the other veterans of war in America were treated to an "elegant entertainment" signifying the pleasure of the king.

L'Enfant sailed in April and was back in New York in time to appear at the society's next meeting in early May. According to some, L'Enfant's last-minute arrival—bearing a package of gold eagles and the official confirmation of Louis XVI's personal endorsement—saved the society from oblivion, for even if the members of the Cincinnati wanted to mollify its American critics, they couldn't very well retract all of the honors that had now been officially accorded to the French soldiers and sanctioned by the French king. L'Enfant had racked up considerable debts, spending freely in Paris and presumptuously ordering a golden eagle for every French member at the society's cost without Knox's authorization, but no one was talking money at the moment, now that the society had been successfully established in the face of considerable resistance.

Along with the other French Continentals, L'Enfant had been granted a military pension by Louis XVI, and from the Americans he could reasonably expect a portion of his back pay, some kind of pension, and a bounty of western land—all of this in addition to whatever monies he was receiving from his family. Not yet thirty, he had ample reason for confidence and optimism, to finally believe that he was on his way to fulfilling whatever abstract promises he'd made himself when he left home seven years earlier. He owned a sterling reputation as an artist and occasional architect. His name and work were familiar to generals, ambassadors, congressmen, and of course George Washington. And though it probably would have mystified L'Enfant to learn it, he would never again return to France. That part of his life was over. He was now an American and would remain in America for the rest of his days.

CHAPTER 4

The Remembrance of My Former Services

On April 30, 1789, George Washington was inaugurated as the first president of the United States. The election in January had given Washington a sweep of the Electoral College and more than 80 percent of the popular vote, but New York City had been preparing for this moment since September of the year before, when it had been made the first federal capital under the Constitution.

The inauguration was the country's first great national celebration, and its greatest architectural attraction was the creation of Major L'Enfant. For six months he'd worked at a torrid pace to direct the expansion and renovation of New York's City Hall so that it could become Federal Hall, home of the Congress of the United States and the setting for Washington's swearing in. The transformation was the talk of the city and its newspapers, including the *New York Morning Post and Daily Advertiser.*

No building under similar circumstances was ever erected with such rapidity, and with such taste and judgment of construction, as Federal Hall. This building, though by far the most extensive and elegant of any in America, has not been six months in raising—and when it is considered that since its first commencement, the most difficult and unfavorable season has been . . . encountered, surely no one will hesitate to pronounce it a rare enterprise and an astonishing performance.

Washington emerged onto the portico a few moments before one o'clock, dwarfing Vice President Adams in front of him. L'Enfant's balcony framed the scene with a wrought-iron rail, four Doric columns, thirteen

Federal Hall, by Samuel Hill, for the June 1789 *Massachusetts Magazine*

raised stars on the frieze, and above it all, filling the pediment, a great American eagle spreading its wings, thirteen arrows clutched in one claw and an olive branch in the other. Thousands filled the streets below, while others hung from windows, perched on roofs, and crowded in doorways. The air was crisp, winter was gone, and summer was about to set in, rain clouds pausing in the distance.

All of Washington's previous incarnations—as citizen, gentleman planter, and soldier—were plain to see in, respectively, his homespun brown suit, his powdered hair, and the dress sword that dangled at his side. For most, it was their first glimpse of the man, and the crowd responded with a roar. The chancellor of the state of New York, Robert R. Livingston, stood and unsuccessfully held out a hand for silence while Samuel A. Otis of Massachusetts, secretary of the Senate, smaller even than Adams, held aloft a Bible borrowed on short notice from a nearby Masonic lodge. Almost no one in the crowd could make out a word of the conversation that passed above, but they could see Washington bow, and at this they gave their excitement full throat. Washington kissed the Bible, and then the chancellor turned to face the crowd and shouted, "Long live George Washington, President of the United States!" Those who couldn't make out the words heard the choreographed roar of artillery from the Battery and saw the American flag rise over the cupola of Federal Hall.

The president went inside to deliver his inaugural address, emerging less than half an hour later to take his place at the front of the day's second formal procession. Accompanied by riders on horseback, congressmen, ceremonial infantry, constables, notable gentlemen, and hundreds of citizens gleefully making themselves part of the parade, Washington wound his way up Broadway to St. Paul's Chapel, at the intersection with Fulton Street, where the forces of heaven were enlisted in the cause of preserving his health and wisdom. As the president was lionized by speaker after speaker, he sat in a pew that afterward would be marked and set aside for his use alone. Whatever pride, humility, joy, or embarrassment Washington felt at finding himself the undisputed center of the nation's attention, he listened with his customary stone face.

Outside, the party had already begun. A day spotted with showers was turning into a starlit night perfect for promenading, and the streets were more crowded than they'd ever been. The crowd ranged from the Battery up Broadway to the northern edge of the urban landscape at Bayards Lane, from Greenwich Street bordering the Hudson over to the East River slips. Bankers, carters, grocers, auctioneers, housewives, washerwomen, book-sellers, clergymen, tavern keepers, slaves, domestic servants, prostitutes, attorneys, tailors, and more—all coursed through the old Dutch company town huddled on the southern tip of Manhattan Island to make themselves part of this historic beginning.

"It was a day which will stand immutable and indelible in the annals of America," wrote Washington's personal secretary, Tobias Lear. Overhead an array of fireworks spun, fizzed, and boomed. Merchant and military ships crowded just offshore, their masts and lines outlined with strings of light, while the windows of private residences blazed with candle lamps. Crowds gathered to gawk at wondrous "illuminations," giant sheets of cloth backlit by lanterns and painted to depict the father of his country in classical tableaux emphasizing his most classical virtues.

At ten in the evening, nine hours after Washington's oath, the street in front of Federal Hall remained too crowded for the use of carriages. Crowds filled the intersection of Nassau and Wall to gaze at the facade that had hours earlier earned architectural immortality. The new home of Congress glowed with its own collection of lanterns, every one of its windows alight, its crowning glass cupola blazing and visible from every quarter of the city. No one had done more than Major L'Enfant to create the theater of the day and to move the new federal government from the realm of words to that of wood, brick, and stone. It was the latest and most impressive achievement in a fast-rising career—which makes it all the more peculiar that he was, on this day of all days, nowhere to be found.

L'Enfant had arrived in New York five years earlier straight from his return trip to Paris. The contrast between the two cities could not have placed the eventual center of American commerce in an impressive light. The future designer of the American capital wouldn't have given a second thought to the plan of New York, because it hardly had one. In the 1780s the city still looked much like the Dutch West India Company town it had once been, despite the fires set in 1776 and 1778 during the British occupation. Thirty thousand people lived within its confines, twenty-three hundred of them slaves. The number of people in New York on the day of Washington's swearing in, swollen by thousands of visitors, was no greater than the popu-lation of the faubourg Saint-Marcel, L'Enfant's childhood neighborhood.

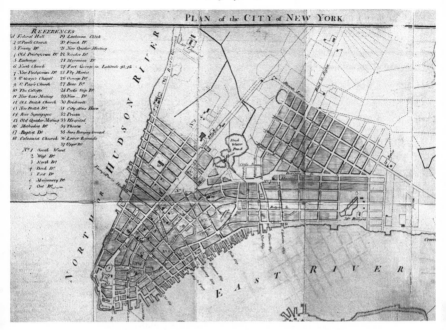

Plan of the City of New York, 1789, by John McComb, Jr.

But if New York was small by European standards, it did have a history more boisterous and variegated than that of any other city in the United States. Its incarnations had already included an Indian settlement, a brawling company outpost, a prim Dutch religious town, a British wartime stronghold, a burned-out battlefield, and now the first home of the federal government under the Constitution. The famed Commissioners' Plan, which would overwhelm Manhattan with its rectangular blocks, was still more than two decades in the future, and meanwhile most of New York was close, dirty, and dangerous. This, at least, L'Enfant would have found familiar. The city's sewer system consisted largely of slaves carrying tubs of refuse on their heads in the hours before dawn and after dusk. Cart and carriage accidents were many and watchmen few, while the gallows, whipping post, and stocks were in constant use, providing punishment and entertainment in similar measure. Another sight familiar to a young man of Parisian birth would have been the rush of construction work pushing the city's boundaries outward. Once out of the charred wake of the British occupation, the urban district had expanded northward by a dozen blocks. New brick colonials had gone up alongside the old Dutch gable-fronts as moneymen and merchants arrived from the states, making Wall Street the most important address in the city and a swarming locus of economic life in the United States.

L'Enfant had begun his private life in New York with a preview of the great public project that would come to dominate his professional career. As the thirteen colonies had pondered the idea of becoming one nation, the possibility of a permanent capital was suddenly something to take seriously, and in late 1783, just before L'Enfant left for France on behalf of the Society of the Cincinnati, the Confederation Congress had considered applications from locales hoping to become the seat of government. A federal city was unlikely to rise before the question of a new constitution was resolved, but that didn't keep L'Enfant from weighing in on the subject once he was back on American soil.

This first recorded evidence of L'Enfant's inclination toward city planning occurred in December 1784, when he wrote at some length to George Washington describing his scheme to establish a peacetime corps of engineers. It was a topic General Duportail and others had already addressed, but L'Enfant made his case as though the idea were entirely his. He outlined the academic background necessary for an engineer, including the "perfect knowledge" of arithmetic, geometry, mechanics, architecture, hydraulics, drawing, and "natural-philosophy," adding that "an engineer should be possessed of good natural parts, of a cool and active disposition." At the heart of his letter was a proposal to name a chief of engineers at the rank of brigadier general, and with this bit of implicit self-promotion out of the way, he arrived at the subject of a national capital. Such an undertaking was the natural province of a corps of engineers and its leader, he wrote; it would be to the "immediate benefit of the United States" to commit to such a corps the design of the public buildings and the plan of the city itself "in such a manner as to give an idea of the greatness of the empire, as well as to engrave in every mind that sense of respect due to a place which is the seat of a supreme sovereignty."

Not for another decade would the federal government authorize even a single regiment of military engineers, but within a few months of L'Enfant's letter to Washington, it had placed the temporary capital in New York City and designated a spot along the Delaware River near Trenton, New Jersey, as the front-runner for the permanent location. L'Enfant then applied to become one of the hypothetical city's three commissioners. In this hope he had to defer to Robert Morris and two Revolutionary War generals, including Alexander Hamilton's father-in-law, Philip Schuyler, but he was chosen to do the first expert assessment of the ground. "I had made considerable progress in the survey," he would later write, "and in the preparation of the plan of a city first intended there, but the project of that national establishment having been given up, I was encouraged to suspect due compensation at some further day."

Much of L'Enfant's time during his first year in New York was taken up with the possibility of a Trenton capital and with his continuing work for the Cincinnati, but soon he began to find what employment he could in, as one description of the day had it, "the arts of design." City directories of the 1780s listed no one under the title of "architect"—the profession would not emerge in America, distinct from carpentry and building, until well into the nineteenth century—but L'Enfant apparently completed plenty of work as a freelance designer. His best-documented projects were two additions to St. Paul's Chapel, which had been built in the mid-1760s to resemble London's St. Martin-in-the-Fields. There he supervised the installment of a memorial to General Richard Montgomery, martyr of the Battle of Quebec; he also designed a florid rococo altarpiece depicting Mount Sinai and the tablets of the Ten Commandments, which was needed to keep parishioners from having to stare out at Montgomery's back during services.

New York had become the nation's political hub when the state's internal battle over ratification of the new Constitution held the rest of the former colonies in suspense. L'Enfant followed the fate of the Constitution with interest, not least because of Article 1, Section 8, Clause 17, which granted Congress the power to "exercise exclusive Legislation in all Cases whatsoever, over such District (not exceeding ten Miles square) as may, by Cession of particular States, and the Acceptance of Congress, become the Seat of the Government of the United States."

He became aware of these words late in 1787, in the same cold season that brought him news from Paris of his father's death at the age of eighty-three. He would later describe these as his salad days, writing that his various sources of income—his "fortune," as he always called it, now augmented by a small inheritance—allowed him to abandon "tavern living" and keep a house and servant. In June 1788 he was enlisted by Alexander Hamilton and other Federalist friends in New York to plan their day of festivities in anticipation of ratification. He made the most of the chance, outfitting a parade down the length of Broadway featuring five thousand tradesmen, some in the exaggerated dress of farmers or Continental soldiers, walking alongside dozens of floats and carrying placards and props advertising their enthusiastic support of the Constitution. The procession was dotted with flags and posters depicting Hamilton, the city's brightest political light and the ostensibly anonymous force behind the influential *Federalist.* The arrival of the largest float, the federal ship *Hamilton,* at the Battery concluded the parade and sent the revelers off for a lavish meal served nearby in a pavilion of L'Enfant's design, a temporary structure featuring seven hundred-foot-long tables radiating outward from a giant circular dais. Three thousand people had attended the feast, which concluded with a display of fireworks on a scale that wouldn't be witnessed again until the evening of Washington's inauguration.

That was July 23, 1788. Three days later New York ratified the Constitution, and though Virginia had preceded it as the ninth and decisive yea, the achievement was considerable. New York, already the home of the Confederation Congress, had become the first truly national capital, and now it had to act the part. The Common Council of the city, likely acting at Hamilton's urging, tapped L'Enfant to create a suitably dignified home for Congress. His ambitious plan for the conversion of the old City Hall into Federal Hall was approved on September 30, apparently, once again, with no serious competition. L'Enfant accomplished the wholesale alterations in six months, overshooting his budget by at least $20,000, 40 percent of the original appropriation, but the appetite in New York for life at the center of things was so strong, the pockets of some of its citizens so deep, and Hamilton's influence so persuasive that objections to the cost were easily mollified. By late April, when the pediment's eagle was hoisted into place in front of a large crowd of onlookers, the building had already become something of a sensation, even before President-elect Washington appeared on the scene.

As a token of its appreciation for his work on Federal Hall, the new Congress designated L'Enfant as a ceremonial "assistant" for the inauguration, reserving him a seat in the House chamber amid military men who had served under Washington during the war. The designation also placed him second in the day's pair of processions, behind a troop of horses, ahead of Washington's canary-yellow carriage with its six white horses, ahead of the assembled members of Congress, ahead of the marching bands and the columns of New York militia in full dress, and ahead of the mass of citizens pouring into the streets behind. If L'Enfant had wanted to march up Broadway with Washington to St. Paul's Chapel, where more of his work was on prominent display, all he had to do was say yes.

For L'Enfant to refuse such an honor seemed impossible, but refuse it he had. Federal Hall was equal to the gravity of the moment, and the citizens of New York were gratified by his work—that much was clear. Nor was creative autonomy the issue: the renovation of the building had been left to L'Enfant from start to end, and despite gaps in the budget, he'd kept the pace from flagging so that the exterior and most of the interior had been finished by inauguration day. Nor is it likely that he was exhibiting a sense of superiority to the other "assistants": many were members of the Society of the Cincinnati, and all were military men, and if L'Enfant reflexively honored one class of men, it was his Continental Army brethren.

It wasn't the last time he would decline such a token of recognition as incommensurate with the magnitude of his services. His father had long been honored not by wealth—despite being surrounded by it—but by his professional association with the Royal Academy of Painting and Sculpture and the War Ministry of Louis XV. So too, it seems, did his son expect to be honored by a more conspicuous acknowledgment of his talents and his personal association with Washington. Money, he believed, would take care of itself: if one always did one's best work for such illustrious patrons, a reputation—and more work—would naturally follow.

His desire had been to receive a separate and singular designation: Peter Charles L'Enfant, architect of Federal Hall. Instead, he had been asked to step out into the mob and go ahead of the president to *direct traffic*. As the *Daily Advertiser* put it, in the same article that noted his refusal, it was "to be entrusted to the Assistants to take proper precautions for keeping the avenues to the Hall open." There may have been more to the honor than this, but clearing a path to a "Hall" not properly trumpeted as his handiwork was not the payment L'Enfant had had in mind. It was simply not *enough*.

So here in the story of George Washington's inauguration, L'Enfant steps out of our view, his sense of honor intact, leaving his place in history unrecorded rather than allowing it to be recorded in such a desultory way, his face absent from the streets of New York City on the evening of Washington's inauguration but his presence written firmly in wood and brick and iron and glass. Here is the first flaring of an intractable image of self in which fame was the most important and only sufficient reward, above money or land or title—which were more than welcome to him, of course, but only as secondary prizes.

Two facts about George Washington stood out so dramatically as to already have become part of the American cultural consciousness: first, he had refused a salary as commander in chief, and second, he was Cincinnatus reincarnated, the gentleman farmer who had gone back to his farm after a victorious war, then returned to assume the presidency only with the greatest reluctance. His reward for a lifetime of public service had been not wealth or position but glory and honor. L'Enfant's belief that such a thread of reputation bound himself to the president would help to keep him in the United States and prevent him from demanding his due until after Washington's death, when he would finally make fully known the depth of his bottled resentment.

The *New-York Journal and Weekly Register* took its readers on a rapturous verbal tour of Federal Hall, describing a building that revealed itself in layers, small rooms alternating with large to delightful effect.

> The whole composition is most admirably contrived for the purpose for which it is intended. The style is bold, simple, and regular; the parts few, large, and distinct; the transition sudden, and strongly marked; and we think the whole has an air of grandeur.

Passing beneath the Tuscan colonnade on the ground floor, visitors entered a low-ceilinged antechamber before passing into a marble-paved vestibule rising three full stories to the cupola overhead. Double doors immediately ahead opened into the grand Representatives' Chamber, called "the master piece of the whole" by the newspaper, a soaring room framed by four corner fireplaces and ringed with two tiers of galleries, public below and private above, its walls sheathed in curtains of blue damask. Stairs on either side of the vestibule led up to a "lobby" decorated with portraits of George Washington and Alexander Hamilton by the artist John Trumbull, beyond which lay the smaller Senate chamber, lined with crimson cloth and neoclassical pilasters of L'Enfant's own invention.

The Massachusetts Magazine, or, Monthly Museum of Knowledge and Rational Entertainment ended its own lengthy description of Federal Hall with praise not only of L'Enfant's work but, ironically, of his forbearance.

> We cannot close our description without observing, that great praise is due to Major L'Enfant, the architect, who has surmounted many difficulties, and so accommodated the additions to the old parts, and so judiciously altered what he saw wrong, that he has produced a building uniform and consistent throughout, and has added to great elegance every convenience that could be desired.

No recognition, however, could compare with a final, private honor that arrived a month later, one that seems to have better gratified L'Enfant's desire for luminous patronage. Early on the morning of June 13 Tobias Lear sent a short note to the architect's rooms informing him that Martha Washington, recently and reluctantly arrived in New York from Mount Vernon to join her husband, would be honored if L'Enfant would present himself at six that evening in order to provide the first First Lady with a personal tour of Federal Hall.

This payment was, at the very least, of a proper kind. We know L'Enfant felt it was because he kept Lear's note for the remaining thirty-six years of his life.

None of the conflicts argued by the First Federal Congress inside Federal Hall was as nasty or as potentially destructive as the fight over the location of the new seat of government. The tug-of-war that had been joined following the British capitulation in 1783 hadn't let up during six years of political posturing and backroom arm-twisting. The capital was a prize as complicated and controversial as the federalism that had given it life, and about all that had been established was the principle of permanence: the gravitas of L'Enfant's Federal Hall helped to tamp down the persistent suggestions that the seat of power might just as well wander the country from city to city like a great legislative caravan.

This was no symbolic battle fought over phantom stakes. On the contrary, it was the most contentious and polarizing question of the new nation, and the rhetoric deployed in the House was explosive. No less influential and brilliant a legislator than the young James Madison rose from his seat to say that Virginia might not have ratified the Constitution had it foreseen a federal capital rising so far to the north. Short of creating a compound national fracture, said others, the argument was at the very least bound to feed the insidious spirit of faction. The practicability, the very existence of the government, hung on the resolution of this question.

Only one consensus was emerging, but it would prove to make all the difference. This was the idea that the permanent seat of government was destined to become the most visible and lasting piece of the first president's legacy. The assumption on all sides was that the seat of government would be George Washington's second home for the rest of his life—and no one at this moment imagined him outliving what would surely be a very long presidency. Representative John Vining of Delaware made one of the few unchallenged statements of the debates when he called the future seat of government a place that would "inherit the President's virtue, and possess his influence," once Washington had left this world and taken his rightful place in the next. The *Daily Advertiser* of September 7, 1789, published a prescient editorial by an anonymous author suggesting that Washington himself should settle the issue "by pointing to a map where the centre of the United States was designated," adding that "he has never given bad advice to his country."

It was at this moment that Major L'Enfant wrote to the president to ask for the most coveted commission of his life. Congress had adjourned for the weekend in the midst of arguments over three river locations: the Susquehanna, championed by Hamilton and most of the other northerners; the Delaware, hobbyhorse of the formidable financier Robert Morris; and the Potomac, in third place at the moment but still very much alive in the crafty and determined hands of Madison. L'Enfant, for his part, didn't care where the federal district was placed, just as long as his would be the hand to design it.

Washington received the major's letter on or shortly after September 11, 1789.

The late determination of Congress to lay the foundation of a city which is to become the capital of this vast empire offers so great an occasion of acquiring reputation to whoever may be appointed to conduct the execution of the business that Your Excellency will not be surprised that my ambition and the desire I have of becoming a useful citizen should lead me to wish a share in the undertaking.

Whether the country could afford at first to build the entire city or not, he continued, "it will be obvious that the plan should be drawn on such a scale as to leave room for that aggrandizement and embellishment which the increase of the wealth of the nation will permit it to pursue at any period however remote." The basic philosophy of Federalism—a fully vested and visible central government with sovereign authority—suffused his opening. Given the letter's eloquence, L'Enfant almost certainly had help with many of the words. This conjecture has led some historians to suspect Alexander Hamilton, who had been nominated four days earlier as secretary of the treasury and whom L'Enfant later credited with helping to secure the federal city commission. Certainly the kind of verbal dexterity and grandeur glimmering in the letter was one of Hamilton's most bankable stocks-in-trade, and L'Enfant would rarely demonstrate it again.

For all of L'Enfant's insistent rhetoric, though, he spent only two paragraphs on the request, as if he already knew there was little chance he wouldn't get the job. In the rest of the letter he returned to the proposition he had made five years earlier, when he had argued for the creation of a peacetime corps of engineers. Then he had suggested a brigadier general chief of engineers without explicitly asking for the job; now he called the position "Engineer to the United States," suggested that such an individual's primary responsibility would be to maintain the country's coastal defenses, and put himself forward as the logical choice, being the last of the original French engineers remaining in America. Having made this request for an appointment that would be "most gratifying to my wishes," he ended by appealing to Washington's fellow feeling.

I shall conclude by assuring you that ever animated as I have been with a desire to merit your good opinion, nothing will be wanting to complete my happiness if the remembrance of my former services, connected with a variety of peculiar circumstances during fourteen years residence in this country, can plead with Your Excellency in support of the favor I solicit.

One week later, on September 19, 1789, the headline of the *Daily Gazette* in New York announced "A Complete Revolution in France" atop the stunning news that the Bastille had been stormed, several of its guards killed and their severed heads placed on pikes, and its prisoners—all seven of them—released. The provocative headline aside, it wasn't quite yet revolution, but the events must have turned L'Enfant's mind toward his mother, who, having been a widow for two years, was still occupying her *logement* in the Gobelins and still very much in the orbit of the monarchy. The reign of violence fast approaching would in fact spare her and the Gobelins, but neither his family inheritance nor his military pension from Louis XVI. It would also destroy much of the documentary evidence necessary for even a cursory portrait of L'Enfant's formative years and a better understanding of his thoughts as he left home at twenty-two. Such materials would have helped piece together a fuller portrait of his relationship with his mother as well; after his father's death they seem to have corresponded only a little—so little, in fact, that one of his cousins would eventually admonish him to pick up the pen more often. Though L'Enfant did on occasion express concern for his mother's situation, he seems to have made no serious plans to visit her.

Three weeks after the extraordinary news from Paris, the Common Council of New York offered L'Enfant a ten-acre plot of land at the city's undeveloped northern edge and the freedom of the city in exchange for his services as the designer of Federal Hall. L'Enfant considered a piece of cheap ground improper recompense for his role in the events surrounding Washington's inauguration, but he snatched at the honorary citizenship. The freedom of New York City was hardly a ceremonial award. Despite his war service and his work on Federal Hall, L'Enfant as a foreigner only now gained the legal right to vote in city elections and to incorporate his trade. The council members expressed their surprise at L'Enfant's truculence regarding the real estate but graciously granted him citizenship and again praised his work for the record. Shortly thereafter the major was offered and accepted a personal commendation from the mayor of the city, but otherwise he remained out of sight until the political battle over the seat of government reached a resolution.

In June 1790, finally, the "residence question" was settled once and for all at Thomas Jefferson's new home at 57 Maiden Lane, four blocks north of Federal Hall. Here, over food and wine, Alexander Hamilton (the quintessential New Yorker) agreed to drop his opposition to a southern location for the federal city as long as fellow dinner guest James Madison (a Virginian to the core) agreed to follow suit by moderating his opposition to federal assumption of state debts incurred during the War for Independence. Not all historians agree that this meeting by itself had such a magical effect, but such an interpretation is supported by subsequent events: in the weeks after the dinner, momentum picked up as legislators emerged from meetings with Hamilton or Madison with not-so-mysteriously changed minds. The Residence Act was signed by Washington on July 16, 1790.

> Be it enacted by the Senate and House of Representatives of the United States of America in Congress assembled, That a district of territory, not exceeding ten miles square, to be located as hereafter directed on the river Potomac, at some place between the mouths of the Eastern Branch and Connogochegue, be, and the same is hereby accepted for the permanent seat of the government of the United States.

The legislation also created a board of three federal city commissioners to supervise the construction of public buildings and—in part thanks to a crafty rearguard maneuver executed by Robert Morris and the other Pennsylvania legislators—named Philadelphia and not New York as the temporary capital. This document also set a deadline of December 1800 for the completion of the President's House and the hall of Congress in the new federal district.

On January 24, 1791, President Washington informed Congress by proclamation of his choice of location along the Potomac, surprising no one: the southern edge of the new federal district would be placed in Alexandria, just five miles upriver from his beloved Mount Vernon. The capital would be built a morning's ride from the president's front door. And though some, including Jefferson, had recommended a smaller and less magisterial annexation, the district would measure out at a full ten miles per side, to encompass one hundred square miles.

At the beginning of March L'Enfant received Jefferson's letter ordering him to head for Georgetown. The rhetoric in Federal Hall, now that the heat and rancor of the previous autumn's debates had subsided, centered on the far happier and nearly unopposed proposition to admit Vermont to the union. Just at the moment when the thirteen original colonies were finishing their transformation into a nation of fourteen states, with more candidates waiting in line, Major L'Enfant departed New York on his way to the forests, farms, woods, and marshes where the Eastern Branch flowed into the Potomac River.

CHAPTER 5

In Every Respect Advantageously Situated

As L'Enfant set to work on the morning after his first day's ride around the site, nothing weighed more heavily on his mind than his upcoming audience with George Washington. The president planned to return to Mount Vernon from Philadelphia before the start of April, and while passing through Georgetown, he expected to speak with the commissioners, the landowners (or, as they were customarily called, the "proprietors"), and Ellicott and L'Enfant. From Ellicott Washington expected an update on the plotting of the district's borders and the placement of the boundary stones, while L'Enfant was to report on his preliminary survey of the ground between Georgetown and the mouth of the Eastern Branch, offering some early options for the placement of the President's House and a meeting place for Congress.

L'Enfant had something more in mind. Determined to go beyond his limited charge and envision the seat of government in toto, he knew he had to encourage Washington to expand his vision of the city. Despite his experience with the president, success was not preordained. He had never before been in Washington's presence with something so monumental at stake, but now, if he wanted to cement the federal city commission for his own and seal their relationship as one of patron and artist, he had to make himself indispensable to the country's one true indispensable man.

On March 11, the day after his first tour of the site, L'Enfant sent a letter to Jefferson apologizing for his slow journey from New York and bemoaning the continuing mist and rain. Then, without taking a breath, he boldly objected to confining the federal city to the precincts next to Georgetown "when considering the intended city on that grand scale on which it ought to be planned." In that location, he explained impatiently, the most important buildings in the nation—in the *world*—would squat on a shallow bar of land with hundred-foot heights looming to the northwest. The seat of government as envisioned by L'Enfant was not going to be so small, so pedestrian, so unsuitable. He was of only one mind. The syntax of his letter is tortured, but not so much that it obscures the point.

> As far as I was able to judge through a thick fog, I passed on many spots which appeared to me really beautiful and which seem to dispute with each other who command the most extensive prospect of the water. The gradual rising of the ground from Carrollsburg toward the Ferry Road, the level and extensive ground from there to the bank of the Potomac as far as Goose Creek—present a situation most advantageous to run streets and prolong them on a grand and far distant point of view. The remainder part of the ground toward Georgetown is more broken—it may afford pleasant seats, but although the bank of the river between the two creeks can command as grand a prospect as any of the other spots it seems to be less commendable for the establishment of a city not only because the level surface it presents is but small, but because the heights from beyond Georgetown absolutely command the whole.

If Jefferson found L'Enfant's attitude surprising, he neither said nor did anything to dissuade him. He saw no reason for L'Enfant's vision to be widely broadcast, however, and ended his return letter with a postscript asking the architect to take care.

There are certainly considerable advantages on the Eastern Branch; but there are very strong reasons also in favor of the position between Rock Creek and Tiber, independent of the face of the ground. It is desired that the proper amount should be in equilibrio between the two places till the President arrives, and we shall be obliged to you to endeavor to poise their expectations.

These words take on special meaning, written as they were by one of America's preeminent practitioners of poised expectations. Jefferson, like Washington, was a master at keeping his thoughts and plans out of plain view, of holding strong opinions in reserve until they could most advantageously be aired. L'Enfant, however, was not known for tact or political skills, and it was typical of him to show all his cards to the secretary as the proceedings began, even as Jefferson played his own extremely close to the vest.

There were at least two important things that Jefferson was not telling L'Enfant. First, the secretary had already submitted his own rough sketch of the city at the president's request, a drawing laying down a very different idea of a capital from the magnificent embryo growing in L'Enfant's letters. In Jefferson's sketch the "federal town" was the model of republican restraint and modesty, made of a small public walk tying together a closely spaced President's House and "Capitol" (Jefferson's preferred term for the Congress House) tucked between Rock and Tiber creeks. The whole of his design was smaller than the settled portion of Philadelphia, even considering the simple grid framework that allowed for expansion of the plan "in future." Jefferson's drawing represented at most about fifteen hundred acres, or roughly a fourth of the territory that L'Enfant and Washington would eventually annex to the needs of the new nation.

Jefferson also kept out of these early exchanges with L'Enfant his deeply held reservations about cities of any size, the corruption and surrender of ideological independence that invariably resulted when men and money were put in such seductive proximity. This opinion was not truly a secret: a sharp-eyed reader of Jefferson's *Notes on the State of Virginia,* first published in England four years earlier and familiar to many well-read Americans, would have noted the secretary's belief that the "mobs of great cities add just so much to the support of pure government, as sores do to the strength of the human body." Jefferson may have been putting more emphasis on "mobs" than on "cities," but his ideal America was in all cases a nation

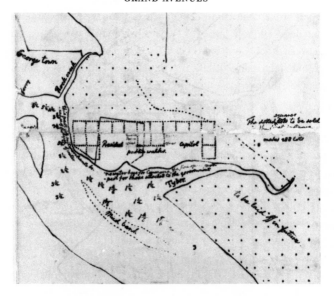

Thomas Jefferson's sketch of the "federal town," 1791

made of farms and small county seats supporting those farms. On a mountaintop in central Virginia he would devote his lifetime to articulating this idea: that a free man at a dignified remove from other free men was man in his highest, most civilized state.

L'Enfant and Jefferson would leave no record of a personal exchange of thinking on the moral effect of cities, and no pitched battle between diametrically opposed urban visions occurred at this stage in the story. After all, Jefferson had produced his own sketch at the president's request, on the assumption that "no offer worthy of consideration" would come from any of the landowners not immediately adjacent to Georgetown. It would be a mistake to confuse his pleasure at the idea of a severely limited capital with an active conspiracy to sabotage larger conceptions. But the fact remains that a city spread exuberantly across many miles in the embrace of a robust federal presence was in no way a Jeffersonian vision, and clearly the major's first instinct represented Jefferson's last option, if indeed it was an option that Jefferson would ever have entertained had L'Enfant's task been his own.

· · ·

As L'Enfant worked over the next three weeks to put something meaningful onto paper for the president, the weather continued to worsen. The nettled architect was temperamentally prone to frustration, and that he did little grousing is a sign of the positive momentum at the start. He'd been preparing for this moment long enough—it had been eighteen months since he'd written to Washington to request the federal city commission and more than six years since he'd surveyed the potential Delaware River site—and he would tolerate no more waiting.

He set out in a determined frenzy, treading where he could tread, seeing what he could see, and learning what he could learn before the president's arrival. The core of the federal district had never been the swamp that schoolbook history has made it out to be, but it did contain patches of soggy land, most obviously at the base of Jenkins Hill, where a collection of vigorous springs came down to refresh the Tiber. It rained long and hard during the first of his precious three weeks, and L'Enfant had nothing to do but to stay on higher, drier ground and extrapolate the features of the landscape where he couldn't traverse it directly underfoot.

His second week of effort saw the rain become snow as L'Enfant worked assiduously to get the major areas "laid down": surveyor's parlance for establishing elevation changes and dimensions, locating major ridgelines and plateaus. He was not doing this work in advance of making a plan, as was the usual practice; rather, his planning and his survey were happening at the same time. For one person to perform both of these roles at once was rare, even unique, but he was able to manage the trick. The deadline approached without any recorded word from the pressed architect other than one more vague update to Jefferson, but when the president arrived in Georgetown right on schedule, L'Enfant was ready.

Washington's diary entry for March 28 is, in the usual fashion of the president's writings, a study in gross understatement.

> Dined at Suter's Tavern (where I also lodged) at a public dinner given by the Mayor and Corporation—previous to which I examined the surveys of Mr. Ellicott who has been sent on to lay out the district of ten miles square for the federal seat; and also the works of Major L'Enfant who has been engaged to examine and make drafts of the grounds in the vicinity of George Town and Carrollsburg on the Eastern Branch.

The entry does not begin to suggest what happened in the conference between the president and L'Enfant. The major was able to lay in front of Washington only what he called "a rough drawing in pencil," but it was still much more than a survey. He made up for any real or imagined deficiencies in his drawing by writing a lengthy "memorandum" outlining the essentials of his progress. Huddled with the president over his single hasty sketch, he talked the city into being.

The subsequent run of events and the evidence of the memorandum itself make clear much of what passed between L'Enfant and Washington that day. One was a man full of words in a language he would forever find vexing, the other a man who rarely spoke when important matters were under discussion, who preferred to read, listen, and deliberate his way through a dilemma. L'Enfant described a city that would cover *all* the ground bordered by the Eastern Branch, the Potomac, Rock Creek, and the cap of high hills to the north. This first point, the same one he had made to Jefferson two weeks earlier, had now been refined into a specific insight: the zones he had been asked to explore should be treated not as several different potential city sites but as one place.

L'Enfant went on, providing a verbal legend for his drawing. He had completed some surveyor's lines to show the shape of Jenkins Hill, the site's wooded center and the high point from which the city would radiate and from which all of its points would be measured. Two new bridges would be necessary, he explained, one near the current ferry dock on the Eastern Branch and the other running southwest out of Georgetown and over the dramatic formation of rocks in the middle of the Potomac known as the Three Sisters. A new street roughly following the ferry road (later to be named Pennsylvania Avenue) would arrow across the city and connect these two bridges, providing a direct connection between the two harbor areas in order to speed the progress of goods and materials into the central construction areas. This large diagonal avenue would also serve as a proto-type for many others, all designed to shorten travel time, encourage growth, and prevent unhealthful crowding. Some would even extend, like the ever-lengthening Champs-Élysées of L'Enfant's youth, well into the rural environs.

And the city would grow, he told Washington in an even more startling proposition, until a million people would live there, until the four thousand acres he had now delimited were not nearly enough to hold the eager influx of residents. The *entire district* would eventually fill—every one of its sixty-four thousand acres, all of its one hundred square miles of land, a footprint larger than any city anywhere in the world. Washington's attempts to placate the squabbling landowners, as well as Jefferson's poised expectations, would be rendered not only unnecessary but irrelevant, replaced with a show of confident and exuberant ambition.

Whether or not Washington even attempted to visualize L'Enfant's dream of a fully populated hundred square miles—a dimension fifteen times the size of any city the president had ever visited—the underlying principle was irresistible, a chance to stop stooping to each individual's private interest and raise his eyes to the wider view. He'd always found such a perspective far more comfortable than an immersion in other people's particulars. Even in these first glimpses of a much bigger canvas, L'Enfant's desire to write something magnificent across the land was helping Washington to see his way up and out of a fog of provincialism and into the clearer air, where he could launch a capital truly worthy of the country. It was a dramatic shift in perspective, sidelining the local in favor of the national, the present in favor of the future, and the familiar in favor of the extraordinary.

A political ideology was also lurking not so far beneath L'Enfant's proposals. His argument for an arrangement of long, converging diagonal streets included some pointed statements about the already venerable American gridiron plan.

> Such regular plans indeed, however answerable they may appear upon paper or seducing as they may be on the first aspect to the eyes of some people, must even when applied upon the ground the best calculated to admit of it become at last tiresome and insipid and it never could be in its origin but a mere contrivance of some cool imagination wanting a sense of the real grand and truly beautiful.

By this L'Enfant meant that the capital would be no Alexandria, no Savannah, no Philadelphia. Some of his objections were simply those of a born-and-bred Parisian. But he also believed, as did Washington, that "grand" and "beautiful" was the only appropriate goal for the federal city and the nation over which it would preside. Not everyone agreed. Jefferson's complaint against grandiose cities was not based in aesthetic displeasure: in his view, centralized government would be abetted by a centralized city, one to which all roads and ambitions would lead, and the larger and more dramatic that city, the greater its attractive—and therefore corruptive—power.

Washington held no such pessimistic views and was a receptive listener well on the way to becoming a ready collaborator in L'Enfant's vision. The president's experience of war had taught him again and again the dangers of depending on the whims and unreliable finances of individual cities and states. He desired a lodestone of national identity, a geographical anchor and point of origination for the American empire. The seat of government would act as a kind but firm and deeply resourceful parent, a city beautiful and inspiring but at the same time made of sinew and bone. Washington believed in life as a kind of stage on which important men played out their roles for the eyes of posterity, and this new place would serve as a backdrop of magnificence in front of which a man's—and a nation's—strength and humility could more readily stand out.

Aside from these proto-Federalist underpinnings, the plan's form also had to be matched to the reality of the topography. The terrain "best calculated to admit" a gridiron was flat, wrote L'Enfant, but the district was not flat. He kept returning to Jenkins Hill, the ideal spot for a congressional building: "From these heights every grand building would rear with a majestic aspect over the country all around and might be advantageously seen from twenty miles off." Here on the high ground the city would be planted, and "thus in every respect advantageously situated, the Federal City would soon grow of itself and spread as the branches of a tree do towards where they meet with most nourishment."

There was plenty here for the president to digest. It seemed hardly possible that L'Enfant's presentation was the result of less than three weeks' work, and Washington recognized the thought and acuity that had gone into it. The president rarely used his diary to record his internal deliberations, and he did not change that practice now. But those deliberations, and his ability to recognize and absorb the expertise of others, were two of Washington's greatest strengths. He had already inaugurated the custom of having his trusted aides and department heads, Jefferson and Hamilton especially, argue their positions and proposals by means of written briefs, so that he might consider their plans and their advice by his own lights and on his own time before announcing a course of action. That L'Enfant was already using memorandums may indicate that Washington had made such a request of him or that Hamilton or someone else had suggested their preparation. Ill suited as this protocol was to the convolutions of his written English, L'Enfant had at least happened upon the method best suited to engage the president's attention.

The next day Washington rose and headed out for a tour of the site with his friends David Stuart and Daniel Carroll, two of the three men already designated as the city's commissioners, but he soon came back unsatisfied thanks to the same troublesome skies that had so hampered L'Enfant. Washington had slept on the architect's presentation, and in the passage of the evening his thinking had undergone an evolution. No longer was the game of "equipoising" anything to continue. Now Washington desired only to, as he put it in his diary, "properly manage" the proprietors.

This approach put the president on familiar footing. He knew just how to "manage" men, by making use of a device that his military experience had taught him: the carefully modulated public audience. He had mastered the art in a hundred moments large and small, and he knew better than any of the other founders (apart from the recently deceased Benjamin Franklin) how to play out a public persona for his own and the nation's purposes.

Still, his meeting with the landowners was now built upon an ambitious platform, and as he did in all such cases, Washington made himself ready. He instructed Jefferson to draft a strict agenda so that things would not devolve into an open debate. Two of the items on this list—the formal appointment of the three commissioners and the presentation of a proclamation setting the exact location of the federal district—were expected and would pass without comment. From there things could get thornier. The announcement of the proposed sites for the Congress House and the President's House—located neither next to Georgetown nor in Carrollsburg but on two previously unmentioned heights, Jenkins Hill and the rise just north of Tiber Creek—would be the first public revelation of the greatly expanded scale of the city. The news would surely create some anxiety, while the next item, a proposal to take the deeds of cession from the landowners, relied for its success on a genuinely optimistic appraisal of Washington's own persuasive powers. Not only would he place in front of the proprietors a proposal for a capital the size of a dozen Georgetowns, but he expected to reach a binding verbal agreement with them *this night* on the terms of acquisition of their lands.

The meeting at Suter's on March 29, 1791, was not an audience for a landed gentleman to skip. Gathered with L'Enfant to listen to Washington were the city commissioners Stuart and Carroll and most or all of the property owners in the federal district. Present were Benjamin Stoddert and William Deakins, Washington's original secret land agents, now freed from their charge and openly able to advance their own prospects, along with other locals of influence, including Robert Peter, James Pierce, Anthony Holmead, James Lingan, David Burnes, Jonathan Slater, Samuel Davidson, William Young, Abraham Young, Charles Beatty, and Clement Woodward. Two other men in the room, Notley Young and Daniel Carroll of Duddington, were far and away the wealthiest in the proposed city. Between them they owned nearly half of the land under discussion. Their business was everyone else's business, and their fortunes were a marker of the entire region's financial health and reputation.

Rounding out the group was George Walker, a Scottish emigrant who would quickly become L'Enfant's greatest supporter. Indeed, they had been thinking along parallel lines for some time. In January 1789—prior to the residence debate in the First Federal Congress, L'Enfant's letter of application to Washington, and the Residence Act of 1790—Walker had written an article for the *Maryland Journal and Baltimore Advertiser* under the pseudonym "A Citizen of the World" in which he proposed the location adjacent to Georgetown and argued for putting all of the city's infrastructure in place before erecting the public buildings. This last belief, especially, showed that he alone among the commissioners and landowners shared L'Enfant's philosophy, and already he was the major's most useful ally.

Washington began his proposal with a little scolding. He pointed out to the proprietors that all of this contention served neither the public interest nor their own. Their attempts to squeeze the city into one spot, each man's *own* spot, were limiting not only the city but their own prospects. They might in fact sink the entire project: Who, after all, would invest broadly in such a small city? By working to raise the price of a few acres and to bring the public buildings to their own lands, they were only doing themselves harm. The landowners, he said, using a Federalist analogy that he wholeheartedly embraced, were like states disputing their individual positions without any understanding of the important advantages that union might bring.

Then Washington added an observation that probably came straight from L'Enfant himself. Philadelphia measured three by two miles; if the capital of one single state occupied so much land, shouldn't the capital of an entire nation be commensurately proportioned? Work on the city had to begin. Major L'Enfant was on the site, knew the site, and had been given instructions to begin putting the plan into its ultimate shape. All that was wanting from the landowners was a financial agreement, and Washington, pressing on, proposed a scheme for reimbursing them for their property and ensuring them a healthy profit in the bargain. Should any of them have reason to quarrel with the president's terms, he made sure they understood that only some of them signing on would be as detrimental to the national interest as none of them signing on. They could join the circle, or they could stand outside it.

Then he gave them the evening to think about it.

The next day, March 30, Washington wrote this in his diary: "The parties to whom I addressed myself yesterday evening, having taken the matter into consideration, saw the propriety of my observations; and that whilst they were contending for the shadow they might lose the substance."

It's hard to believe that no hint of amusement or pride supported this summation. Certainly there is satisfaction in his tone, even elation, for the success of Washington's public audience meant that the federal city was set to move forward with the momentum that only the prospect of landowners willing to sell, and sell soon, could provide. A fast start was all the more important because many Americans still viewed the idea of a federal city, so prized by the president, with indifference or skepticism. Washington's desires and decrees aside, other locales were still angling to replace the seat of government along the Potomac, Philadelphia most loudly and confidently. Given the choice of moving to a construction site or remaining in the nation's wealthiest and most sophisticated city, most members of Congress, it was widely understood, would prefer to stay put.

Washington's letter to Jefferson, written the next day, set the specific terms of the land agreement and offhandedly announced the considerable expansion of L'Enfant's responsibilities.

All the land from Rock Creek along the river to the Eastern Branch and so upwards to or above the ferry including a breadth of about a mile and a half, the whole containing from three to five thousand acres, is ceded to the public on condition that when the whole shall be surveyed and laid off as a city (which Major L'Enfant is now directed to do), the present proprietors shall retain every other lot.

For such part of the land as may be taken for public use, for squares, walks, etc., they shall be allowed at the rate of twenty five pounds per acre.

It was finally official: L'Enfant was "now directed" to plan the capital—and at a startling size. "Five thousand acres" was an area that begged credulity, comparable to the footprints of Paris and London and as large as the occupied portions of New York City, Boston, and Philadelphia *combined*. L'Enfant had not been concerned with contending groups of landowners, because his conception of the city was a wave that subsumed them all.

The landowners, for their part, had little cause for complaint. They were now in possession of one of the sweetest land deals in America's accelerating history of sweet land deals, and all of it hinged on the sweep and expanse of L'Enfant's plan. This was a bargain potentially rich in cash; ground that had been made of forests and tobacco farms was suddenly transformed into lots in the national capital. The property owners were now looking at a potential legacy of great wealth, and in an age awash with airy and irrational speculation, this scheme had George Washington standing behind it. Suddenly most of these proprietors were eager to join George Walker in wholeheartedly supporting L'Enfant. And suddenly they weren't competing so earnestly to attract the public buildings to their own pieces of property, possessing the business sense to understand that they had just been changed from competitors into partners. As Washington wrote to Jefferson, "The enlarged plan of this agreement [has] done away with the necessity, and indeed postponed the propriety, of designating the particular spot on which the public buildings should be placed."

To say that the proprietors were dazzled by the president would be to go too far: he was, after all, a fellow tidewater Virginian and a familiar face. And notwithstanding Washington's presence, concerns still lurked beneath the bonhomie. Successfully launching a city so large would depend disproportionately on putting money in their pockets through speedy and lucrative lot sales, as many would lose the income from their crops as they waited for the proceeds from those auctions. The proposition was pinned neither on predictable profits nor on steady income; rather, it was a new kind of financial arrangement in the public interest sold through the force and charisma of the president, one that happened to coincide with their own dreams of great influence.

L'Enfant's job was technically still that of a surveyor. After all, Washington had described the task of planning the city, in true American fashion, as one of sizing and shaping lots in preparation for a public offering of property. But as the delineation of lots *was* the shaping of the city, the major now felt secure in his position. Besides, subdividing these lots was going to be a great deal more complex than performing the same task would have been in a city such as Philadelphia. L'Enfant and Washington were now thinking in terms of a plan expressing a truehearted nationalism, while most of the proprietors saw a potential pile of dollars and little else. The pairing was not troubling for the president. The open-eyed marriage of ideal to interest was a theme he believed in utterly, and the successful uniting of the two was, to his mind, a superb beginning.

If L'Enfant had felt frantic before—given three weeks to formulate an idea and create a rough sketch—he was now charged with a task as enormous as any ever given to a city planner in any era. He now had two months at most to produce the design of the capital in all its complexity, to move from the concept to a fully executed city plan by which lots could be sold, streets carved out of the soil, and public buildings placed and built. If he had been granted a threefold increase in time, it had come with a hundredfold increase in expectations.

L'Enfant wrote immediately to Jefferson explaining the outcome of his conference with the president.

> I had the satisfaction to see the little I had done agreeable to his wish—and the confidence with which he has been pleased since to honor me in ordering the survey to be continued and the delineation of a grand plan for the local distribution of the city, to be done on principle conformable to the ideas which I took the liberty to hold before him.

He next requested a list of the necessary "public buildings." That list began with the Congress House and the President's House, certainly, but it would also, after additions by Washington and L'Enfant himself, come to include such structures as the federal courts, the city armories, a nondenominational "national church," and a naval station. He then asked Jefferson, so recently returned from Paris, for city plans and lots of them, specifying London,

Madrid, Paris, Amsterdam, Naples, Venice, Genoa, and Florence, along with "particular maps of any such sea ports or dock yards and arsenals as you may know to be the most complete in their improvement."

With this message to Jefferson sent, he turned his attention to Alexander Hamilton, to whom an update was apparently long overdue. In the simple act of writing to Washington's secretary of state and his secretary of the treasury during the same week, the designer found himself poised between two men who were fast coming to genuinely hate each other and whose political battles would symbolize and prefigure many of the important schisms in American thought and policy for more than two centuries to come. The difference in the letters he wrote is extraordinary and telling. The one to Jefferson was an expression of professional enthusiasm written to a government figure of artistic taste, a source able to provide important resources. The other, to Hamilton, was written as to a friend and patron of some intimacy.

> I need not assure you I shall do my best to contribute to this for besides what honor may reflect on me from the endeavor, I have to answer the confidence with which the President has been pleased to rest upon me, in directing I should delineate a grand and general plan for the local distribution of the city.

Hamilton was a dreamer too, seeing in the world great systems of cause and effect, imagining all-encompassing ways of tying the fortunes of wealthy and politically influential individuals to the needs of the federal government. He had encouraged L'Enfant's bid for the federal city commission, and reading about his friend's grand ambitions would not have alarmed Hamilton. Indeed, one unanswered and probably unanswerable question is to what degree Hamilton spurred those ambitions. In 1788, at the very height of his acclaim as Publius, semianonymous coauthor of *The Federalist* and the most indefatigable promoter of the Constitution, Hamilton had helped to make L'Enfant a rising star by putting the architect in charge of New York City's raucous ratification celebration. They were not frequent correspondents, but Hamilton was L'Enfant's patron in a far more personal way than Washington.

Hamilton had also recently asked L'Enfant to produce a set of designs for the first American coins, but those illustrations would have to wait. News was spreading that the Pennsylvania legislature had appropriated money to build a new Congress House and President's House there. This information only added an extra urgency to L'Enfant's work. To Hamilton he extolled the virtues of the federal city's location, making sure his friend understood that the idea of expanding the site and scuttling local rivalries was his own and not Jefferson's or Washington's, a claim that may or may not have been entirely true. The major ended by expressing sentiments of loyalty and obligation that seem almost filial.

> If I had not already intruded too long upon your patience I should here thank you for the good disposition the President has manifested towards me but you do me I promise that justice to rest assured I love to retrace to you whatever fate I wish to befall on me and therefore shall not weary you with useless acknowledgements for the prospect I have here.

It was a genuinely grateful, even self-effacing, sentiment, one of the few in all of L'Enfant's correspondence.

Washington wrote L'Enfant on April 4 to include the small sketch plan Jefferson had produced the month before. This was the first time L'Enfant would have seen the secretary's gridiron design for the federal city, and one might wonder if he immediately reread the draft copies of his earlier letters to Jefferson and Washington, worried that he'd insulted Jefferson by his reference to the "cool imagination" that would prefer such a simplistic pattern of streets.

That is very unlikely. L'Enfant was neither a writer of tactful prose nor an easily chastened man. A respect for his own artistic judgment, he believed, must certainly have already settled the matter. It would not have surprised L'Enfant to learn that Jefferson and most other Americans would want to follow the example of Philadelphia. That type of city was all that most everyone seemed to know on this continent, and he would not have held it against Jefferson for believing there could be no better way.

On April 10, six days later, L'Enfant received Jefferson's reply, which expressed the secretary's pleasure that "the President has left the planning of the town in such good hands"; it was accompanied by a roll of maps, depicting Frankfurt, Amsterdam, Strasbourg, Paris, Orléans, Bordeaux,

Lyon, Marseille, Turin, and Milan. "As they are connected with the notes I made in my travels and often necessary to explain them to myself," Jefferson wrote, "I will beg your care of them and to return them when no longer useful to you, leaving you absolutely free to keep them as long as useful."

L'Enfant may never have met Jefferson before they made this exchange of letters. It is difficult to imagine a world where the high and low tides of Jefferson's life and politics are not widely known—and hotly debated—but that was the world L'Enfant inhabited. The major might have associated him with the Declaration of Independence, but during the last decade of the eighteenth century that credit was reason for admiration but not yet immortality. L'Enfant might have known that Jefferson had supplied the design for the Virginia state capitol, a virtual copy of the Maison Carrée at Nîmes, one of Jefferson's small canon of favorite French buildings. But Jefferson's dramatic expansion of Monticello and his visionary plan for the University of Virginia were still years away, and neither man's correspondence contains any hint of creative friction between the two.

Jefferson was as informed about and interested in architectural matters as anyone in the United States, and he proceeded to advise L'Enfant on the design of the "public buildings" with the same mix of authority and deference one would expect from Washington himself.

> Whenever it is proposed to prepare plans for the Capitol, I should prefer the adoption of some one of the models of antiquity, which have had the approbation of thousands of years, and for the President's House I should prefer the celebrated fronts of modern buildings, which have already received the approbation of all good judges. Such are the Galerie du Louvre, the Gardes Meubles, and two fronts of the Hotel de Salm.

Jefferson's letters would have already made it clear to L'Enfant that the secretary was a tried-and-true neoclassicist. He was a devotee of Marc-Antoine Laugier's *Essay on Architecture,* the French Enlightenment's clarion call to architectural arms, a repudiation of all building forms developed after the fall of the Roman Empire. The Galerie du Louvre was Claude Perrault's massive eastern facade for that complex, the supreme example of the Sun King's own precocious allegiance to classicism. It was the most famous building front in Paris, through which L'Enfant may very well have walked on his way to his lectures and drawing classes at the Royal Academy. Ange-Jacques Gabriel's twin Garde-Meubles mirrored each other and dominated the north side of the Place Louis XV, the public square connecting the Tuileries to the Champs-Élysées. As a boy L'Enfant had watched Gabriel's great colonnades and the square beneath them emerge to transform the public face of Paris.

The search for a villain in L'Enfant's story has led some historians straight to Jefferson. According to such a reading, this and all of Jefferson's subsequent letters were simply false fronts. The theory usually assumes that Jefferson had read L'Enfant's memo of March 26 and its scathing quote— "a mere contrivance of some cool imagination"—and interpreted this as a gross impertinence aimed squarely at himself, a jab brought on by L'Enfant's disregard for Jefferson's quick sketch of a federal "town."

The best evidence, however, strongly suggests that L'Enfant wrote his memo disparaging the gridiron plan before he ever saw Jefferson's drawing; and Jefferson was hardly the only person in favor of a simpler scheme. Nor was Jefferson likely to have been ready to devote so much time and thought at this stage in clandestine opposition to a designer he barely knew. There was plenty going on in the secretary's life, and not just the lingering culture shock of his return to America six months earlier or his appointment to an administrative position he did not especially want.

In the spring of 1791 Jefferson was wrapped up in a quixotic campaign to standardize the multiple American currencies, weights, and measures under a single metric system. Also at the front of his mind was his uneasy consideration of Hamilton's second *Report on Public Credit* and an unsuccessful attempt to topple Hamilton's Bank of the United States before it could open its doors. And this is all to leave aside his prodigious correspondence, his ongoing obsession with the purchase of expensive foreign furnishings and unusual scientific objects, and, for that matter, his tendency toward migraines and other debilitating maladies.

L'Enfant and Jefferson were by all appearances embarking on a polite and even congenial correspondence, bound by their professional interest in architecture and their mutual experience of Paris. If we are to listen to the charges of plots and sabotage to come, we should also pay attention to the amicable words and spirit of collaboration now.

. . .

Through all of April and May L'Enfant was a dynamo, directing the work of his assistants, putting down stakes on the ground to mark off the sites of the public buildings, exhorting the proprietors to clear their woods, and running preliminary lines on the wide avenue connecting Congress to the President's House. Benjamin and Joseph Ellicott arrived to rejoin their brother Andrew and in the process greatly increased the surveying acumen on the site, despite the departure of Benjamin Banneker. Banneker's decision was regrettable—he brought considerable astronomical expertise to his work and was probably the only African American whose contribution to the project during L'Enfant's tenure did not come in the form of forced or underpaid manual labor—but now he left for good to tend his Baltimore County farm and to resume his authorship of the remarkable set of almanacs that would become his foremost claim to history's recognition.

L'Enfant's trunk, meanwhile, was beginning to fill with notes and preparatory sketches as he returned to his rooms each evening for the solitary portion of his work. He might have glanced into Jefferson's quiver of city plans for help with a detail here and there, but nothing indicates that he consulted them at length. L'Enfant had made that request to gain an understanding of the relationship of waterborne commerce to large cities, but most of the maps Jefferson had located for the designer's use were not of port cities. Jefferson had generously emptied his map cabinet, but L'Enfant would have found little use for the random selection he'd been provided.

Pencil and eraser in hand, he bent over his slowly emerging master drawing with a compass, rule, triangle, and other instruments close by. What he'd described to the president at the end of March had been an outline, an evocative piece of imagination, but Washington would now be expecting a document of more practical use. No matter how tiring L'Enfant's day had been, back in his rooms he needed to concentrate, all the time thinking about the growth of the city, working back and forth from plan to terrain to plan. Each square half inch of his drawing had to be stood on, measured, and experienced at full scale before it was committed to the plan.

L'Enfant wasn't the only individual interested in the emerging shape of the federal district. A brand-new seat of government, whatever other reactions it might elicit, was a great curiosity, and outsiders of many different origins and callings began to apply to the president, his planner, the commissioners, and the landowners for personal tours of the site. Too busy to personally sell the city to potential investors, L'Enfant seems to have limited himself to congressmen and other distinguished parties.

One such illustrious visitor must have provided L'Enfant with special satisfaction. John Trumbull, like L'Enfant, was a member of the Society of the Cincinnati and an artist who had come to his success after an eventful but unremarkable stop in the Continental Army. Two years younger than the major and the son of a former governor of Connecticut, Trumbull had marched on Boston with the first Connecticut regiment formed following Lexington and Concord. He'd subsequently been made one of General Washington's first aides-de-camp, partly on the strength of his family connections and partly because he'd shown himself adept at drawing fortifications—one of the skills, of course, that had once brought L'Enfant's father to the attention of the French War Ministry. Trumbull, however, soon quit the army to set up in Boston as a full-time artist—at a time when assuming such a vocation was tantamount to declaring oneself idle and rich. While the Trumbulls were hardly idle, they were certainly rich, enough so that when John finally convinced his father of his seriousness, he'd been sent to London and then to Paris to see the museum collections there and meet the best painters Europe had to offer.

During a dinner at Jefferson's Paris home, the idea for a magnificent painting of the signing of the Declaration of Independence had been hatched. While in France Trumbull had also visited L'Enfant's former Royal Academy classmate Jacques-Louis David at his instructor's studio in the Louvre. There Trumbull had viewed the completed canvases of *The Oath of the Horatii* and *Belisarius,* just days before witnessing the storming and destruction of the Bastille. In the wake of that cataclysm he'd carried letters from Lafayette to Washington across the Atlantic, and now he was consumed by his work on the *Declaration,* crisscrossing the states collecting portraits of the signers in order to attach them to the headless bodies he'd already painted into the picture. He'd collected a dozen faces during the two years in New York City between Washington's inauguration and L'Enfant's departure for Georgetown, and there L'Enfant would have had many opportunities to meet Trumbull and uncover the common threads in their young and eventful lives.

Both had served at different times in George Washington's officer corps, Trumbull directly under the general and L'Enfant by way of Steuben. Both had drawn the general's portrait, and both knew him to be an insightful and appreciative patron of their work. The connections did not end with the president. Both had been taken prisoner by the British during the war, L'Enfant in Charleston and Trumbull in London, the latter on a trumped-up charge of espionage in response to the hanging of Benedict Arnold's collaborator John André. Trumbull had volunteered to design the Cincinnati medals before the job had been given to L'Enfant. And both had been an ocean away from home upon the death of their fathers.

Most of all, though, the two were linked through their ambition: Trumbull wanted nothing in the world more than to make a name for himself to posterity through his *Declaration,* while L'Enfant had the federal city to design. In their fever pitch of desire to leave lasting artistic monuments to the great events of their era, he and L'Enfant were unique, the closest of kin.

It was May 1791, and Trumbull was passing through the Virginia coastal plain on his way back to Connecticut after foraging a few portraits in the South, including one of Henry Laurens in Charleston. L'Enfant brought Trumbull to the place he surely brought all of his visitors: Jenkins Hill, described by the painter with unfortunate brevity as "a thick wood" despite all the cutting well under way. The moment would have been worth a painting: two official iconographers of the American political experiment standing side by side and comparing notes. One was looking backward to consecrate the nation's birth, while the other was looking forward to a time when a million people might make the capital of the United States the greatest city in the most important country in the world. But in many ways they were doing the same job.

CHAPTER 6

A Plan Wholly New

Few visitors who had ever ridden the long approach to Mount Vernon possessed an architectural eye equal to that of Major L'Enfant, who bore precious cargo to George Washington's estate on a day near the end of June 1791. Not even their first meeting at Suter's had taken place with such a sense of moment: he'd met his second impossible deadline in the past three months, and now he was coming to display his first detailed, large-scale plan of the federal city.

Washington had returned to his estate a few days earlier from his belated postinaugural tour of the southern states and was anxious to learn what L'Enfant had accomplished. While the president had been dining with dignitaries and waving to the well-wishers lining the streets in Richmond, Charleston, Savannah, and numerous smaller towns, L'Enfant's frenetic activity had continued without pause. Twelve weeks of the most concentrated urban planning ever accomplished were behind him when he ferried across the Potomac and rode through Alexandria on his way to the home of the president.

Visitors to Mount Vernon on horseback entered through the estate's unassuming white wooden gate, nearly a mile west of the house. Those who recorded their first arrival at this spot often noted the neatness of the grounds: tidy fences, uncluttered earth, and agreeable cultivation, trees trimmed and kept free of understory. Beyond the gate a dirt path sloping downward into a thick wood served as a sort of foyer, and Washington had taken care to make this outdoor entry hall as gracious as the one inside his house. Regularity and dominion were the message: such a pervasive aura of domestic order on such a broad scale was almost a novelty in rough-and-tumble early America.

The immensity of the grounds, an estate that included five farms pieced together across more than eight thousand acres of property, was not possible to encompass in one glance. But once they passed through the western gate, visitors encountered an extraordinary vista. Here the line of sight carried up and over thirty-six hundred feet of rolling meadow before alighting on the center of the front of the house. In this moment a well-traveled guest would realize that the approach to Mount Vernon was like no other in the country. The vista was elongated by the corridor of flanking trees, a disarming play of distance and perspective that made the house seem larger than it was. Larger than life from afar, agreeably modest at close view: this was a decidedly Washingtonian impulse, a subtle play of form and landscape that a man with L'Enfant's sensibilities couldn't help but recognize.

The path descended through a stand of young oaks, twisting and turning into a small valley that bottomed at a winding rivulet sixty feet below the gate. Rising through another half mile of forest and grassland, visitors arrived at the estate's hourglass-shaped Bowling Green, where the earlier long vista was compressed into a more readily absorbed tableau, the house only six hundred feet away and flanked by densely planted and roughly symmetrical woods, or "Wildernesses," at either side of the central lawn. These miniature woods were an arborist's delight, populated with specimens of Spanish chestnut, tulip poplar, magnolia, catalpa, weeping willow, and spruce, all concealing a kitchen garden to the south and the greenhouse and slave quarters to the north.

The house at Mount Vernon would have seemed quaintly homemade to

Mount Vernon, by George Isham Parkyns, ca. 1804

any European with L'Enfant's artistic training and experience. While from a mile distant it appeared to be classically symmetrical, the closer one came, the more one realized that its windows were arranged on the front facade slightly askew, an unself-conscious concession to the placement of the rooms inside. The finish on the front was rusticated trompe l'oeil, wood siding covered over with sand-speckled paint, corners and edges beveled to give it the appearance of stone. Most interesting, the cupola topping the entire ensemble was perched almost, but not exactly, over the front door, missing the centerline by a seemingly whimsical total of eighteen inches.

Smartly kept yet eminently practical, well situated but not lordly: visitors accustomed to the courts of Europe tended to choose sides about Mount Vernon, either to dismiss it, their prejudice for splendor too entrenched, or, fully in the grip of the myth of the man, to become moony. Baron von Steuben, an occasional guest at Mount Vernon in the decade after the war's end, opined to Stephen Duponceau in confidence that "if Washington were not a better general than he was an architect the affairs of America would be in a very bad condition," while Duponceau managed to subscribe to a full range of interpretations, appending that the house "might be considered handsome and perhaps elegant but at present the most that can be said of it [is] that it is a modest habitation, quite in keeping with the idea we have of Cincinnatus and of those other great commanders of the Roman Republic."

Even the dwelling of George Washington, then, could be converted into a classical virtue. Major L'Enfant was hardly immune. He'd been instrumental in the creation of the Society of the Cincinnati, institutionalizing Washington's Roman associations for posterity in that order's medals and certificates. But to this paradox—the humble and majestic as one and the same—L'Enfant would have brought a very different kind of perspective from Steuben or Duponceau. For the major was in the midst of an artistic process aimed at writing that paradox into the earth so that the president could walk in it, live in it, and govern in it.

Indeed, the plan of Mount Vernon was a kind of counterweight to the Versailles of L'Enfant's youth. Both were country residences of rulers set a morning's ride away from their capital cities, and each was a place inherited from others but expanded over decades into the unmediated expression of one man's conception of his historical self. Mount Vernon, as an arrangement of structures and open spaces on the land, mattered to L'Enfant because he was designing a city for its owner. Though no official announcement had yet appeared, everyone seemed to know that the name of the city would be "Washington" if one group of people had their say, or "Washingtonopolis" should another faction prevail.

The most dramatic feature of Mount Vernon, far exceeding its house or any of its forests or farms, was the bucolic sweep of the Potomac, as picturesque here as any stretch of the Mississippi or the Seine. The relationship between the new federal city and the river running past Mount Vernon was complex and deeply meaningful to Washington because the Potomac was very much *his* river, the touchstone of so many important moments in his life. George Washington's dreams of the Potomac were powerful and primal, perhaps the only true dreams of his life. In bringing the federal city to the tidal plain of Virginia and balancing the southernmost point of its diamond on the town of Alexandria, he was coming home. At the same time he was introducing the river to the wider world and to its own potentially glorious future. He was bringing the presidency and the entire federal government to the shores of his youth.

L'Enfant certainly could not have known how many of the threads of the president's life were woven together in the Potomac; not even Washington himself quite understood its grip on his own imagination. The river that flowed serenely past Mount Vernon's steep eastern yard was not just superior scenery. It made Washington, the most practical of men, insensible and wild eyed. Much more than the command of the Continental Army or the presidency, the Potomac was his passion.

"No estate in United America is more pleasantly situated than this," he wrote. "It lies in a high, dry, and healthy country 300 miles by water from the sea on one of the finest rivers in the world." Born in a modest house built by his father a few miles downriver, Washington in the fourth year of his life moved with his family up to Epsewasson, the site on which perched the unassuming single-story home that would grow over three decades to become the Mount Vernon of L'Enfant's visit. Here, eventually, Washington became familiar with the day-to-day exigencies of the water: swimming from one shore to the other, handling the boats, and observing the particular nature of river commerce. He came to an understanding of tides and the ways the river behaved in good and bad weather. He learned to row with and against currents, and with each passing year he believed more strongly in the Potomac's inexorability.

At sixteen Washington became a regular visitor three miles south of Mount Vernon at the estate of the all-powerful Fairfaxes, where he became enraptured of Sally Cary Fairfax, two years his senior and married to one of his best friends. For the rest of his life Washington recalled the sumptuous Fairfax mansion perched high over the Potomac, called Belvoir—"beautiful to see" in French—as the font of his own aspirations. In 1749 Washington assisted his older brother Lawrence and the Fairfaxes in the survey that laid out Alexandria, the river port he would come to think of as his hometown. In 1753 Lawrence succumbed to tuberculosis, and in 1761 Lawrence's widow passed away, leaving Mount Vernon to Washington. Suddenly the young colonel, fresh off his troubles during the French and Indian War and newly married to the wealthy widow Martha Dandridge Custis, owned a substantial piece of shoreline and was on his way to becoming one of the region's wealthiest and best-known men.

Soon he had started to imagine what might happen to the region's economy and his own fortunes if Alexandria and Georgetown continued to prosper, if the number of sailing ships gliding past his windows and loaded with goods and men continued to increase. In June 1770, when the boy Pierre Charles L'Enfant had not yet entered the Royal Academy of Painting and Sculpture in Paris as a student of his father, Washington was introduced to a business proposition that he would doggedly pursue for the rest of his life. Thomas Johnson, an entrepreneurial lawyer and future governor of Maryland, came to the strapping former regimental colonel to ask for Virginia's help in a speculative subscription scheme based on improving the commercial possibilities of the Potomac. Investors in the Potomac Navigation Company, explained Johnson, would help the two colonies pay to clear the river, lock it, dam it, reroute it, and portage it, all in order to make it a lucrative shipping lane, their public shares reimbursed out of tolls and taxes.

Washington responded to this overture one month later with a private letter whose every effusive word L'Enfant would have understood perfectly. The president's writing about the Potomac was like almost no other surviving prose of his: it was clearer and more evocative, more prolix and full of emotion—or at least containing emotion—and even sometimes dappled with metaphor and a kind of proprietary pride. Only for this river would Washington use five words where one would do; only the Potomac would the president so relentlessly *endorse.*

> There is the strongest speculative proof in the world of the immense advantages which Virginia and Maryland might derive (and at a very small comparative expense) by making [the] Potomac the channel of commerce between Great Britain and that immense territory tract of country which is unfolding to our view—the advantages of which are too great and too obvious, I should think, to become the subject of serious debate.

Washington believed that the river's potential for commerce was unlimited and envisioned the entire enterprise *en grand.* As he told Johnson, "I am inclined to think that, if you were to exhibit your scheme to the public upon a more extensive plan than the one now printed, it would meet with a more general approbation; for so long as it is considered as a partial scheme so long will it be partially attended to.

"A more enlarged plan," Washington added, would provide "a means of becoming the channel of conveyance of the extensive and valuable trade of a rising empire." He was willing to wager a good part of his wealth and reputation on the success of the Potomac Navigation Company and on his belief that the river would inevitably become the nation's great trade route between the Mississippi River and the Atlantic Ocean. The progress eastward from the Ohio River to the Potomac was simple, to his mind, though in practice it would have required a series of mind-bending and backbreaking portages through the mountainous country that now comprises West Virginia and southwestern Pennsylvania, then down through an interminable series of locks to the junction of the Eastern Branch. The upriver journey required technology that did not yet exist, but what were Americans if not inventive?

Such a route needed a magnificent port of entry, and with his selection of the federal city site Washington hoped to personally ensure one.

> There is such an intimate connection in political and pecuniary considerations between the federal district and the inland navigation of the Potomac, that no exertions, in my opinion, should be dispensed with to accomplish the latter. For, in proportion as this advances, the city will be benefited. Public and private motives therefore combine to hasten this work.

At this spot just above Alexandria and just below where the tidewater met the fall line—where oceangoing trade would meet vessels from the interior—the country's greatest commercial center would blossom. And finally there was an ideological component to his plans.

> The opening of the navigation of [the] Potomac is, perhaps, a work of more political than commercial consequence, as it will be one of the grandest chains for preserving the federal union. The western world will have free access to us, and we shall be one and the same people, whatever system of European politics may be adopted. In short, it is a work so big that the intellectual faculties cannot take it at a view.

In 1785, two years after accepting the presidency of the Society of the Cincinnati, Washington had accepted the same title in the Potomac Navigation Company. The tangled story of the federal city's residence question—its caustic north-south divisions, the famous dinner at Jefferson's home, the backroom compromises—suddenly and neatly unsnarls if we simply follow it from the president's point of view. In this reading, the arrival of the federal city on the Potomac represented the magnetic convergence of George Washington's public and private interests. To chart the story of the seat of government from its conception in 1783 to L'Enfant's arrival in Georgetown in 1791 is to see it inexorably moving closer to the plantation at Mount Vernon.

The final step in the capital's journey to the tidewater Potomac was the president's decision to ask Congress to approve an alteration of the original Residence Act, which had decreed that the federal city must be placed on the Potomac *entirely* north of the Eastern Branch. Washington, in making his selection the following year, ignored this stipulation and decided to annex the town of Alexandria as well.

> Now, therefore, in pursuance of the powers to me confided, and after duly examining and weighing the advantages and disadvantages of the several situations within the limits aforesaid, I do hereby declare and make known that the location of one part of the said district shall be found by running four lines of experiment in the following manner, that is to say: Running from the court house of Alexandria, in Virginia, due southwest half a mile, and thence a due southeast course till it shall strike Hunting Creek, to fix the beginning of the said four lines of experiment.

In mid-April 1791 a Masonic ceremony had taken place on Jones Point, a curling peninsula marking the southern tip of Alexandria. Here the members of Alexandria's lodge, led by Commissioner David Stuart but minus L'Enfant (who was not a Mason and who was, anyhow, busy elsewhere on the site), had dedicated the first of their brother Andrew Ellicott's boundary stones with applications of wine and oil, consecrating the emerging district and, in the bargain, cementing the marriage of Washington's "public and private motives." When the boom in international navigation and commerce came, all of it would pass by Washington's door on its way northward to the federal city.

L'Enfant might have been aware of the relationship between Washington's personal residence and the nation's capital, but undoubtedly he was more keenly concerned with the formal composition of the estate, the way the front of Mount Vernon communicated with an open lawn, flanked by stables, workshops, slave quarters, gardens, and all the other aspects of his thriving farms. The arrangement of buildings in landscape adjacent to important waters: this was the way the major's mind was working.

George Washington's customary manner of receiving guests was not to sit in his house and wait idly for them to arrive. Unlike almost all of his fellow Virginia estate owners, including Jefferson, he did not rely on overseers when he was present and able to make the rounds himself. When visitors arrived, they would be greeted by a servant or member of the family and often had to wait for the president to come from his farms dressed in clothes reflecting a morning or afternoon of work: a plain coat, knee breeches, and black boots. Washington would then move to his personal chambers just off the entry hall and return after a few minutes wearing a clean shirt and a plain coat and white silk stockings, his hair powdered, his face washed, once again the president. Martha or one of the other members of the household would often fill the intervening time conversing with the guests in the Passage, the central hall that passed from front to back and in which Washington conducted the daily business of his farms.

The West Parlor, just off the Passage, was where Washington generally received visitors who needed more than a moment of his time. One entered through a door frame made of Ionic pilasters into a wood-paneled room painted a deep sky blue. The fireplace here, like all those in the house, was another of the president's practical oddities, built at an angle in the corner of the room, topped by an overmantel faced with an oil painting of sailing ships. It was a room well suited to private talks on public business, and the West Parlor was the most logical location for this all-important exchange between patron and planner.

What L'Enfant laid in front of the president, to judge by his accompanying memorandum, is best described as an advanced draft of his first design, a progress plan accompanied by a set of explanations. Washington was an accomplished amateur surveyor and architect himself, but he had never been to Europe and did not own Jefferson's collection of city maps or share the major's everyday experience of living in a city of a half-million people. The president, whose greatest talent was not his ability to generate but rather to absorb, understand, and then execute, was about to learn something wholly new about the way a city might come together out of its myriad components.

L'Enfant's *parti*—that is to say, the essential diagram of his plan grasped at a glance—was simple enough: a grid overlaid with a system of public squares linked by radiating diagonal avenues. The Congress House and President's House were set on the two highest points in the territory, providing a pair of geometrical and geographical anchors for the city's road map. But side by side with these grand gestures were subtleties in the plan of the federal city. These subtleties, more than anything, were what L'Enfant needed to explain to the president. No longer making the case for the necessity of his services, he was now making the case for a great city in all its glory and in its minute particulars alike.

As always he began by discussing scale, the single determination enabling all the others. The plan presented to the president was not detailed block by block; rather, it was designed to show "the situation and distance of objects" and the geometric drama of those situations and distances. L'Enfant two months earlier had proposed that the city stretch itself to fill four thousand acres. Now, after his early summer of work, he had with the president's approval projected his plan across six thousand acres, over nine square miles. L'Enfant had not only covered these six thousand acres with lots, streets, and public reservations, but he had also devised a novel way to be sure the city would fill with *people.*

[The work] should be begun at various points equi-distant as possible from the center; not merely because settlements of this sort are likely to diffuse an equality of advantages over the whole territory allotted, and consequently to reflect benefit from an increase of the value of property, but because each of these settlements by a natural jealousy will most tend to stimulate establishments.

The finely tooled linchpin and the great conceit of his proposal, rather Jeffersonian for someone allied with Alexander Hamilton, was his "squares," those variously shaped open spaces where the city's diagonal avenues converged. The success of the plan counted on people settling these places first, and to that end he proposed that one of the open spaces be given to each of the original thirteen states and another to newly admitted Vermont. Congressmen and other high officials from each state would claim the most desirable lots on the squares themselves to create a series of impromptu embassies. Other residents and their servants would claim lots on the surrounding streets, which, in a remarkable feat of geometric precision, grew narrower as they moved farther from each square, an innovation most likely designed to decrease the amount of traffic and prices of the lots for these less influential, less wealthy residents.

How this feature of the plan might have worked in the long term is impossible to say, but in theory it was a remarkably optimistic fusion of state-centered republicanism and nation-centered Federalism. Pride of place would be imported from fourteen state capitals and fused directly into the inner workings of the federal city, invigorating its system of arteries, the presumption being that this pride would harness itself to speedily develop each of the squares. The city would start not as a pair of giant buildings looming over all subsequent development but as a series of small "towns," each with its own storefronts, its own traders, mechanics, homes, and taverns. The squares would naturally become separate self-perpetuating entities: no state, L'Enfant maintained, would want its neighborhood to fall too far behind the others, and in the meantime the scheme would ensure an immediate influx of population, as all the states would surely find a number of patriots willing to purchase nearby lots. Fourteen hamlets growing slowly together to form the seat of federal government: it was a poetic metaphor for the knitting together of the country, expressed here in line as emphatically as in words.

L'Enfant's plan abounded in squares, many more than fourteen. The others, he told Washington, would provide appropriately dignified settings for all manner of civic places and institutions: for sundry learned and fraternal societies; for a large nondenominational national church housed in a sort of American Pantheon; and for smaller churches of various religious denominations. Some would contain fountains and memorial columns, and some would be reserved for uses as yet unforeseen. Each square would be visible from the next along the city's diagonal avenues; none was more than a half mile from its nearest counterpart, a distance L'Enfant knew, probably from his study of optics at the Royal Academy, as the limit of visual comprehension.

Only now, with the growth of the outer precincts explained, did L'Enfant make his argument for Jenkins Hill as the centerpiece of the entire plan, branding it in his famous phrase "a pedestal waiting for a superstructure." Here was a promontory worth the effort, no matter how much labor would be necessary to clear the spot of its trees and vegetation and make it sufficiently level for the great federal square and the legislative chambers he planned there. A second high ground a mile and a half distant toward Georgetown, just above the Tiber Creek, was designated for "a presidential palace" in a location selected to give its tenant an "extensive view down the Potomac, with a prospect of the whole harbor and town of Alexandria." And for the president, whether or not L'Enfant articulated the point, to see Alexandria was to see a piece of home.

Future generations of observers were to become infatuated with the placement of the Capitol and the White House in constitutional equilibrium, the legislative and executive branches given perfect geometrical balance. It is a neat piece of symbolism and certainly the most popular interpretation of the plan, but it is probably wrong. L'Enfant never in all his writing about the city referred to a constitutional "separation of powers," and he made it clear from this point forward that the junction of the two buildings was less important than their respective individual relationships to Washington's beloved Potomac. "From the first settlement of the city they would stand to ages in a central point," he wrote, "facing on the grandest prospect of both branches of the Potomac with the town of Alexandria in front, seen in its full extent over many points of land projecting from the Maryland and Virginia shores in a manner as adds much to the perspective."

The imposing distance between the President's House and the Congress House L'Enfant explained with a single statement, a rationale extracted not from any founding document but developed entirely to preserve the Roman dignity that he and his fellow Continental Army officers had always attached to General Washington. "No message to nor from the President," he wrote, "is to be made without a sort of decorum." The three departments— Jefferson's State, Hamilton's Treasury, and Henry Knox's War—were "contiguous" to the President's House in a parklike arrangement to allow the chief executive ready contact with his most important advisers. The connection between president and Congress, the avenue that was later named Pennsylvania, would be a street full of social activity, interrupted midway in its progress by a grand fountain. This was to be the city's center of learning and amusement, an avenue "all along side of which may be placed play houses, rooms of assembly, academies and all such sort of places as may be attractive to the learned and afford diversion to the idle."

Thinking perhaps of the Bièvre River curving behind his childhood home, but also considering the need to move goods through the city and create a more efficient transportation link to upriver regions, L'Enfant proposed that Tiber Creek be made into the first stretch of a great through canal, bringing the water of the Potomac to the Congress House and then south out to the Eastern Branch. At the foot of Jenkins Hill it would burst forth as a grand cascade, a fountain as large and impressive—and as advantageous for the health of the city's denizens—as any in Rome or St. Petersburg.

All of this work—the grid, the overlaid avenues, the state squares, the public buildings, the fountains, the canal—surrounded and provided the setting for L'Enfant's most expansive idea, his grandest avenue in a city full of grand avenues. It was at this meeting with the president, at this stage of the design, that L'Enfant first unveiled what he called his "public walk," a "vast esplanade in the center of which, and at the point of intersection of the sight from each of the Houses, would be the most advantageous place for an equestrian statue, which with proper appendages and walks artfully managed, would produce a most grand effect."

This description is the initial entry into the historical record of what eventually became known as the National Mall, a reservation of public space that would remain the largest governmentally administered green place in America until the designation of land for New York's Central Park in 1853. "The whole will acquire new sweetness," he wrote, "being laid over the green of a field well level and made brilliant by the shade of a few trees artfully planted."

The moment when Major L'Enfant left Washington's company to accept his horse and ride back toward the estate's western gate can fairly be viewed as the very moment the federal city finally took shape. The rest of its story, full of ever-increasing human drama and pathos, is on one face simply a question of how much the city would live up to or fail this concept. And for those willing to pore through L'Enfant's various memorials, proposals, explanations, and other writings, that concept is remarkably clear and complete.

Where that design came from, however, has always been a much more difficult question to answer. Of all the guessing games surrounding L'Enfant's life—not least, why he came to America and why, given multiple chances, he couldn't head off repeated personal and professional catastrophes—the question of the sources of the federal city's plan was to become the most inscrutable and tantalizing. What were the progenitors of the City of Washington in the District of Columbia? Was the city conceived in an ecstasy of untrammeled monarchism, or were its parents respectable democratic folk at heart?

The argument and curiosity are ours, however, not George Washington's. The estate and house at Mount Vernon proved that somewhere in the president lay the soul of an architect, and he was anything but a passive observer of the process; yet the subtleties and details and especially the sources of the city plan were entirely L'Enfant's. Washington neither expected nor received more than a cursory explanation of the artistic roots of L'Enfant's work. This is a tribute to Washington's willingness to trust L'Enfant as the considerable artist he was, but it is also a documentary silence to deeply regret. One wonders if such an exchange might have been recorded had the making of the federal city commenced during the presidency of Thomas Jefferson. Although such an alternate history is entirely improbable, it is tempting to imagine. When in early April the major had asked Jefferson for plans of European harbor cities, he had been quick to clarify his motivation for doing so.

> I would reprobate the idea of imitating and that contrary of having this intention it is my wish and shall be my endeavor to delineate [in] a new and original way the plan the contrivance of which the President has left to me without any restriction soever.

This sentence was L'Enfant's first and only recorded statement of the plan's progenitors—or lack of them—and it would receive much attention in the two centuries to come. At the very least, it seems to explain why he never discussed the antecedents of his design: he was concerned with making a new place out of old models—"a plan wholly new"—much as he'd accomplished in his renovation of Federal Hall. His true interest was in leaving his own name to posterity.

We have no reason not to take L'Enfant at his word, but then he hadn't lived his life in a vacuum. It does him no disservice to follow in his footsteps and retrace the experiences and vistas of a lifetime spent in capital cities: first in Paris, then in Philadelphia and New York, and now on the raw ground of the new American seat of government. The basic gridiron lattice of his plan had hardly originated in the United States, but it had been so fervently adopted here—experienced firsthand by L'Enfant in Charleston, George-town, and Philadelphia—that it is tempting to call the federal city plan the major's homage, or at the least his accommodating nod, to the dominant mode of planning in his adopted country. Or perhaps, given L'Enfant's famous expressions of disdain for the "cool imagination" that would em-brace such a plan, we can find something devilishly symbolic in his use of a grid that he literally sliced up.

Both of these propositions, however, are too convenient. The grid underlying L'Enfant's Washington was put in place as a framework for the more dramatic elements of his plan. In the arrangement of avenues and spaces superimposed on that framework, the plan was at heart not an American *shape.* Historians of city planning classify L'Enfant's diagram as baroque: ceremonial vistas and broad avenues dramatically linking monu-

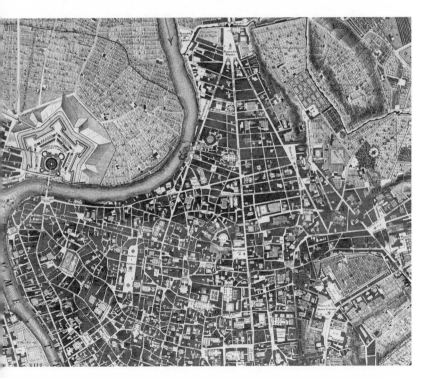

Detail from *Rome 1748,* by Giambattista Nolli

mental spaces. And the baroque owed its first allegiance not to property values or to ease of development but to the drama of the topography and its desire to make a few spots preeminent over all others.

The world's most famous example of this style and the one most obviously available to L'Enfant was Rome. The city had been virtually reincarnated two centuries earlier during the short reign of Pope Sixtus V, who granted the architect and planner Domenico Fontana broad powers to clear

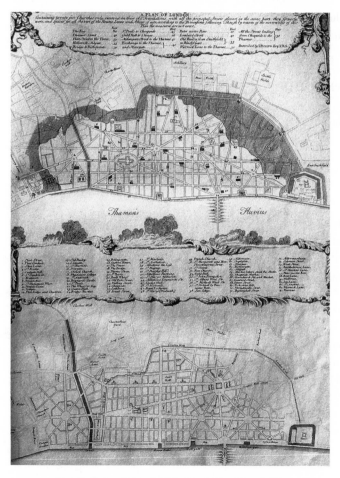

Unrealized plans for London following the Great Fire of 1666,
by John Evelyn and Christopher Wren

out public squares around seven important churches, mark those squares with obelisks, and link them by way of long and wide boulevards slicing across the city, often ignoring the street pattern underneath. It was a new way of thinking about an urban environment. Neither a commitment to Greek rectilinearity nor a resignation to medieval happenstance, the new Rome sought to use its street plan as a stage on which a small number of places were granted preeminent dramatic roles.

Rome was the most studied city of the age and had many progeny, including two important but unexecuted baroque plans for rebuilding London in the wake of the cataclysmic fire of 1666, one created by the city planner John Evelyn and the other by renowned astronomer and architect Christopher Wren. Both plans made St. Paul's Cathedral the launching point for a trio of dramatic vistas, and both sought to undo the tangle of streets that had helped the inferno to spread so quickly. Thanks to his father's mentoring—and perhaps to any time he might have spent perusing the city plans and models stashed in the Louvre—L'Enfant is not likely to have reached the age of twenty-two without having seen and digested these archetypes.

Another famous expression of the baroque was also lodged in L'Enfant's memory, of course, and critics of his plan of Washington have required only a short step to move from the American capital to the absolutist will that made Versailles possible. The Mall as viewed from the west side of the Capitol does indeed strongly recall the greensward of Versailles as viewed from the west side of the château. But this formal kinship is largely the result of decisions made not during L'Enfant's eleven months of work on the federal city but more than one hundred years later. The Washington-as-Versailles interpretation also ignores a basic difference between the two spaces: nowhere in the westward view from the château of Versailles was one able to catch sight of a single square yard of ground that a French subject could visit without the king's permission. But the Mall was designed, in a phrase that its champions would later make famous, as "a people's park," an expression of the democratic accessibility of American government.

Versailles was totalitarian, a controlled experience of stopping and starting, while the center of L'Enfant's city was a "system of movement" designed as an open invitation to all comers. Whatever physical resemblance the major's "Grand Avenue" might later have come to have with the esplanade at Versailles—especially since, contrary to L'Enfant's plan, Washington, D.C.'s

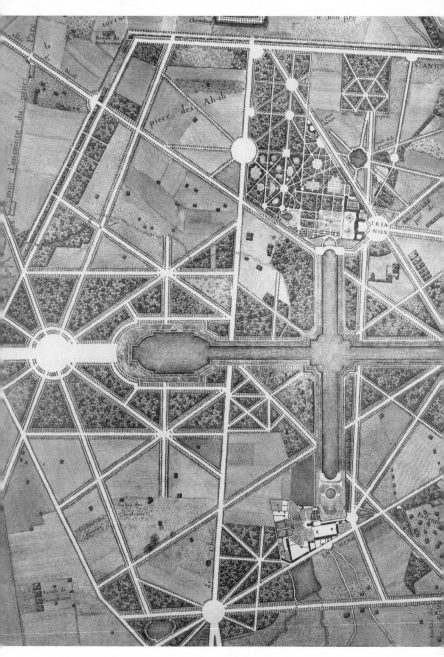

Plan de Versailles, by Jean Delagrive, 1746

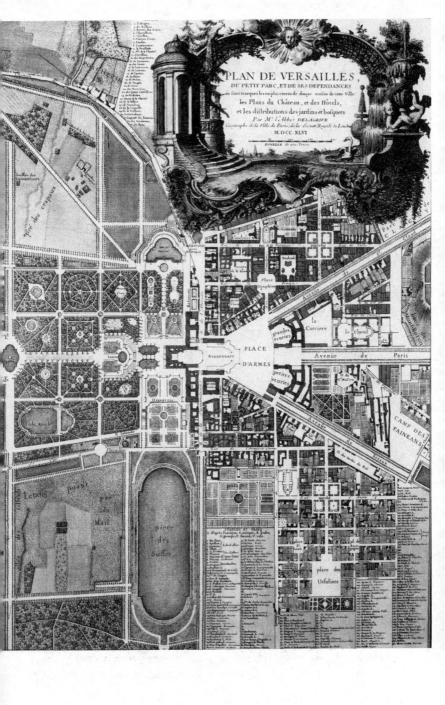

PLAN DE VERSAILLES,
DU PETIT PARC, ET DE SES DEPENDANCES
ou sont marqués les emplacemens de chaque maison de cette Ville
les Plans du Château, et des Hôtels,
et les distributions des jardins et bosquets
Par M. l'Abbé DELAGRIVE
Geographe de la Ville de Paris de la Societé Royale de Londres
M.DCC.XLVI
ECHELLE de 400. Toises

"Avenue" would never include a roadway slicing down its center—it was at the moment of its creation much more the civic cousin of the Tuileries Gardens and especially of the Champs-Élysées, another grand avenue built not for repose but for kinetic activity, a popular favorite with rich and poor, with residents and provincial visitors alike.

L'Enfant's design of the federal city can also be read as a reaction to the squalor and compression of Paris: a sensible grid overlaid with spacious avenues instead of an oppressive and unhealthy medieval template that could be opened to air and light only with great difficulty. To picture a city of one million people was out of George Washington's ken, but L'Enfant could easily imagine a city organized with geometric regularity yet remaining a growing, organic thing. For L'Enfant, a city could hold a million people and still be both sensible and beautiful.

The birth of the design of the city of Washington, like the birth of L'Enfant, may have occurred in Paris, but its ultimate expression was wholly American. At a time when the most broadly representative legislative body of France had become famous for meeting in a tennis court, the design of the American federal city granted pride of place to the Congress House and not to the President's House. Where the king's bedroom was placed on the central axis of Versailles, enshrining the rule of divine right transferred via primogeniture, here in L'Enfant's plan the home of Congress took center stage.

Architectural scholars have carefully traced these and other possible patterns of influence, while conspiracy-minded amateurs have tried gamely to explain everything by looking for Masonic symbols in the geometry of the plan. Without subscribing to any particular interpretation or posthumously initiating L'Enfant as a Freemason, this much can be said: his plan of the American capital displayed all the sophistication of the European baroque in combination with a good dose of George Washington's republican sensibilities. It also used the topography of its site to make a statement about the future of the country. Washington was a man of truly national orientation, and he could see in L'Enfant's plan an unreconstructed optimism about America.

Designer and patron believed that America was an empire such as the world had never seen, one that would reach out with a firm but benevolent hand and claim a continent for its own enlightened purposes. The early news of revolution out of France was enough to suggest that America was an empire with great symbolic reach as well. If L'Enfant's squares represent the plan's commitment to the spirit of separate governing entities made one, the best way to read the national iconography of the plan is to stand on the crest of Jenkins Hill and look over the great plain below, over the Potomac and over the Virginia shore beyond. If the vista from the President's House overlooking the southward flow of the Potomac was undeniably private— George Washington's life story and love of his home embedded in the plan— the great westward view from the front of the Capitol was an entirely public statement of American destiny.

The National Mall was designed to be a great civic meeting place, the greensward of Versailles turned on its political head, the Champs-Élysées reincarnated and renovated in the cause of democracy, a horizon held in trust for the American people. The idea may have been grandiose, but so was Major L'Enfant, the supremely confident European immigrant. The progress westward from past to future was no abstract philosophy but a very real journey he'd already made.

On June 28, 1791, one week after their meeting at Mount Vernon, George Washington and Major L'Enfant rode across the site so that the president could stand for himself on the promontories marked for the public buildings. With them rode the surveyor Andrew Ellicott, who in the wake of L'Enfant's conference at Mount Vernon was moving into a different and more subordinate role. Now that the plan had been accepted, Ellicott's survey would be conducted in service of L'Enfant's vision, and the lines would be run according to L'Enfant's directions.

Washington's purpose in making this tour of the site was to put his final imprint on the plan before L'Enfant went off to create a definitive version. The president requested that the planner eliminate a few of his diagonal avenues and their concomitant squares in order to reduce the overall reservation of less lucrative public land. Washington met with enthusiasm the idea for a great federal plaza and Congress House upon Jenkins Hill, but after riding up to the position of the President's House, he asked that L'Enfant move that building westward to higher ground. The contest here was between the longer vista down the Potomac and the greatest possible elevation, and Washington, it turned out, preferred the latter. L'Enfant had apparently struggled with this decision and had no problem making the alteration; it would fit neatly into his conception in either case, something the president seems to have understood.

The following day, June 29, in a near duplication of the scene at Suter's three months earlier, Washington gathered the proprietors together to listen to L'Enfant describe his scheme. As the president noted in his diary, "A plan was also laid before them of the city in order to convey to them a general idea of the city," and that "it was with much pleasure that a general approbation seemed to pervade the whole."

Not all of the proprietors were entirely sanguine about the work in question, though. Daniel Carroll of Duddington, the wealthiest man in the district and nephew of the commissioner also named Daniel Carroll, was building a large house south of Jenkins Hill and had already dug its foundation. Carroll of Duddington apparently asked at this meeting when he would learn if his mansion was outside or inside the plan's reservation of public land. L'Enfant told him that such a determination was impossible until the survey reached that section of the territory. Work on the house, therefore, would have to remain in a state of suspension.

Washington departed early the next morning, a little after four, for Philadelphia, but he left behind a set of detailed instructions for the commissioners. The first task at hand was to craft the newspaper advertisements for the initial sale of lots.

The President having approved the sites of ground for the public buildings to be erected in pursuance of the Act of Congress for establishing the temporary and permanent seat of government of the United States, the commissioners appointed in virtue of that act will meet at George Town on Thursday the seventeenth day of October next and proceed to sell at vendue a number of lots in the best situations in the Federal City.

The *George-Town Weekly Ledger* regularly ran more enticing notices for dry goods. The lack of quality publicity seems peculiar; perhaps the commissioners assumed that the very fact of the city's existence was enough to generate the necessary excitement. The creation of the federal district was finally under way, and nothing, it must have seemed, could be too great an obstacle to the eventual realization and prosperity of the capital. That view was shared at this moment by Washington and most of the landowners in the district, not least the always enthusiastic George Walker, who published an anonymous article in the *Maryland Journal* praising the plan's "exalted genius, elegance of taste, [and] extensive imagination."

The surge in optimism seemed to overpower almost everyone—that is, everyone except L'Enfant himself. As the crowd dispersed from Suter's onto the streets of Georgetown, the major was agitated, for the first time in real doubt as to the city's prospects. The announcement of an October lot sale, he thought, had set loose a demon that would not rest until it achieved the ruin of the entire plan.

CHAPTER 7

The Wheel to Give Motion to the Machine

The height of summer had arrived, and George Washington, Thomas Jefferson, and James Madison were convened in Philadelphia in the middle stretch of an eight-month adjournment of Congress to do some hard thinking about money. It was the only thing about which everyone would always agree: without money, the federal city was just a high-sounding set of words and an enticing collection of lines on paper with no prospect of rising. Where interested parties differed starkly was in their assessment of how the government might generate the necessary funds.

While Major L'Enfant continued to crisscross the site trying to fix everything in its place so that a fully detailed engraving of the plan could be made, the president and his advisers had been waiting in Philadelphia for their planner to pay them a visit. There they had been outlining the terms of the lot sale and a set of building regulations for the city, and they needed to see the most recent version of L'Enfant's design. On August 18 Jefferson wrote to request the major's overdue presence and to add a second, more peculiar request.

> The President had understood for some time past that you were coming on to Philadelphia and New York, and therefore has delayed mentioning to you some matters which have occurred to him . . . If you are detained by laying out the lots, you had better not await that, as a suggestion has been made here of arranging them in a particular manner, which will probably make them more convenient to the purchasers, and more profitable to the sellers. A person applied to me the other day on the subject of engraving a map of the federal territory. I observed to him that if yourself or Mr. Ellicott chose to have this done, you would have the best right to it—do either of you intend this?

L'Enfant would eventually develop the habit of carrying a selection of letters and notes and ledgers with him as he moved from place to place: not a great number and never more than a single trunk's worth, some were letters from others, some drafts or copies of his own. Most were mementos of his tenure as the designer of Washington, D.C. A few were important certificates of honor or letters of commendation, but the majority dealt with matters on which he felt he'd been wronged. No monetary value was ever assigned to them during his lifetime or afterward, but to historians interested in Washington, D.C., and its planner, they are priceless.

Many of these letters and materials, now held at the Library of Congress, bear annotations by L'Enfant: underlinings and stars and bracketed sections of text. A few are dotted with marginal notes in the faintest of script, only a sentence or two in length, serving as brief rebuttals, rhetorical arguments, and reminders. Written to and for himself alone, they often provide us our most intimate window into his state of mind. One such note was added to the end of Jefferson's otherwise unremarkable letter. Next to the name "Mr. Ellicott," L'Enfant's marginal note in fine pencil whispers an argument and an accusation back across many long years: *What right could this man have thereto?*

The major had, in fact, already engaged with a Philadelphia engraver named Narcisse Pigalle for the production of an engraved copy of his plan, but that was not his complaint. What unsettled him was Jefferson's assumption that the map of the city was not L'Enfant's exclusive property—and, by extension, his exclusive progeny. The letter seemed to indicate that Jefferson, despite his expressions of unqualified satisfaction with L'Enfant's work, did not grasp the very basic professional relationship between planner and surveyor. Did the secretary not understand that the measuring out of the city was not the design of the city? Could he not comprehend that every line, word, and marking on the plan had been made by L'Enfant and that the fruits of that labor belonged to no other person?

The explanation may have been as uncomplicated as Jefferson's ignorance of what was actually happening at the site. By the time L'Enfant headed for Philadelphia, Jefferson had not yet set foot in the federal district during the major's tenure there. L'Enfant and Ellicott may have seemed to him less like separate men with distinct tasks and more like a team, brought together by the president to move in concert for the realization of one goal. Snatching part of the credit for the plan from L'Enfant's hand and offering it to Ellicott might have been as innocent a gesture on Jefferson's part as failing to inform Georgetown's mayor of L'Enfant's arrival in advance. L'Enfant would eventually have ample reason to think of Jefferson's letter as the beginning of something shadowy and conspiratorial. But for the time being he had larger problems before him.

Jefferson was right: the major had indeed been "detained by laying out the lots." The most significant problem for L'Enfant in putting together a drawing detailed enough to set out individual lots was the pace of the main surveying work. This ancient skill had by the end of the eighteenth century reached a state of considerable technological precision, using rods and chains for taking physical measurements, plane tables and circumferentors and theodolites for determining relative angles, and sextants and zenith sectors for positioning by the heavens. But no tool available in 1791 could help Andrew Ellicott and his brothers see through trees, take exact measurements on boggy ground, or make up for a shortage of capable assistants as they worked in separate teams to finish the boundary line and to create accurate outlines on the ground indicating the many "acute angles and intersecting lines" of L'Enfant's plan.

The weather had calmed after the stormy spring, so at least Ellicott's men could work through most days. But surveying terrain that was in key sections forested meant delays while the trees were cleared. Slaves and hired hands felled trees atop Jenkins Hill and around and along the avenue connecting the Congress House to the President's House, letting the valuable lumber lie until it could be stored or sold. Ellicott and his crew were running the lines of L'Enfant's streets and squares and public spaces, but the boundaries separating private lots were the responsibilities of the proprietors, which meant more delay, as the limited number of available surveyors went from site to site.

Just before L'Enfant was to leave the federal district for Philadelphia, Ellicott's team ran the line along the east side of what would become New Jersey Avenue at the request of Daniel Carroll of Duddington, who was ever more impatient to resume raising the walls of his manor house just south of Jenkins Hill. The line struck the house, as its owner had feared. Ellicott spoke to the impatient landowner, and apparently the two of them worked out an agreement that the street would be narrowed by ten feet to save the house.

Daniel Carroll of Duddington was not dim—he did not take Ellicott's word for it. He went to find L'Enfant, but the planner had already gone north. Carroll's workmen were on the site, and he had no idea when he'd be able to get time with L'Enfant in private to work out the matter. He decided to resume work on the house and let the conflict come when it might.

If in 1791 the unbuilt federal city was an emblem of the nation's promise, if New York was beginning its ascent to the helm of American commerce, if Boston was adding new chapters to its history of intellectual ferment, if Savannah represented patrician gentility and refinement, then Philadelphia still stood as America's apex of urbanity and sophistication. The host city for the First Continental Congress in 1774 and the Constitutional Convention thirteen years later, the Pennsylvania capital was now for the third time the vigorously beating political heart of the country.

Like New York City, Philadelphia had been occupied during the War for Independence (though for a far shorter period); but it had not burned, as had New York, and so it was one of the few cities in America that retained some real architectural tradition. Its lamplit streets, many guttered with wood and paved with pebble and brick, were lined with sidewalks set off by posts and faced by two- and three-story early colonial redbrick row houses, some of which had already been home to a half-dozen generations. The docks and quays of the Delaware River overflowed with business, especially now at the height of summer, more tonnage running through this port than Boston or New York.

If it was a place to appeal to the appetite for bustle, it was also a place to slake the thirst for debate. Philadelphia was a reading town, full of libraries and bookstores and at any given time home to at least a half-dozen single-proprietor newspapers, some beginning to take sides in the battle between Hamilton's Federalists and their incipient opponents. Many were still reprinting nearly every bill before Congress in its entirety. If an American wanted to feel cosmopolitan and politically connected, in step with the tenor of the times, he or she went first to Philadelphia. It was a crossroads like no other, full of successful hotels and a famously healthy sense of self-importance.

Above all, Philadelphia was the undisputed social bastion of the country, a place where family mattered but new money was welcome, where the mix of politics, religion, and merchandising was potent and flavorful and often went on late into the night. Balls and discussion groups and small salons created the country's most vivid sense of a national gathering, a city where a well-dressed southern belle might flirt with a prim New England gentleman, where a politician in search of power might huddle with a newspaper publisher in search of influence or a shipping magnate in search of a good cigar. A Quaker might freely discuss theology with a Catholic, a Presbyterian, a Baptist, or a Jew; one could find abolitionists alongside rabid supporters of slavery, struggling shopkeepers and burgeoning western land barons, and hear a bewildering variety of tongues, including English, French, Spanish, Portuguese, Dutch, and Swedish. And the city had even, finally, joined the chase for speculative riches: the Bank of the United States on Chestnut Street was only six weeks old and already attracting investors in numbers beyond even Alexander Hamilton's considerable expectations.

The city's reservation occupied thirty-six square miles, but its populated zone filled only two, forty thousand people occupying six thousand residences pressed against the banks of the Delaware. The twelve hundred settled acres of the city were still one-fifth the size of what L'Enfant was proposing for the new seat of government, but Philadelphia was large and active enough that Jefferson could call it "the old Babylon" without too much overstatement. William Penn had originated the city a century earlier as a "holy experiment" in political and religious freedom for his fellow Quakers, but he'd made it a model of ultra-rational urban planning as well by

Plan of the City and Suburbs of Philadelphia, by A. P. Folie, 1794

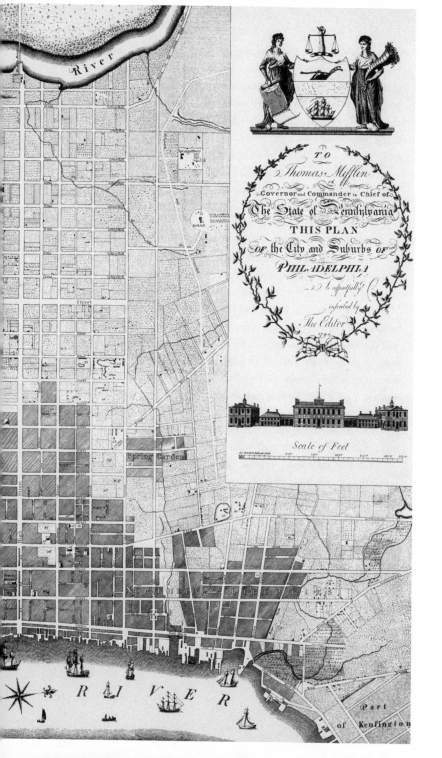

TO
Thomas Mifflin
Governor and Commander in Chief of
The State of Pennsylvania
THIS PLAN
of the City and Suburbs of
PHILADELPHIA
is respectfully
inscribed by
The Editor
1792

Scale of Feet

River

Spring Garden

NORTHERN LIBERTIES

R I V E R

Part
of Kensington

appointing three commissioners and giving them a fateful set of instructions. "Be sure to settle the figure of the town so as that the streets hereafter may be uniform down to the water from the country bounds," he wrote, a philosophy echoed in Penn's 1681 invitation to English settlement: "Every purchaser and adventurer shall, by lot, have so much land therein as will answer to the proportion which he hath bought or taken up upon rent." If L'Enfant's design was a symbolic embodiment of American empire touched by European exuberance, here in Philadelphia Quaker simplicity was etched into the ground: practical, cheap, and financially and legally transparent.

The plan of Philadelphia was easily held in mind. The layout was dominated by High Street, which cut a clean, uncompromising line down the middle of the city and connected the Delaware with the winding Schuylkill twenty-four blocks to the west. George Washington lived on the south side of this main thoroughfare, seven blocks back from the river in a house provided by Robert Morris. The national legislature met two blocks away from Washington's house in Congress Hall, the House of Representatives on the ground floor in a simple high-ceilinged room dominated by a horseshoe dais and the Senate in a smaller chamber one story up. Hamilton and his Treasury Department dominated an entire block on Third Street, while Jefferson and his small collection of State employees occupied one room in modest quarters on Eighth, near where the developed portion of the city gave way to neat, square gardens and unfinished blocks. On his arrival L'Enfant rented quarters at 112 Second Street, within sight of the water and no more than thirty minutes' walk from any other spot in the city.

Philadelphia's sense of civic pride was tied tightly to its pleasure at being the capital, now and—so it was assumed—in the future. The confidence that the seat of government would never in all of eternity move to Georgetown and vicinity went past hope to desire and became entrenched belief, so much so that the idea of a federal city somewhere down on the southern end of the Potomac seemed more and more like a fool's dream. Philadelphia acted like the capital because it believed it would always be the capital. John Trumbull had written of New York in 1790 that "all the world was assembled there." One year later it was true of Philadelphia. To this assemblage of humanity was now added Major L'Enfant, who brought with him not only the finished version of his plan but also an idea about paying for the new federal city that would make it different from all other cities in the world.

James Madison was hardly a new voice in the development of the seat of government, but to L'Enfant he was a sudden and perhaps disquieting physical presence, a diminutive man dressed in black who radiated hard, incisive thought and drew a stark contrast with the towering Washington and the rangy, infolded Jefferson. That Madison had a role in the federal city was not a surprise for many reasons, the most obvious of which was his pivotal involvement in the project since the beginning. His skill in oratorical stalling during the debates of 1789 and 1790 in L'Enfant's Federal Hall had been crucial in bringing the capital to both its current and its eventual locations. At more than one moment, in fact, only the procedural acumen of Madison had saved the possibility of a Potomac site.

But there was much that L'Enfant and Washington did not know about their companions at this meeting. Madison and Jefferson, already an inseparable team for close to a decade, were now rapidly and somewhat secretly expanding their political network in an all-out attempt to beat back the perceived villainy of Alexander Hamilton, a man Jefferson had never trusted but with whom Madison had written *The Federalist* in support of ratification of the Constitution. That goodwill had evaporated, and Madison and Hamilton were now engaged in a personal and political falling-out as absolute as any American politics would ever witness.

In May and June Madison and Jefferson had traveled together through much of New England on a botanical expedition that included a meeting with Hamilton's enemy George Clinton, the governor of New York, and another with the influential poet and journalist Philip Freneau, whom the pair successfully encouraged to come to Philadelphia to take a State Department sinecure so that he might set up a newspaper in open opposition to the Federalists. Freneau had reached the city just a few days ahead of L'Enfant to assume his clerk's position and begin the clandestine conversations with Jefferson that would result in the launch of the *National Gazette* on All Hallows' Eve.

But for all of the tensions and intrigues growing under the surface, the founders still liked to present themselves as a cohort of political men who could look ideological differences in the face and hammer those differences out through the force of personality and common cause. Though both Madison and Jefferson would soon enough turn against George Washington and later, during their presidencies, show little appreciation for Washington's conception of the federal city, they were here now to attend to the matter of getting the land sold.

With L'Enfant finally on hand, the entire group first revisited a set of building regulations that Jefferson had proposed almost a year earlier in his commentary on the Residence Act. L'Enfant and Jefferson, with their shared Parisian perspective, were Washington's two most capable advisers on this issue, and both were inclined to use the more genteel precincts of the French capital as a model of pleasing regularity. Houses, they now determined, would not be allowed to rise above a height of forty feet. Disastrous fires in New York and London had taught all of them to demand that structural walls be made of stone or brick, while most of the other regulations were typical for the time, related to setbacks, shared foundation costs, vaults, and projections into the street.

These regulations attended to, the three men turned to the plan itself. This was L'Enfant's third presentation of his design, but it was the first time that Jefferson and Madison had seen the layout of the city firsthand, and both expressed general satisfaction with the scheme. The next business was the delimiting of property boundaries so that a sale of lots could happen. That, at least, was the view of Washington, Jefferson, and Madison. But L'Enfant had grave concerns about scheduling a lot sale for October.

Three days earlier, in preparation for this meeting, L'Enfant had written another of his long and detailed memorandums. He knew what the rush to sell lots meant, and he was worried, enough so that before leaving for the meeting he had compiled a painstakingly detailed list of reasons against it. He had no procedural questions; rather, the plan and prospects of the city, as he saw it, were in enormous and immediate danger. Seven pages of text all argued one point: don't do what you're about to do.

The sale, L'Enfant began, was premature. His plan had been approved, but, he wrote, "there still remains the fulfillment of the wish to see the execution of the plan effected to the full attainment of your object." The major was eager to see the sale advertised in all the states, well and early; to skip this step meant the sale would attract only locals, those with existing equity in the federal district, in what smacked of a thinly disguised speculative opportunity for a small group of men who wouldn't improve the lots they purchased, seeking only to "engross the most of the sale." This lack of publicity, in combination with the low down payment required, a paltry 8 percent, meant that the sale would encourage only these speculators and not potential residents.

Speculation held more dangers. Why, asked L'Enfant, wouldn't an investor from Philadelphia come down and spend a little money to stall the project and be sure his lands elsewhere held their value? Anyone, for that matter, could do plenty of damage by buying lots and letting them sit, good intentions or no. L'Enfant asked for the insertion of a binding arrangement by which buyers would agree to build on their new lots.

Still another consideration was obvious to L'Enfant. Work on the new city had barely begun, and as yet the site lacked the slightest visible hint as to what it would become. The surveys weren't complete and wouldn't be complete by October. How could the commissioners expect to sell lots accurately representing the boundaries between properties without the lines drawn? Selling lots now was a formula for nothing but endless adjudication. The city did not need to be finished to attract investors, but it surely needed *something*.

"Being persuaded that money is the wheel to give motion to the machine," L'Enfant wrote in a very Hamiltonian phrase, "I shall now call your attention to advantages which may be expected from borrowing a sum on the credit of the property itself." His solution: the federal city should be financed with large loans secured against the half of the city that was already in federal hands. Such loans would provide funds for work on the roads and public squares, while at the same time each of the fourteen states could be given a group of lots surrounding its particular square, or be offered those lots cheaply, to encourage the collegial competition that was the core of L'Enfant's distributed model of development. Not only states but religious societies of all denominations could be granted lots at no charge in order to attract worshipers, "a move from which infinite advantage must result." A heterogeneous piousness and overweening state pride, two distinctly American characteristics, would provide the first fuel for the creation of this distinctly American city.

The rise in property values, L'Enfant argued yet again, would be worth the sacrifice in time. The memorandum was a plea for patience from a congenitally impatient man. His vision centered on first laying the groundwork for the purchase of lots, rather than allowing the purchase of lots to drive all subsequent decisions. In addition to seeding the city with state offices and churches, he wanted to create a context for commerce. This meant getting the canal completed so that men, goods, and building materials—money, in other words—could move easily into, out of, and around the site.

L'Enfant then turned to the central piece of his plan, his "Grand Avenue."

> The making of the public walk from under the Federal House to the Potomac and connected with the palace . . . will be productive of equal advantages with the foregoing as it will give to the city from the very beginning a superior charm over most of those in the world as it will likewise be an improvement over all in point of convenience of distribution.

The key was to begin constructing the city with this great "public walk," a kind of Greek agora and European garden park at the same time. If it were finished before lot sales took place and finished well, he argued, such a public reservation would lend an ease and magnificence to the city that no other city in America and very few in the world could match. His thinking anticipated the wild popularity of urban interruptions such as Central Park and represented a devotion to the made landscape a century before the professional denotation "landscape architect" would finally replace the less appropriate "gardener."

The major understood that much of what he was proposing would seem unconventional or even impossible to his audience. These methods, "so out of the ordinary for developing a town," he wrote, probably would not gain the approval of many interested parties. He was not naïve as to the reason—"as it may effect public speculation in public property many will decide against the idea"—but L'Enfant was convinced that this was the best way and indeed the only way to go forward. To use lot sales simply as a source of funding for first expenses would be to cripple the capital from the very beginning.

This was an extraordinary meeting, attended by the president after whom the capital would be named, the first two presidents to spend their entire terms in office as its residents, and the visionary planner who could see not only its shape but its future as if he were reading the finished script of the next one hundred years. L'Enfant now was arguing for a fundamentally public city—in opposition to the motivations behind almost every other

American place—and to that end he was committed to the development of the public areas before the sale of the private. Let buyers see what they were missing, he was saying, not miss what they were seeing.

No minutes were taken. Perhaps the text of the major's memorandum was delivered to Washington at a separate moment and only outlined at the meeting, but plenty of evidence in the statements and actions that follow suggests that the greater part of L'Enfant's objections had been aired. On August 26 Jefferson and Madison were given the plan by Washington and left to huddle over it in response to "certain matters," a process including a second meeting with L'Enfant that also went undocumented. Later Jefferson would refer briefly to "the sentiments developed at the conferences here and approved by the President." Whose consensus he meant is hard to say, but it was not L'Enfant's. For the "sentiments" of the others—including Washington—were clearly to dismiss L'Enfant's entire argument.

The plan was suitable. The engraving would proceed. And on October 17, less than two months thence, the sale of lots would go on.

Jefferson and Madison hurried ahead to Georgetown to the meeting of the city commissioners scheduled for September 8. The best evidence that L'Enfant's objections had been aired and were under consideration is a list of questions posed to the commissioners, some of which closely mirrored L'Enfant's own concerns. These queries have a decidedly perfunctory sound: "Will circumstances render a postponement of the sales of lots in the Federal City advisable?" The commissioners' response: "Not advisable." Would it be "necessary or prudent" to secure a large loan? The commissioners: "Doubtful."

After meeting with Jefferson and Madison, the commissioners wrote to L'Enfant, who had stayed behind in Philadelphia to attend to the engraving, to let him know that they had made several minor decisions. These were the kind of cosmetic choices that L'Enfant seems to have shown no special interest in claiming but that do so much to create the history and character of a city.

> We have agreed that the federal district shall be called "The Territory of Columbia," and the federal city "The City of Washington": the title of the map will, therefore, be "A Map of the City of Washington in the Territory of Columbia." We have also agreed the

streets be named alphabetically one way, and numerically the other; the former divided into North and South letters, the latter into East and West numbers from the Capitol.

No longer was L'Enfant engaged to create a nameless "federal city" or "seat of government." It was with this directive, and not with the Residence Act of 1790, that a place called the City of Washington in the District of Columbia was finally born.

The commissioners agreed to the proposed date of October 17 for the lot sale, providing L'Enfant with his fourth nearly impossible deadline in only five months. And this deadline came with specific instructions provided not by the president but independently by the commissioners. They instructed the major to check with a brick maker named "L'Brunt" to approve the man's bricks and make terms for their purchase, and they asked L'Enfant to indicate a new postal route on the outskirts of the city. Then, for the first time, the commissioners asked for the plan itself.

If you have no contrary directions we wish about 10,000 of the maps to be struck on the best terms, and as soon as possible, leaving what number the President pleases subject to his order; one-half the residue to be left in Philadelphia subject to our order, and the other half transmitted to us. We shall honor your order for expenses.

With this letter from the commissioners, then, events began to accelerate. In July L'Enfant had contracted Narcisse Pigalle to deliver several copies of the plan in time for the lot sale, but Pigalle had thus far failed to do so, blaming the tardy delivery of the copper plate onto which the engraving was to be carved. Copper plates large enough, smooth enough, and malleable enough to properly take the impression of an engraver's stylus required time to produce, but Pigalle seems to have led L'Enfant to believe that everything was on track, perhaps out of fear of losing the high-profile job. Publicity for the sale had been slack, as L'Enfant had feared, and by the beginning of October only a handful of newspapers had run notices. No one was sure just how many lots would land on the auction block. By October 17, Andrew Ellicott had accurately platted only a few acres northwest of the President's House; after returning half of this property to the proprietors, per the original agreement, the commissioners were left with about forty fully surveyed lots to sell. Ellicott, like L'Enfant, had argued for first laying out squares far from the public buildings to discourage speculators, but the commissioners paid him no more heed than they had their planner. In no way were the commissioners prepared for any kind of impressive lot sale, but they were bound by their notices to go ahead.

PROCLAMATION

OCTOBER 17, 1791

The President of the United States doth hereby order and direct that the sale of lots in the City of Washington to commence this day be of such lots as the commissioners or any two of them shall think proper—that the same sale shall be under their direction and on the terms they shall publish.

The day of the lot sale dawned with the return of miserable weather. More than one resident of Georgetown would record the early-arriving blast of snow and sleet as the worst storm the town had experienced in its forty-two years; whether or not this was literally true, many potential buyers doubtless skipped the auction because of impassable roads. The idea all along had been to hold the sale on the very ground of those lots that Ellicott had already divided, as a way of demonstrating firsthand some kind of progress and evoking the drama of the landscape. It was an idea L'Enfant favored, as investors on the site would purchase physical property and not abstract, entirely speculative lot numbers. The rain, never his friend, was doing him no favors now.

In the absence of an on-site auction, the crowd of bidders and observers retired to Suter's. No official records were kept beyond financial tallies, but plenty was written and said afterward. After the initial proclamation was read, another was introduced setting out the lot-improvement and building regulations. Missing from the realized version was L'Enfant's demand that buyers be required to build on their lots within a certain time frame. The door was now wide open for pure speculation.

Washington, Jefferson, and Madison were present for the reading of these proclamations but for almost nothing else. Their conspicuous departure left a dramatically different mix of authority at the site. The three men left on the first afternoon of the sale for the reconvening of Congress in

Philadelphia only six days thence, leaving behind the French minister Jean Baptiste Ternant, whose presence L'Enfant surely appreciated. The major knew Ternant well from their coincidental attachment to Baron von Steuben at Valley Forge and from the minister's time as a colonel under Nathanael Greene in the southern campaign of the War for Independence, when he had visited L'Enfant in Charleston both before and after his capture by the British. Ternant was preoccupied with slave uprisings in the West Indies and probably appreciated the chance to share a few reminiscences in his native tongue with an old revolutionary acquaintance.

Pigalle's failure to deliver an engraving on time was troublesome enough, but Washington's hasty departure was a stroke of impossibly bad luck. The president, who had assumed all along that he would be available and present for the entire lot sale, had simply misread Congress's calendar. He had calculated the "fourth Friday of October," designated as the opening of Congress for the fall, as the thirtieth instead of the twenty-third, a wildly uncharacteristic lapse that was to have awful consequences for L'Enfant. Had the date of the lot sale been arranged properly so that the president could be present, many troubles could have been prevented.

The procedure for selling lots was simple and familiar to these men, most of whom had participated in dozens of land auctions during their professional lives. As was customary, a common room was decorated with the paraphernalia of real estate transactions, prime among them a list of lots for sale and plats of those lots. A rough sketch of the city was posted, but no large-scale plan was on display. No one, least of all the president himself, had made a prior request for the display of L'Enfant's large plan. The forty four-thousand-square-foot lots Andrew Ellicott had laid out represented a minuscule fraction of the land that would eventually go up for sale, though all the evidence suggests that Ellicott had worked unceasingly and that this was the best anyone could reasonably have hoped for. L'Enfant stood by to provide verbal descriptions of how these plats fit into the overall scheme.

The auction soon became a study in disarray. Some men were present to buy, some to gawk, and some possibly to scuttle things: Washington himself later referred to rumors floating around Georgetown on the day of the sale that Congress would never come to the Potomac. So many bidders wanted to talk about lots other than those Ellicott had platted that, at one point early in the sale, the commissioners asked L'Enfant to go to his rooms and return with his draft of the full-scale plan. He refused their request, but quietly. Neither the commissioners nor L'Enfant saw any benefit in quarreling before the potential buyers, and the matter was dropped. By the third day no one else was coming through the door, no local proprietors deciding to reinvest in their territories, no shadowy representatives from distant and wealthy purchasers. Though the sale could have gone on as long as there were interested parties, the fiction of an auction without bids could not continue.

In three days' time thirty-five lots had sold for prices ranging from about $150 to $400, for a total of a little over $7,000. The largest buyer was a former Continental officer and member of the Society of the Cincinnati named Jacob Welsh, who bought five lots for Philadelphia businessman Samuel Blodget. James Gilchrist, also of Philadelphia, spent over $1,000 for four lots, while Nicholas Kirby of Baltimore spent half that amount for three. Most other buyers were locals or relations of locals and bought single lots. Probably in a show of confidence and good faith, L'Enfant had put his name onto this list by purchasing for himself a premium lot near the President's House on the second day of the sale, paying one quarter of the price down. L'Enfant also arranged for a proxy bidder to successfully procure Tobias Lear his lot, a southern exposure on the great connecting avenue now named Pennsylvania.

It was difficult in the immediate aftermath of the sale to make out what had really happened. It was a disaster; it was not a disaster. It had exposed the entire project as a sham; it had proven the project's viability. The average sale price represented a staggering increase over the previous top value of $50 an acre, but only thirty-one lots had sold to private individuals, almost all of them on credit. And the credit terms—8 percent down—were generous to say the least. What money the federal city made was mostly in the form of promises for payment. More troubling yet, the commissioners themselves had bought four of the lots to raise the auction price. These were not "real sales" because the commissioners were not bound to follow through with payment.

The outcome was exactly as L'Enfant had foretold in his meeting with Washington, Jefferson, and Madison. Yet he came away from the sale somewhat gratified. In his letter of October 19 to Tobias Lear immediately after the sale, L'Enfant was reasonably happy insofar as the case for a large loan had only been bolstered.

L'Enfant's receipt for his purchase of lot number 30, Washington, D.C., October 1791

As far as the sale has gone it has been middling good considering the excessive badness of the weather which much lessened the concurrences, but however pretty large may be the sum it will procure, I cannot say I am otherwise pleased with it but in as much as it set the business in a proper train and will undoubtedly give the whole property a value—as is essential to facilitate a loan being made adequate to the work in contemplation.

In this opinion L'Enfant was supported by George Walker and most of the other proprietors, who were becoming convinced that L'Enfant's way of doing things afforded them the best chance of making large profits and achieving long-term success, while the commissioners were intent on moving everything along in small, more certain steps no matter what might become of the landowners' expansive hopes. L'Enfant was anxious now to return to Philadelphia and supervise the production of an accurate engraving that could be properly displayed as a way to attract the large loan he knew was necessary.

In the meantime, though, his troubles suddenly escalated, without his knowledge. After ten days' consideration the commissioners arrived at the conclusion that the sale had been a complete failure and that the sole cause of this failure was Major L'Enfant.

The commissioners' first two communications to Washington after the sale were pessimistic but did not single out the designer as a primary reason for the troubles. David Stuart had written privately to the president on the second day of the sale bemoaning the weather and the inability to conduct the auction on the ground, but he hadn't mentioned L'Enfant. The sale complete, the commissioners met on October 21 to go over the results, and at this meeting they began to think more intently about the planner, writing somewhat cryptically that "from several intimations we consider the business as resting more on us than heretofore; this is an additional motive for us to wish a clear understanding of the terms on which Major L'Enfant renders his assistance."

The "terms" they wished to understand here were in part financial, as the letter continued by proposing that L'Enfant be put on a salary of about $2,500. It was now seven months since the work had begun, but this letter marked the first discussion of pay. It was clearly not an effort to recognize the designer's contribution. The commissioners knew, as did L'Enfant, that once they paid a man, they could better control him. He'd taken no money nor asked for any to this point, and he had spent a great deal of his own in hiring and providing for workmen. To accept a salary might, at the very least, make it easier for others to diminish the expected reimbursement for those expenses at the project's end. At the most it might lead the commissioners to claim the final outcome of L'Enfant's work—the plan itself—for themselves.

Still, the commissioners did not mention the withholding of the map, and never did L'Enfant think of his decision to withhold it as a mistake or even a provocation. His motives, whatever they were, had gone well beyond intransigence or truculence. He was refusing to let go of his hope for a loan, and it was this difference in philosophy that was really creating the fissures, not a sale whose middling results were rather obviously attributable to the weather. The commissioners were acting exactly as their meeting with Jefferson and Madison had established they must act—the city must pay for itself each step of the way, the speed and scope of its rising always proportionate to the cash they generated. They'd been told that the federal government should not go into debt to build the capital, while L'Enfant, despite lacking the power to do anything about it, still believed exactly the opposite.

L'Enfant had another reason for considering himself blameless. If potential buyers had asked for a plan, he believed, it was his plan to provide and no one else's. No less an authority than Jefferson had supported this right. The plan was not a communal document; it was a piece of work produced exclusively and at great pains by him. The city was nothing without his expertise and vision, and he believed it was not his role to retrieve and display a plan that was still inexactly matching site to ground. His refusal, he held, had been his right as the city's sole planner, as only he could say with authority when the drawing was ready.

L'Enfant felt that to let people set their own hierarchy of desirable lots based on a crude impression of the placement of public buildings was folly at a stage when the territory was still undergoing so much surveying and when the untutored eye might jump to ridiculous assumptions or fail to understand that the plan was not just a collection of lines on paper but the visual representation of an entire chronology of settlement and development. His greatest fear was that the most important lands would be bought, held, and not developed, a sequence that would destroy his distributed system and render all of his work pointless. The commissioners essentially ignored this aspect of L'Enfant's vision, either from a disbelief in its practicability or from their inability to understand what the planner was talking about.

Only on October 29, ten days after the close of the sale and six days after the commissioners' previous letter, did Stuart write to Washington complaining of L'Enfant's refusal to share the plan and blaming the poor sale solely on that decision. Stuart's letter no longer exists, but Washington's response makes clear that the accusation had been forcefully made. Washington wrote back to Stuart to express a guarded confidence in the city's prospects and to defend L'Enfant's temperament. The president's letter is a curious mix of condemnation and defense, and seems to allude to many letters and conversations that have gone unrecorded.

> It is much to be regretted—however common the case is—that men who possess talents which fit them for particular purposes should almost invariably be under the influence of untoward dispositions or are sottish idle or possessed of some disqualification by which they plague all those with whom they are concerned . . .
>
> Since my first knowledge of [L'Enfant's] abilities in the line of his profession, I have received him not only as a scientific man, but

one who added considerable taste to his professional knowledge; and that, for such employment as he is now engaged in, for projecting public works, and carrying them into effect, he was better qualified than any one who had come within my knowledge in this country, or indeed in any other, the probability of obtaining whom could be counted upon.

I had no doubt, at the same time, that this was the light in which he considered himself, and, of course, that he would be so tenacious of his plans as to conceive that they would be marred if they underwent any change or alteration; but I did not suppose that he would have interfered further in the mode of selling the lots than by giving an opinion with his reasons in support of it.

Washington's letter did not equivocate. It was unsparing and unsentimental, giving L'Enfant neither more nor less than his due. It expressed an assessment that the president would hold on to through difficult times to come, and in the meantime its dissection of the artistic temperament—a temperament nearly absent from all of Washington's experience of the pragmatic, commerce-minded United States—was remarkably perceptive and objective.

The comments also illustrate one of the best and most American things about Washington: that he did his utmost to evaluate people in terms of their unique skills and not their upbringing, manners, or politics. But by "suppos[ing]" that L'Enfant would not "have interfered further in the mode of selling the lots than by giving an opinion with his reasons in support of it," he misread his planner. He seems to have failed to calibrate L'Enfant's sense of subordination or to realize that L'Enfant's greatest loyalty was not to anyone or anything other than the plan itself.

L'Enfant, of course, had his own view of the affair, one that required no one's forgiveness of his "artistic temperament." He had finished seven months of exhausting work to imagine the city in great detail, the greater part of which the commissioners could not comprehend. L'Enfant had at his back his studies with his father as well as his academy training, many years of the finest artistic preparation, while no one else on the site had had so much as a single minute. He also had a track record of perseverance in important public works, to which Washington and Alexander Hamilton could attest.

Ultimately his view was simple. He'd given his reasons for delaying the lot sale and had seen his opinion ignored. He had participated in an auction he knew would go nowhere, and he had withheld a plan that he knew was not yet accurate, without doubting for a moment that he had the authority to do so. As Washington wrote his response to David Stuart, the question at hand for the commissioners was still a matter of how to clarify relationships and bring the planner into line. No one other than L'Enfant had suggested that the project was in jeopardy, but the stakes were about to become much, much higher. L'Enfant's temperament would soon become the central issue in the making of the city.

CHAPTER 8

The Whole Leveled and Thrown to the Ground

L'Enfant had kept a vigilant watch on the bricks since March, when he'd first seen them piled beside a gaping foundation hole along the ridge of Jenkins Hill. As he measured out the great federal square he would give over to the Congress House, and as he began to plot the twelve wide avenues radiating out from the site like a massive sunburst, he understood that this mansion in the making was bound to cause trouble.

As he knew too well, the bricks, the hole, the land, and the slaves working the construction site were the property of Daniel Carroll of Duddington. Fourteen hundred acres in three roughly equal parcels—almost a fourth of the territory covered by L'Enfant's plan—belonged to Carroll, who was nearly a decade younger than the major but already in control of his generous slice of an enormous family fortune. The land on which the "paper town" of Carrollsburg had been laid out was his, as was the entire western ridge of Jenkins Hill. The expanse of these holdings made him unique, as did the significance of his surname.

The Carrolls, one of the nation's oldest and most influential families, boasted John Carroll, the bishop of Baltimore, who two years earlier had founded and begun to build the educational academy that would eventually become Georgetown University. The clan also included the only Catholic and the wealthiest signer of the Declaration of Independence—Charles Carroll, cousin to Duddington's father—and was descended from another Charles Carroll, of Ireland, who had emigrated in 1688 hoping to find a political and economic environment less dominated by British prejudices against "papists." Daniel called himself "Duddington" because his nearest relative was an uncle also named Daniel, one of the three commissioners of the federal city. This blood tie filled out the long slate of reasons, then, that L'Enfant could have chosen no worse adversary than Duddington at any stage of the proceedings.

Even without a Carroll genealogy in hand, one could see clearly that the owner of these neatly stacked bricks was a man of means who desired to build one of the largest and grandest mansions in the lands given over to the federal district. But as the major's plan of the city evolved, it had become just as obvious that this house was likely to protrude into an important public space. The scale of L'Enfant's plan was that of the Champs-Élysées and the encircling boulevards of Paris, which meant that its streets would be wide enough to encompass walkways, two double rows of elms, and carriages moving in both directions with room to spare. The diagonal avenues reached a width of 160 feet as they approached Jenkins Hill, the kind of staggering dimension that helped to turn twelve hundred of the plan's six thousand acres into roadways and that ensured that many of the buildings now standing in the district would soon find themselves in the paths of congressmen in their carriages.

Every owner of land inside the district's hundred square miles knew that Duddington had become, thanks to L'Enfant's placement of the Congress House, the most advantageously positioned man in the city. As if he needed the leg up, many might have said, for which Duddington might have felt at least some gratitude. But he did not. His fortune was secure with or without L'Enfant's intervention. For the major to challenge Daniel Carroll of Duddington over his home was to join in a symbolic battle for control over the heart of the city, and L'Enfant, though he seemed not to know it, lacked the proper weapons for the fight.

At least four different versions of the affair of Duddington Manor exist in some detail: L'Enfant's, Duddington's, the commissioners', and George Washington's. Where all of the stories agree is that the survey conducted by Andrew Ellicott in late August did show that Duddington's house protruded into one of L'Enfant's primary avenues. Also in little doubt is the basic chronology of events. What has never been resolved is the age-old legal question of exactly who said what to whom, and when, and why.

Duddington's version maintained that Ellicott, after discovering the infraction, gave him assurances that the plan of the city was "mere fancy work" and could be altered with ease. L'Enfant would have been aghast to hear it: his plan was neither fanciful nor changeable, and he had never suggested otherwise. Had the major been available on that day, he might have explained to Duddington and Ellicott and anyone else unfamiliar with the details of his scheme that his streets did not run vaguely from one general zone to another. Rather, they jogged and bent in order to carefully control lines of sight, and they were interrupted often by great civic squares that depended for their placement on the natural rise and fall of the land in combination with the rigorous and painstaking geometry of circles, diagonals, and right angles that he had built into the plan. Reconciling the landscape and his complex street pattern had taxed L'Enfant to the limit of his abilities. But he had triumphed, and now to tamper with the fruit of this labor was out of bounds, a non-negotiable petition by any man other than George Washington.

The line of the future New Jersey Avenue apparently hit Duddington's house by a negligible amount, but an adjustment of even a few feet in this spot would have necessitated an adjustment of nearly a hundred feet by the time the road met the Eastern Branch, and that kind of alteration would have wreaked havoc with the whole plan. Besides, as L'Enfant understood things, the house was Duddington's problem, not his own. He had given the man more than one warning. Duddington, in L'Enfant's telling, was only indulging an intransigent sense of self-importance. Far more obstacles than this mansion alone stood in the way; roads, farms, houses, slave shacks, woods, and fences all over the territory would have to vanish so that the city might appear. To give in to the demands of one supplicant meant that all supplicants deserved an audience, which would have meant a city design in need of constant undersigning by committee and absorbed at all moments with the arbitration of hundreds of small boundary claims. Better in that case to let every landowner begin laying out his own streets in whatever fashion he saw fit, or just plow the hills into a rectilinear grid plan, call the city Washadelphia, and be done with it.

Duddington, for his part, had agreed to wait before finishing his house, but not indefinitely, and with the major gone to Philadelphia, he decided to wait no longer. After failing to find L'Enfant that August afternoon, and without speaking to his uncle or to either of the other commissioners, he had ordered the work resumed. Much might have changed if Duddington had been able to bring the planner to the site—at the very least, George Washington might have been able to intervene earlier—but things did not play out that way, and by the time October arrived, the walls were up and the roof under way. Duddington believed in the possibilities of L'Enfant's federal city, but he believed even more in spacious quarters for his growing family: his wife, Ann, was about to give birth to another child, their fifth, and Duddington Manor was the place where all of the Carrolls would gather to watch the seat of government and their own fortune grow.

On his return to the federal district in mid-November, L'Enfant wrote to Duddington to say that the walls of his house would have to come down. The plan had been accepted in Philadelphia by the president and his advisers and was being prepared for engraving. There could be no alterations now, whatever Andrew Ellicott had or had not said. The necessity of demolition was unfortunate, but it had been Duddington's own choice to proceed without an assurance from any figure in authority—not from L'Enfant, from Washington, or from his own uncle.

The commissioners' next meeting took place on, of all dates, Friday the thirteenth. L'Enfant told David Stuart that he had written to Duddington with the news that the manor house would have to come down. As Stuart later reported the exchange, L'Enfant promised that he had written Duddington in an accommodating manner, and he felt in his pockets for the draft of the letter, only to find that he did not have it with him. Stuart answered that he had no quarrel with L'Enfant's position, provided all further action remained in abeyance until the commissioners could conduct a review and make their determination. He told the major that the commissioners would meet again the following Friday, at which time they would mediate the house dispute, in possession of both L'Enfant's letter and Duddington's defense.

In the meantime, Duddington responded to L'Enfant's letter by saying that whenever his house "should be deemed an obstruction in consequence of buildings in that part of the city, it should be taken down." This was not L'Enfant's sense of the affair. Any obstruction of the plan as drawn was an obstruction in fact, and so the planner, ignoring Stuart's instructions, responded that it would be taken down at once. Duddington appealed directly to George Washington—again bypassing the commissioners—and immediately rode off some thirty miles to Annapolis to obtain an injunction against L'Enfant's plans from the Maryland court of chancery.

On his way to Chesapeake Bay, then, is where we find Duddington on the morning of November 20, 1791, as a crew led by Benjamin Ellicott and surveying assistant Isaac Roberdeau rode up to commence the dismantling of his house. There they conferred with Duddington's own workmen, who seem to have had no problem accepting L'Enfant's authority and even offered their help in order that the materials could be saved for reuse. The "destruction" of Duddington Manor thus became a slow and polite affair, the two squads working side by side and piling the timber neatly nearby. By the end of the morning the house had been shorn of its roof; then the hands proceeded to the walls, one course of bricks at a time.

This careful demolition went on for three more days, until Duddington returned to the federal district from Annapolis bearing a summons requiring that L'Enfant appear in the Maryland court. Someone somewhere, perhaps a relative in Georgetown or a traveler moving eastward on the Bladensburg Road, told Duddington that he'd better get over to Jenkins Hill, and fast. Riding up to the sight of three months' progress undone, he confronted Roberdeau and Ellicott with his injunction and then asked to see L'Enfant, only to learn that the planner was again absent, having left once more for the sandstone quarries south of Dumfries along the Potomac, forty-five miles away.

Roberdeau and Ellicott apparently refused to acknowledge the jurisdiction of Maryland law in the federal district—a completely inaccurate legal interpretation on their part, as the Residence Act left Maryland law in force until 1800—and so Duddington headed off in high dudgeon to find the commissioners and get them to do something about what was nearly a fait accompli. Duddington was dismayed for another reason: as the commissioners later reported to Washington, "we have been much hurt at insinuations that [L'Enfant] acted by authority from you," insinuations that had to have come from men on the site. This was no misrepresentation: L'Enfant did indeed believe that he was acting in the president's name, exercising authority that, in L'Enfant's mind, was implicitly vested in the city planner.

L'Enfant was still not present when the commissioners met in emergency session and delivered a directive to Roberdeau and Ellicott on Wednesday the twenty-fifth.

> We are informed that you have been directed to pull down Mr. Carroll's house—We are sorry a measure of such magnitude and such delicacy should have been decided on without our instructions—We therefore find ourselves under the necessity of requiring you to desist.

But when Duddington returned to the building site, he could do nothing. The stop-work order in his hand meant little, as the house was once again a hole in the ground and a pile of bricks, much as L'Enfant had first seen it in March. Two days later, on Friday the twenty-seventh, Stuart and Carroll conducted their weekly meeting in an unaccustomed state of crisis, minus the often-absent Thomas Johnson, acutely conscious that a great deal more than a house was at stake.

Like Washington, they feared bad press and the advantage it would provide for opponents in Philadelphia and elsewhere to the north who were waiting for the federal city project to fall flat on its face. This fear put the commissioners in an unwieldy position, because the supremely assured planner they were suddenly trying to subdue considered those opponents irrelevant. A properly initiated city, L'Enfant believed, would bring all of these ludicrous tussles to a halt.

After the commissioners' second meeting of the week, another eighteenth-century accident of timing provided the major with what he thought was the strongest possible defense for his actions. The president's mail, as it turned out, was reaching Philadelphia a full week behind the controversy. When on the twenty-eighth Washington responded to Duddington's appeal of the twenty-first, he did so without the slightest idea that the demolition had not only begun but was essentially complete.

Washington's response to Duddington displayed his typical evenhand-edness. He began by saying that he had no interest in involving himself in the matter and referred the owner to the commissioners for the resolution of his claim. The president could not stop there, though, worried as he was about the Philadelphia newspapers and perhaps cognizant that Duddington had only one commissioner to appeal to, as Thomas Johnson was not present and Duddington's uncle Daniel Carroll had recused himself because of the obvious conflict of interest. Though it directly contradicted his instructions that the commissioners alone should arbitrate the dispute, Washington proposed a solution made of two options: first, the commissioners could finish the demolition and then move and rebuild the house the following spring at public expense out of the proceeds of lot sales, in line with the street and in conformity with the building regulations; or, second, Duddington could rebuild the house on the current foundation at his own expense and occupy it for six years, after which time it would be removed and allowance made only for the value of the walls at that time.

The president followed with a letter to L'Enfant enclosing a summary of his proposed solutions and, unaware that workers were already chipping away at Duddington's mortar, did a little paternal cajoling.

> As a similar case cannot happen again (Mr. Carroll's house having been begun before the Federal District was fixed upon) no precedent will be established by yielding a little in the present instance; and it will always be found sound policy to conciliate the good-will rather than provoke the enmity of any man, where it can be accomplished without much difficulty, inconvenience or loss.

The argument, forged of incontrovertible Washingtonian wisdom, clearly sided with L'Enfant even as it chided him for his behavior. Nowhere did Washington intimate that the house of Duddington had any intrinsic right to stand. Meanwhile, the mischances continued, messages skipping their targets and mischievously overlapping to sow confusion and distrust in every direction. The commissioners' letter reporting their meeting of the twenty-fifth, when they had issued the stop-work order, reached Washington only on the thirtieth, two days after the president's gentle admonition to L'Enfant.

Suddenly, with the commissioners' news in hand, the entire affair was before Washington. A quick glance at the post dates would have shown him that L'Enfant had received the president's caution only after all the damage to Duddington's house had been done, but the sequence of delivery must have made it all too easy to feel that L'Enfant had deliberately ignored his advice. Washington immediately conferred with Jefferson and Madison, the latter of whom was also a friend of the Carroll family, then wrote to Duddington asking him to hold off on filing suit while Jefferson drafted a letter to the commissioners and another to L'Enfant. Jefferson's draft to the planner was written to take the signature of the president, so it is impossible to know with whom the sentiments originated. But the anger was doubtless new and real and belonged to both.

> I wished you to be employed in the arrangements of the federal city. I still wish it: but only on condition that you can conduct yourself in subordination to the authority of the commissioners . . . to the laws of the land, and to the rights of its citizens.
>
> Your precipitate conduct will, it is to be apprehended, give serious alarm and produce disagreeable consequences. Having the beauty and harmony of your plan only in view, you pursue it as if every person and every thing was obliged to yield to it; whereas the commissioners have many circumstances to attend to, some of which, perhaps, may be unknown to you; which evinces, in a strong point of view, the propriety, the necessity and even the safety of your acting by their directions.

Suddenly, an ultimatum. These words, written by Jefferson and signed by Washington, made the first concrete suggestion that L'Enfant's time in the federal district might come to a premature end. But even allowing for such omens, Major L'Enfant still had ample room to see his way safely through. All of Washington's advisers on the matter of the federal city—Jefferson, Madison, and the commissioners—continued to take to heart the president's repeated conviction that L'Enfant was the only man for the job. But now the president's wishes seemed to be the only thing preventing these advisers from dismissing L'Enfant. L'Enfant correctly assumed that the shield of presidential favor still existed, but he did not realize how thin that shield was becoming.

The commissioners' letter of November 25 to Washington was both a reflection of their appreciation for L'Enfant's talents and another portent of the end of the major's work on the project.

> Anticipating your feelings on this subject, and fully apprised of the Major's fitness for the work he is employed in, we cannot forbear expressing a hope that the affair may still be so adjusted that we may not lose his services.

The discussion moved swiftly from the propriety of L'Enfant's conduct in dismantling the house to the arguments for and against his removal from the project. George Washington, now the fulcrum of the question, was trying as best he could to call forth an outcome advantageous to all parties. To the admonitory letter drafted by Jefferson, the president added a single conciliatory paragraph designed to reflect the commissioners' laudatory sentiments and to mollify the major's temper.

> I have said, and I repeat it to you again, that it is my firm belief that the gentlemen now in office have favorable dispositions towards you, and in all things reasonable and proper, will receive, and give full weight to your opinions: and ascribing to your zeal the mistakes that have happened, I persuade myself, under this explanation of matters, that nothing in future will intervene to disturb the harmony which ought to prevail in so interesting a work.

This house sticking out into the street was less prominent on L'Enfant's list of concerns than it might have been, and given everything else he was expected to be doing, this paragraph may have convinced the major that the Duddington affair was about to blow over. He now made a third trip to the Acquia quarries to negotiate for the stone there, and only after he returned from this foray on December 4 did he receive Washington's admonitory letter of the second. Rather than accept a verdict suggesting that he was in the wrong, L'Enfant wrote to the commissioners on December 6 to robustly defend his actions.

L'Enfant's letter to the commissioners may show the planner at his impolitic zenith. He began by pointing out that during the summer he had written Duddington twice on the matter of his house. Since L'Enfant felt himself to be in the right—and felt himself supported in this belief by Washington's letter to Duddington of November 28—he maintained that the entire onus of appeal had been on Duddington. The major's sense of unfairness may have been justified, but it permeated the letter to the point where he lost his senses. A writer more attuned to the idiosyncrasies of the English language and the political interconnections lodged deep in the soil of the tidewater Potomac might have set down his quill before making this next point.

"It was proper," L'Enfant wrote of the demolition, "[and] I proceeded to it of right and with as much confidence as in directing a tree to be cut down or a rock to be removed where obstructive to the operation." The major, thoroughly carried away by his conviction of the justice of his cause, then turned his self-defense into a gauntlet thrown recklessly at the feet of the commissioners: "I account how one of the gentlemen of your board close connection with Mr. Carroll of Duddington must have interested you in the event and led you to conceive the undertaking delicate and of consequence for you to determine upon."

By parsing the syntax carefully, we might see this merely as an acknowledgment of the difficult position into which all of the parties involved had been thrown by the affair of Duddington Manor. But such was not the commissioners' interpretation. The intimations of nepotism and favoritism were crystal clear to them, even if the construction of the sentence wasn't.

On this score L'Enfant was not alone. He may even have been aping the opinions of George Walker and certain other proprietors who resented Duddington's "close connection" to a commission they saw as operating mostly in support of the speculative interests of two or three of their closest and richest friends. If Walker felt that the commissioners had treated Duddington's house as a special case based only on his advantageous personal connections, L'Enfant not surprisingly agreed.

The next day the major replied to Washington with his own version of events. He did not insult the president by pretending his action had been routine, "since I find that [the house] being destroyed will in some respects oppose your paternal goodness." L'Enfant then did what he would do for no other person over the course of the entire project: he apologized. He said he was sorry that he had proceeded to the destruction of Duddington's house and even added a wish to undo the action. But he also told Washington that being "under impossibility of doing this my regret is tempered from a trust that you are sufficiently satisfied that I proceeded from principle."

L'Enfant next pointed out that an appeal to the commissioners would have been pointless, as there had been no commission present to appeal to. Thomas Johnson was still absent as he attended to his responsibilities on the high court of Maryland, while Daniel Carroll had apparently told L'Enfant in person that he would perform not as a commissioner in this case but as a legal adviser to his nephew. Although Carroll passed the test of ethics, he left L'Enfant with recourse to just one man, David Stuart. Two commissioners were legally necessary for a quorum, but this was not really L'Enfant's argument. Rather, in no instance would he consider himself subordinate to any single man other than the president himself.

By opposing himself so starkly to the commissioners, the major was initiating an acid test of Washington's patronage, pure and simple. And by doing so he'd also made clear his inability to comprehend that Washington's patronage might extend elsewhere. It may seem inconceivable that L'Enfant did not foresee the trouble he would incur by taking these actions and writing these words, but he did not.

The demolition of the house of Daniel Carroll of Duddington has been used ever since as the best evidence of L'Enfant's willfulness, of his intransigence and arrogance. But to notice his earnestness is just as important. No action in all of George Washington's experience was taken with fewer ulterior motives. What possible personal advantage could L'Enfant have hoped to gain? The Duddington incident was a means to no end but a fully realized capital—what Jefferson and Washington had called "having the beauty and harmony of your plan only in view." In ordering the destruction of Duddington Manor, L'Enfant had flaunted his authority and shown an astonishing amount of presumption. But he had also chosen the integrity of his design over every other consideration.

It was the major's ninth month on the site, yet only now did he receive any explicit statement of the working relationship between himself and the commissioners. Even during and after the lot sale L'Enfant had seemed to think of them as nothing more than a board of administrators reporting to George Washington along a different line of authority—managers and moneymen distant from the designer's necessarily broad and directorial charge. He would never bring these three very powerful and well-connected men correctly into focus, not even after his dream of watching his grand federal city grow majestically beside the Potomac died in large part because of that blindness. This failure would cost him time, money, and perhaps a portion of his right mind.

Back in September 1789, one week after L'Enfant had written to George Washington to put himself forward as designer of the capital, Congress had established the existence of a federal city commission serving at the pleasure of the president, and it had also outlined the commissioners' vaguely defined but clearly limited powers: to purchase and accept grants of land and to see to the construction of suitable federal government buildings. The Residence Act of the following year, which placed the city on the Potomac at the Eastern Branch, mentioned "such plans as the President shall approve" without giving the commissioners any role in the creation or endorsement of such.

> And be it further enacted, That the said commissioners, or any two of them, shall have power to purchase or accept such quantity of land on the eastern shore of the said river, within the said district, as the President shall deem proper for the use of the United States, and according to such plans as the President shall approve, the said commissioners, or any two of them, shall, prior to the first Monday in December, in the year one thousand eight hundred, provide suitable buildings for the accommodation of Congress, and of the President, and for the public offices of the government of the United States.

Both directives gave the choice of the commissioners to the president, and when Washington finally made his selections, he drew on his long intimacy with the area and its important men. Two of the original commissioners had a lifetime's worth of personal connections to George Washington, and all three were bound together and to the president through their common stake in the Potomac Navigation Company.

Thomas Johnson was Washington's contemporary, age fifty-nine at the time of L'Enfant's arrival, and the intersections between the two were legion. In 1770 Johnson had inflamed Washington's interest in the development of the Potomac as a commercial route to and from the West. Five years later, as a member of the Maryland delegation to the First Continental Congress, he had nominated Colonel George Washington of the Virginia regulars for the post of commander of the Continental Army. For two years during the war he served as Maryland's first governor, and in 1789 Johnson had become the second president of the Potomac Navigation Company, succeeding Washington. He owned thousands of acres up and down the river, though very few of them within the federal district itself.

Washington and Johnson were opposites in both personality and appearance. Johnson was a pit bull of a man, small and strong though not especially athletic, and he tended to speak bluntly and often on just about anything that came to his mind. He was brusque and impetuous and swore a great deal, though his warmth also found expression in an overflowing personal generosity to friends and family. Washington's reason for placing Johnson on the commission went beyond their mutual interest in the development of the Potomac. Johnson had energy and executive experience and was also an astute lawyer grounded in Maryland land law, which made him helpful in arbitrating the project's myriad and sometimes byzantine property conveyances.

David Stuart was even more closely connected to the president. A resident of tidewater Virginia since birth, he was family, married to Martha Washington's widowed daughter-in-law. He also served as an occasional physician to Washington, oversaw many of his business affairs, and was an active member of the Potomac Navigation Company. Considerably less correspondence survives between Washington and Stuart from this period than between Washington and Johnson, for the simple reason that Stuart and the president were so much more often in private conversation.

Finally, there was Duddington's uncle, Daniel Carroll of Rock Creek, who lived in Montgomery County, north of the district, on his own slave-holding plantation. Carroll had declined to take his appointment as a commissioner until March 4, 1791, when his congressional term expired, and he seemed to have doubts about the appropriateness of his service thereafter. The previous year, as a member of the Virginia delegation to Congress, he had been one of those to change his vote to support Alexander Hamilton's assumption plan, in order to place the capital city close to his own home, and that decision had cost him his next election. Carroll had spent his last weeks as a congressman trying to procure a large loan to ensure the survival of the Potomac Navigation Company, and he too owned thousands of acres along the Potomac north and south of the federal district.

Another thing the three men had in common was a manifest lack of skill or experience as designers. None was an architect or an urban planner, not even of the amateur variety. Their expertise was advancement in politics and commerce. As the president had told L'Enfant, the commissioners had "many circumstances to attend to, some of which, perhaps, may be unknown to you," but they had never been asked for comment or consultation on the design and knew next to nothing of its depth and particulars. They had met L'Enfant for the first time only in mid-April, well after his presentation of his initial ideas to Washington at the end of March.

As these three men came to fault L'Enfant for the meager returns of the lot sale and to distrust the planner's ambitions, L'Enfant had found reason to reciprocate the blame. He felt it was the commissioners and not the president who had forced the rush to announce a sale. He believed that the commissioners had pressed unreasonably for the October 17 date and that George Washington and his city had ultimately been compromised by the commissioners' unwillingness to consider the major's objections, as expressed by request of Washington and through a set of specific questions from the president and secretary of state.

The typically naïve L'Enfant may have been engaged in some scapegoating of his own, of course, but ultimately the conflict was not about withholding a drawing or even about a house blocking the line of a street. L'Enfant's distress was caused by the sudden placement of the commissioners at the very middle of an enterprise that required a sophisticated understanding of the language of line and geometry. Here, in the unwillingness of Johnson, Carroll, and Stuart to cede total control of the design to its creator, L'Enfant's professional contempt was ignited and never died. To his mind, the artist who had brought forth the design was the only person qualified to implement it, to make sure each step in its development was taken properly. Any other understanding negated the need for a plan or a planner in the first place.

In Paris, the city of L'Enfant's youth, great projects went ahead according to the will of one designer, a man trained and carefully chosen for the work at hand. When a Le Brun or Le Nôtre or Gabriel had needed to effect his designs, the permission and authority to do so had been implicit and total. No city official stopped to question the workmen clearing out the Cour Carrée of the Louvre or making room for the streets that knifed in and out of the Place Louis XV between the Tuileries and the Champs-Élysées. L'Enfant had watched these urban projects take shape and knew that the fate of an individual residence had been cause neither for delay nor for excessive thought. He took from that observation a belief that a city was bound to wither when it stopped to consider an inconvenience to any one person.

There is ample reason not to accept this philosophy at face value. In America, L'Enfant was operating in a democracy, not in a realm of absolute power; moreover, in any system the worth of a great building or a great city must be weighed against the human cost of its making. History did not assiduously record the eventual destination of the poor who were displaced from the Cour Carrée of the Louvre. But the contest for control of L'Enfant's design and the planning of Washington, D.C., never made concessions to conscience. It was all a matter of individual will, a European artist intoxicated by the majesty of his charge pitted against three men whose own very American commission was mainly concerned with the making, counting, and saving of money.

Before the Duddington affair, the president had never made it clear to L'Enfant that he was to consider himself subordinate to the commissioners. Only in late October—and in a message to Washington, not to L'Enfant—had the commissioners finally asked for a clarification of the "terms" under which the planner was to work. Only then were the terms finally drawn, and starkly. So it is sensible to ask: Where exactly did this sudden "line of demarcation" come from?

Washington forwarded L'Enfant's letter of December 7, 1791, to Jefferson with the expectation that the secretary would evaluate and report on the validity of L'Enfant's argument for removing the house. Jefferson from the start had acted as a kind of additional, overarching commissioner, fulfilling many of the same functions as Johnson, Stuart, and Carroll but from a more rarified vantage point. His contribution had so far been largely legalistic: carefully parsing the Residence Act to determine the exact rights granted the president, advising in the creation of the deeds of conveyance, and setting out the building regulations and the conditions of the lot sale. Jefferson had received his training in such contractual law under George Wythe, the preeminent legal scholar he had first encountered as a student at the College of William and Mary. This training, and Jefferson's talent with the pen, were what made John Adams so memorably declare him the obvious choice to write the Declaration of Independence, in the same way Washington had so obviously been the choice to lead the Continental Army—and, one might add, in the same way the design of the federal city had seemed to belong so naturally to L'Enfant.

Jefferson's usual tool in writing was neither Adams's cudgel nor Hamilton's scalpel but rather a sort of cool flame that could turn white hot given an appropriate occasion. Underlying his discursive and copiously intelligent prose was often a barely regulated emotionality that could make him seem like a zealot, even by the founders' standards. Such was the mode of the Declaration of Independence, especially before that document was judiciously edited by the Second Continental Congress, and of his recent unsuccessful rebuttal of Alexander Hamilton's second *Report on Public Credit.* Seen in the context of such herculean efforts, his dismissal of L'Enfant's crudely expressed defense was a minor affair, and Jefferson tossed off his judgment in a hurried prose that nonetheless was designed to inflict maximum damage on the planner's pretensions of justness. Washington had defended L'Enfant's right to demolish the house, but he had found fault with the planner's manner and timing in doing so. Jefferson, in contrast, picked apart the planner's right to take down the house in the first place.

In his "Opinion relative to the demolition of Mr. Carroll's house by Major L'Enfant, in laying out the Federal City," dated December 11, 1791, Jefferson's first and basic conclusion in favor of Duddington's position was the fact that the plan at this stage was entirely contingent. This notion, of course, would have astonished L'Enfant, who might have responded that the plan had already been shown to Washington *three times* and that in August it had been declared ready for engraving in Jefferson's very presence. To alter the plan now would destroy it by shattering its interlocking parts and would render null all that time L'Enfant had spent on the ground. Hardly an abstract sketch or a mere idea, the plan had been painstakingly put together for very specific reasons.

Jefferson's second point would have made L'Enfant's blood boil even higher, had he been privy to the logic. "Sales to individuals or partitions decide the plan as far as those sales and partitions go," wrote the secretary. "Till a sale, or partition, or deed, it is open to alteration." For L'Enfant, it was bad enough that the lot sale had gone ahead, but to suggest that the plan should follow the outcome of the sale and not vice versa was to argue that a designer was unnecessary. Jefferson, despite his words of praise for L'Enfant's scheme, could never quite abandon his preference for the rectilinear grid over any geometry that might make building lots more difficult to sell.

Jefferson continued by attacking L'Enfant at his weakest and most vulnerable point: the English language. For the major had written to Washington, saying that "there was no more necessity for applying to [the commissioners] than there is to call for their sanction in cutting down a tree." It was a typically careless and overblown metaphor in a private letter, but Jefferson sank his teeth into it as if rebutting a veteran barrister's carefully constructed summation. Even "if Major L'Enfant is right in saying he had as much authority to pull down a house as to cut down a tree," argued the secretary, "still he would feel a difference in the punishment of the law."

An equally experienced lawyer—Hamilton, say—would have noticed that Jefferson was skirting the issue. To assume the need for punishment was, after all, to assume the existence of a crime. Jefferson was "sure" that L'Enfant had received no authority to pull down houses, but neither had such authority been explicitly denied, and in fact Washington's own letter of the twenty-eighth to L'Enfant had made it clear that as far as the president was concerned, such authority *did* exist. As he'd told L'Enfant, the question was one not of right but of proper procedure and recompense. Jefferson, on the other hand, was taking all legal authority whatsoever away from L'Enfant.

Jefferson then turned mind reader. L'Enfant, he wrote, had *known* he was in the wrong but had torn down the house nonetheless simply to "gratify private resentment against Mr. Carroll." Leaving aside the question of where Jefferson could possibly have picked up this idea, other than from Duddington or the commissioners themselves, we return to what increasingly seems the real target of Jefferson's censure: Major L'Enfant's truculent personality. "The style in which he writes the justification of his act," Jefferson continued, "shows that a continuation of the same resentment renders him still unable to acquiesce under the authority from which he had been reproved."

Then, out of nowhere, Jefferson went on to concede the main point to L'Enfant.

> I do not accurately recollect the tenor of the deed; but I am pretty sure it was such as to put much more ample power into the hands of the President, and to commit to him the whole execution of whatever is to be done under the deed; and this goes particularly to the laying out the town: so that as to this, the President is certainly

authorized to draw the line of demarcation between L'Enfant and the commissioners.

In the creation of the deeds of conveyance, the authority of the commissioners and the planner had been subordinated to Washington equally. In other words, L'Enfant and the commissioners had no legal relationship except that which the president decreed. For six months now L'Enfant had been treated as an autonomous contractor placed along a line of authority with only two poles: himself and the president. Time after time Washington had huddled alone with L'Enfant to discuss the plan before going to the commissioners. To none of those conferences had Johnson, Stuart, or Carroll been invited; in none of the city's planning, until the preparation for the lot sale, had they taken a creative or even an organizational hand.

L'Enfant never in his life read Jefferson's judgment, was never even informed that Jefferson had been told to create the document that would eventually became the core of the argument against his continued employment. L'Enfant's ignorance of the forces arrayed against him often seems distressingly willful, but in this instance the fault was not his.

The denouement of the Duddington affair occurred rather strangely in the form of two letters. The first was a message from the commissioners to Jefferson. Clearly some kind of accommodation had been quickly reached that allowed the commissioners to disavow all potential legal action against L'Enfant and to give the Duddington matter no more thought: "As we are likely to get every thing happily adjusted between Mr. Carroll and him, it will be most prudent to drop all explanation." This equanimity on both sides was probably based on the news that Duddington had agreed to abandon his chancery suit, which the commissioners, especially his uncle Daniel Carroll, seemed to think of as the real crux of the matter. One week later Washington, now in possession of Jefferson's legal opinion, sent a note by messenger to the Department of State, expressing his pleasure at the sudden rapprochement: "I am very glad to find that matters, after all that has happened, stand so well between the commissioners and Major L'Enfant. I am sorry, however, to hear that the work is not in a more progressive state."

Given the heat that had so recently passed between the major and the commissioners, this pair of brief communications is almost surreal. No surviving documents reveal a summit between L'Enfant and the commissioners, but clearly something of the sort had taken place, either in person or by proxy. Meanwhile, Duddington, having dropped his chancery suit, agreed to the first of Washington's solutions: the commissioners would rebuild his house the following spring in accordance with the line of the street and at federal expense; the price tag was later calculated at £1,680, or about $5,000.

This resolution might have pleased the commissioners, but nearly all of the proprietors signed to the original deed—some of whom were even now abandoning plans for buildings destined to collide with L'Enfant's streets and avenues—erupted. Ten of them gathered at once to request the retraction of the proposed compensation for Duddington.

> Understanding that Daniel Carroll Esquire of Duddington has lodged a claim with you for the full value of his house lately taken down by order of Major L'Enfant, we have and request that you will not apply any of the money granted for the improvement of the City of Washington to the payment thereof. By this however we do not mean to reflect on Major L'Enfant's conduct, but on the contrary are

Photograph of Duddington Manor, completed in 1796 after the original house was dismantled.
Anonymous, ca. 1880

of opinion that his zeal, activity and good judgment in the affairs of the city merit the thanks of the proprietors and well deserve the approbation of the public.

This quick and unqualified support gratified L'Enfant, although he fully agreed with Washington's solution and wished for no further confrontation with Duddington. He was saved from having to choose sides by the snail's pace of the law: the proprietors next appealed to the U.S. attorney general's office, beginning a process that might not resolve for months or even years.

This development left L'Enfant free, as he saw it, to attend to the president's wish for dispatch. Washington had importuned him to get the engraving of the plan done quickly in order to put the city into "a more progressive state." Without putting too fine a point on it, Washington seems to have been providing L'Enfant an entrée back into his good graces, letting him undo or rectify perceived scenes of controversy, including his supposed scuttling of the first lot sale, the suspicions that he'd purposefully obstructed or delayed the engraving, and the destruction of Duddington Manor.

To again move forward without quibbling over these matters must have felt good, and L'Enfant's next order of business was to get back to Philadelphia to prepare the authorized version of the plan for engraving and to complete his designs of the President's House and the Congress House. Before departing, L'Enfant wanted to make sure that his assistants knew exactly what to do in his absence, and so he sat down to write out the winter work instructions. If Washington wanted things put into "a more progressive state," he reasoned, his men couldn't very well sit still for the next four months.

He wrote to the young surveyor Isaac Roberdeau, his primary assistant, telling him to proceed immediately to the quarries on Acquia Creek in order to erect a proper set of barracks and begin exporting the stone at once. L'Enfant's own charge to get on with the design and construction of the public buildings was on his mind. He would need stone and would send measurements when the drawings got that far along. If the weather became too difficult for cutting, L'Enfant said, the men could clear away the rubble. The message was clear: just don't stop working.

As for the city itself, barracks were necessary there as well, temporary housing for as many as eight hundred men, many of them slaves to be taken on loan for wages paid to their owners or itinerant laborers working for next to nothing. Four spots were to take priority: the square in front of the Congress House, the square in front of the President's House, the canal opening near the mouth of Rock Creek, and the territory between the two government buildings destined to become Pennsylvania Avenue. Another priority was the felling and removal of trees from the woods designated as public reservations. Axmen were to cut and clear these areas, laying the wood lengthwise and leaving wide alleys so that other workers could move around more easily and so that Ellicott's surveyors could obtain their lines of sight.

Apply to the commissioners for money or supplies, he told Roberdeau, but if that body was unavailable or if "in the execution of this order some delay should appear, let nothing interfere with the work; it must be pursued without interruption." George Washington was anxious to see things moving along, and so things *would* move along, with or without the commissioners. Like architects and planners through all of history, L'Enfant found that his two most pressing imperatives—to make significant progress and to satisfy the project's administrators at every step—did not easily mesh.

Whatever his virtues and sins, no truer statement could be made about L'Enfant than this: he didn't know how to leave well enough alone. In this case, he didn't know enough to get out of the federal district and let his assistants get on with fulfilling his winter instructions. Instead, he took quill in hand one more time and wrote to the commissioners regarding the second-wealthiest man in the proposed city after Daniel Carroll of Duddington. The message couldn't have made the commissioners more comfortable.

> One of the streets lately to be run being unavoidable to strike on the house of Mr. Notley Young and of course render it a nuisance in the city, I have the honor of informing you of the circumstance and to request you may adjust matters with Mr. Notley Young so as to ensure the house may be removed when necessary.

"I see no necessity at present to proceed to the removal," he added, as if the determination were still, after all that had happened with Duddington, his to make.

Covering all his bases, L'Enfant wrote the same message to George Washington. The major may well have thought he had done things properly this time around, and no immediate censure was forthcoming, but still the president must have furrowed his broad brow. Hours before his departure for Philadelphia, L'Enfant wrote yet another message to the commissioners, asking for their support of Roberdeau, who would communicate to them the details of L'Enfant's instructions. Finally, he found Benjamin Ellicott and asked him to continue to update the plan as the smaller surveys came in and to forward the fully accurate drawing to Philadelphia the moment the platting of lots was finished. These arrangements made, L'Enfant headed north on Christmas Day.

CHAPTER 9

Measures of the Most Immediate Moment

The start of 1792 seemed innocuous, even hopeful. Six weeks after the unsatisfactory lot sale, L'Enfant's plan was finally news. Publishers were still waiting for an engraving or woodcut of the design so that they might print an image of the plan, but in the meantime newspapers from New York to North Carolina were priming public interest by printing L'Enfant's textual explanations of the many core elements of the city. Reading Americans now for the first time learned some of the particulars of a project they'd only heard of.

They read of an equestrian figure of George Washington, of a column one mile east of the Congress House "from whose station all distances of places through the continent are to be calculated," of another column "to celebrate the rise of a navy," of a nondenominational national church, of five grand fountains "abundantly supplied in the driest season of the year," and of fifteen state squares—for Kentucky was now on its way into the union—

marked in grand Roman style by their own "statues, columns, obelisks, or any other ornaments." Without a drawing of L'Enfant's plan to consult, readers were left to imagine the arrangement of the "Grand Cascade," the "Public Walk" ascending to the "Federal Square," the "President's Park," and the "Grand Avenue, 400 feet in breadth and about a mile in length, bordered with gardens." People found their own faith or skepticism confirmed in these written descriptions: a shining city of monumental spaces and myriad advantages on the one hand, a boondoggle for the ages on the other. Many viewed a metropolis housing the federal government as an entirely abstract novelty and formed no opinion whatsoever.

Based in his rented rooms on Second Street, L'Enfant was busy promoting the interests of the federal city while he waited for Benjamin Ellicott to send along his elucidation of the plan. Elevations of the Congress House and the President's House were emerging from L'Enfant's drawing board, though not as quickly as some people, Washington and Jefferson included, would have preferred. John Trumbull, stopping in Philadelphia to paint a full-length portrait of Washington in military dress before returning to New York and the canvas of his *Declaration of Independence,* paid him a visit to view the early sketch work. The disappearance or destruction of these drawings makes it impossible to place L'Enfant in his proper relationship to the history of the Capitol, but Trumbull did record much later in his autobiography that the idea of the "great circular room and dome" had originated with L'Enfant.

The next lot sale had been proposed for June, a time frame to which both L'Enfant and Andrew Ellicott had reluctantly agreed. To head off a second speculative fiasco, L'Enfant was racing to find financial anchors for the public portions of the plan. He engaged in wishful conversations with Theophile Cazenove, representative of the Holland Land Company and a friend of Commissioner Carroll, about a rumor—forever dear to the major's heart—of Dutch bankers looking to invest in something so broad in scope and potentially huge in returns as the federal city. These meetings, which may have sometimes included Alexander Hamilton, were not secret, but nothing indicates they took place at the behest of anyone with the authority to negotiate debt on behalf of the federal city.

As the new year gained steam and no news to the contrary arrived in the post, L'Enfant held tight to a mental picture of the federal city site as a machine with many interlocking parts about to surge into motion. The surveying and clearing of forested areas was progressing. Once all the lines were run and indicated on the plan by Benjamin Ellicott and forwarded to L'Enfant for engraving, the planner expected that the pace of work would accelerate beyond Washington's powers of imagination. If the president wanted dispatch, he would get it, on a giant scale.

That was his view of the matter. On the site, however, a very different mood prevailed. While L'Enfant waited in Philadelphia, impatient but optimistic, his primary assistant was scratching and clawing simply to keep the project alive.

The essential fact about Isaac Roberdeau seems to have been his remarkable temperamental resemblance to Major L'Enfant. Roberdeau was so like his supervisor and mentor, in fact, that L'Enfant might well have noticed his own reflection in the face of this young man who was so anxious to please, quick to temper, and utterly convinced of the greatness of the emerging plan of the city of Washington. This confidence was not misplaced: however severe the traumas that would result from his impetuousness, Roberdeau's personal loyalty to L'Enfant and the project would exceed that shown by anyone else, by several orders of magnitude.

The Roberdeau home on Water Street in Alexandria, just one block off the Potomac, was headed by Daniel Roberdeau, a grandson of French Huguenots and an immigrant, like Alexander Hamilton, from the French West Indies. A signatory of the Articles of Confederation, he'd been present with his family in Philadelphia during the winter of 1778, while L'Enfant was there working on Steuben's Blue Book. Having amassed his wealth in timber and sugarcane, he owned a distillery at the foot of Wolfe Street, just a block from his own house. He and George Washington had been on friendly terms since their first encounters during the war and continued to pay each other the occasional social visit.

Daniel and his wife, Jane, were the parents of seven children, the oldest of whom, Isaac, had four years earlier returned from a course of study in engineering in London to continue his training in Virginia as a surveyor and astronomer. Isaac had quite naturally applied for and received work when Andrew Ellicott first arrived, but once the other Ellicotts joined their older brother in April and May, Isaac seems to have made a smooth and mutually desired transition into L'Enfant's employ. By January 1792 the two men, planner and assistant, had become fast friends, so much so that L'Enfant began to vouchsafe messages of endearment from Roberdeau to one Miss Blair of Front Street, a helping hand that would contribute to the pair's engagement and marriage.

Roberdeau had accepted L'Enfant's winter work instructions with no premonition of trouble, but just after the dawn of 1792 several things happened to draw him deep into the contest for control of the federal city. To begin with, on New Year's Day Thomas Johnson arrived in Georgetown from his home in Frederick, Maryland, bringing the three commissioners together for the first time since the lot sale in October. Johnson wished to assert his will on the project immediately, and to this end he scheduled a meeting for January 3, a Tuesday. The declaration brought Roberdeau to Georgetown, as he planned to lay before the commissioners L'Enfant's "demands for the operations of the winter" so that those operations could commence.

On his arrival in Georgetown the day before the meeting, Roberdeau ran across Johnson and Daniel Carroll and handed them L'Enfant's winter work instructions so they could give them a glance overnight. Everything seemed to be in readiness, but no meeting took place January 3. Nor did the commissioners gather on Wednesday or Thursday or even their customary Friday morning. All the while Roberdeau waited with increasing impatience and confusion. Whatever the commissioners were doing—and no explanation was given—he was not about to stay in Georgetown indefinitely. Worried that the winter work would not get off to a proper start if he were delayed another week, Roberdeau left on Friday for the Acquia quarries to fulfill L'Enfant's first instruction.

The Acquia quarries held the best easily available stone the region had to offer, a rich deposit on Brent's Island in Acquia Creek, thirty miles southwest of Jenkins Hill and accessible by way of the Potomac. The twelve-acre island had once belonged to the Fairfax family, but since the beginning of the eighteenth century the quarries had been the property of the Brents, who had been supplying stone for tomb markers and building trim ever since. Their copious reserves of "freestone," as the coarse-grained stone was called, had been used in constructing the Cape Henry lighthouse, the first on the Chesapeake Bay, and were even present in the front steps of Washington's Mount Vernon home.

L'Enfant had been in Dumfries in November, when the Duddington mess had begun to spill over, preparing to purchase two of the quarries there from the Brent family in the name of the federal government. He had closed the bargain early in December, ensuring, though he could not have known it, a supply of raw materials that would be used for the next century of building on the Capitol and White House. Now the president wanted things in motion, and so, according to L'Enfant's instructions, Roberdeau had to begin the quarrying: "The exporting of stone must be begun at once on both quarries; they must be opened at once all round the island and on the main [land], on the whole front adjoining to the creek. The stone must be taken down as it comes and of any size and in a great quantity as the time will admit."

This task was uppermost in Roberdeau's mind when, as he was leaving Alexandria on Friday, he happened upon Commissioner David Stuart coming along the road. The coincidence is not so difficult to accept, given the limited size of the world they inhabited, but the encounter was nonetheless strange and providential. For now the commissioner insisted that Roberdeau turn around and head to Georgetown for an emergency meeting that very afternoon. Stuart and Johnson had read L'Enfant's instructions and were of the opinion that the hands should be discharged until spring, resolved as they were "not to employ people at the public expense without being satisfied of the propriety and necessity of incurring that expense."

This was not what Roberdeau had expected to hear. And upon hearing it, he made a fateful choice. Inexplicably trusting that the decisions regarding winter work on the city would not be made until his return, he told Stuart that he would continue to the quarries and handle the important business there. He would be happy to meet with the commissioners the following week, he added, at which time he would present an estimate of supplies and tools necessary for the winter work and a system to best procure them, all presumably to leave them convinced "of the propriety and necessity of incurring that expense." Roberdeau left the encounter determined to satisfy the commissioners but also not to dismiss a single man without L'Enfant's orders. Stuart, meanwhile, could only stare at his back in disbelief.

Roberdeau's arrangements at the Acquia quarries took less than two days to complete, but on the return road a second chance encounter taught him that he might have paid better attention to the first. Riding his horse between Alexandria and Georgetown in the later hours of Sunday, he came across a southbound stage bearing the project's commissary, a man named Valentine Boroff, who had also assisted L'Enfant with issuing directions to the hands. In a state of high agitation, Boroff reported news that seemed hardly possible: after a single meeting and without awaiting Roberdeau or consulting L'Enfant, the commissioners had ordered all of the hands discharged. What was more, they had threatened to prosecute Roberdeau should he or any other worker touch any "public tools"—the shovels, the picks, the buildings themselves—before the spring.

Essentially, the commissioners were shutting down the federal city project for several months. As Roberdeau saw it, they had waited until L'Enfant was away in Philadelphia and his assistant thirty miles to the south before doing so—after putting him off for a week. If L'Enfant's choice to tear down Duddington's house without waiting for the commissioners' opinion had seemed willful and capricious, this action was a proportional shock in kind. Roberdeau gave Boroff his horse and sent the commissary galloping back to the city with urgent directions to tell all the hands to stay on the site. Should these men disperse, to their homes or to other itinerant work many states away, they would be very difficult to round up again.

Roberdeau took the stage back to Georgetown; he arrived in the evening and was greeted by chaos. "The commissioners had discharged the commissary, the overseers, and all the hands," he wrote to L'Enfant, adding, "And with the rest I received a written discharge."

L'Enfant's primary assistant, the man charged with personally seeing that the major's complex arrangements went forward, had been fired. By discharging the "hands," the commissioners apparently meant not only the slaves and hired laborers but almost everyone, leaving only L'Enfant and Andrew Ellicott's surveying crew on the job. With one unilateral directive, they had returned the federal city to the state it had occupied at the end of March 1791, the previous year, before a single street had been staked out, a single spade's worth of earth dug.

Roberdeau reacted to the commissioners with an outpouring of remarkably L'Enfantian emotion.

The agitation I was thrown into by this movement was inconceivably great. I rushed into the commissioners' apartment and vindicated my conduct most strenuously as acting under your orders, which to me are sufficient. Unfortunately I was thrown off my guard and insulted them in a public and indecent manner. This treatment from a young man to persons more advanced in life was inexcusable, particularly as Governor Johnson was peculiarly aroused.

If there was one person in the states of Virginia and Maryland, much less on the federal city commission, who would have not received such an outburst with equanimity, it was Thomas Johnson, a fireplug of warm and close emotions whose arrival on the site had precipitated the commissioners' preemptive actions. Roberdeau was audacious, setting himself against three old and trusted associates of the president of the United States; but, then, he was a true believer in the prospects of L'Enfant's capital, as well as the son of an accomplished public figure.

But Roberdeau also understood at once that he had crossed a line, and in the evening he apologized to the commissioners one by one. The three men, including the volatile Johnson, apparently accepted these apologies with some grace and asked Roberdeau to meet with them in the morning. Mystifyingly, Roberdeau took this as a sign of their impending capitulation and sent another note to Philadelphia telling L'Enfant that he expected to see the commissioners' "late resolutions put aside." If not, he continued, he would do everything he could to keep the hands in place and would, he wrote prophetically, "be answerable for the consequences.

"The country already rings with the idea that all the hands are to be discharged," Roberdeau added. These men were on contracts, doing piecework; they had counted on what meager income might be in the offing and were now miles from any other source of similarly steady employment. The commissioners, they knew, were accustomed to using physical labor as a highly disposable commodity and would have few concerns about the prospects of the men cut loose from a project they must have imagined would keep them occupied for years.

The morning after his outburst Roberdeau laid before the commissioners a conciliatory letter he had written the night before. He presented L'Enfant's plans for the winter and extolled the quality of the newly purchased public quarries at Acquia. He emphasized L'Enfant's instructions to erect barracks now in preparation for spring, because if they did not use the colder months for preparation, they would be unable to use the spring for much at all. In addition to gathering workers, L'Enfant and his assistants had established accounts with willing suppliers who were already providing goods. Many tons of dirt had to be moved out of the foundation hole of the Congress House rapidly, and so a skilled maker of spades, shovels, and axes was necessary. To that end Roberdeau supplied the promised list of tools and recommended the engagement of a blacksmith, adding to the pile of debts that he and L'Enfant were incurring in their assumption that someone would reimburse them generously in the end.

So far little in Roberdeau's letter had given the commissioners reason for alarm; they might well have viewed L'Enfant's plans for the winter as nothing more than a set of suggestions best ignored. But then Roberdeau closed his note with a sentence that even the major himself, a master of the poorly considered phrase, might have constructed a bit differently.

If all the hands are discharged, the wood which was been for the barracks will be stolen or burnt, and before the spring operations commence the better part of the stakes, which at present are the only marks in the city, will be thrown down and destroyed.

Nothing in Roberdeau's character or conduct for the rest of his life suggests that this remark was anything except an expression of exasperation and dismay. But the commissioners immediately concluded that Roberdeau's references to theft, arson, and vandalism constituted a triple threat of sabotage.

At nearly the same moment, Roberdeau received a note instructing him to return to Andrew Ellicott's employ. Thinking they now had a contrite and malleable young man in their hands, the commissioners had drafted a notice hiring Roberdeau away from L'Enfant and telling him to "date your new connection with us from your receipt of this letter." His new assignment was to "perfect the marks of the squares in the city . . . forwarding as Major Ellicott expects of you the survey of the waters in the territory." Roberdeau noticed immediately the complete absence of L'Enfant from the rearrangement of authority, and his response surely added to the commissioners' anxiety.

I [received] your favor of this day, and am sorry to inform you that I cannot comply with your sentiments as therein expressed, my orders from Major L'Enfant being so positive and contrary to them. My conversation with you the last evening was, I ardently hope, fully satisfactory, and my letter to you this morning was truly dictated by the purest principles viz the prosperity of the City of Washington, the honor of the commissioners, and the execution of my orders from the Major; until by him I am discharged, from whose authority soever he holds his rank in this business, I should not think myself justified in neglecting his orders as my superior.

On receiving this defiant letter, the commissioners threw off the last vestiges of nicety. They fired Roberdeau for the second and final time and reported the situation to Jefferson, who on January 27 sent a letter to Daniel Carroll proposing that he hire a man to make daily rounds of the wooden stakes marking out the streets and lot divisions. Carroll replied that such surveillance was already well under way. "When the commissioners were compelled to discharge Mr. Roberdeau," he wrote, "they employed a careful person with instructions 'to pay attention to the posts and marks in the Federal City.' "

Finally, amid this spreading contagion of disorder and distrust, Roberdeau received a letter from L'Enfant, written at least a week earlier, instructing him to begin leveling the top of Jenkins Hill. This message indicated a most amazing thing: not a single one of Roberdeau's letters had reached him. Roberdeau's hope had been that L'Enfant would ride back from Philadelphia and put things to rights himself. But the major obviously did not know the first thing about the actions of the commissioners. Roberdeau had been tossing his messages into a void. No one could have blamed him for thinking that this was happening not to the project or to L'Enfant but to himself alone.

"I much fear some of my letters to you have miscarried," he wrote to L'Enfant, "or you would not be ignorant of the length to which the commissioners have inveighed against me." But he kept writing, a lengthy message once every couple of days. Meanwhile, he continued to resist the commissioners, finally putting himself afoul of the law for his troubles. Roberdeau's letter to L'Enfant of January 27 included in his offhand way, midway through his fifth paragraph, the information that he was now "in the hands of the sheriff upon the writ of trespass" for his efforts to find out what was happening on the site, a territory six thousand acres in size onto which he was now not legally permitted to step.

This incarceration could not last long and was not meant to. Roberdeau was quickly given a furlough, then cleared of wrongdoing early in February. Perhaps his father had intervened, but the release of Roberdeau at that point requires no such explanation. The commissioners were about to solve the problem that had put him in jail in the first place.

Later L'Enfant would accuse the commissioners of intercepting his mail to keep the planner and his fury away from the federal district as they established total control of the project. But the mail was not a reliable proposition during eighteenth-century midwinters, and letters might be miscarried as the result of robbers, bad roads, drink, weather, chance, or any combination thereof.

Tardy posts had kept George Washington from understanding the true nature of the Duddington case until he had provided L'Enfant with righteous justification for his actions. Now, in a similar vein, the fickle mail kept L'Enfant in Philadelphia and gave him just what he required: time and freedom from immediate crises so that he could write. In his rooms on Second Street he had been diligently tallying numbers and constructing long lists to express concretely the work and materials and men that would be needed over the next four years to move the capital from idea to actuality.

L'Enfant submitted this information in an untitled report to President Washington dated January 17, 1792.

> The approaching season for renewing the work at the Federal City and the importance of progressing it so as to determine the balance of opinion on the undertaking, to that side to which it already favorably inclines, require that exertion should be made to engage in it from the beginning in such a degree of vigor and activity as will disappoint the hopes of those who wish ill to the business, and encourage the confidence of the well disposed. It becomes therefore necessary to call your attention on measures of the most immediate moment.

He knew that he was about to trespass on the commissioners' prerogative and acknowledged as much to Washington. "Knowing you wished never to be applied to on the subject of business entrusted to the management of the commissioners," he wrote, "I would decline troubling you at this moment, when other affairs must engross your time." But the urgency of the matter, he said, necessitated bothering the president. L'Enfant had simply had it with the piecemeal approach. The project needed forward momentum, and he was the man to provide it. Without that momentum he was worthless to them and the project certainly was worthless to him.

L'Enfant now did something he had never done before, no matter how oppressive the circumstances: he gambled with his own employment.

> Wishing then that matters should be determined in such manner, as may insure harmony amongst the parties concerned, and being convinced it would not be safe to rely wholly on the exertions of the managers of the business, I feel a diffidence from the actual state of things to venture further in the work, unless adequate provisions are made.

L'Enfant had always considered it very important to have a plan in place to raise the considerable monies necessary for work on the city's public spaces. After the failure of the first lot sale, he assumed that such a fund-raising plan was forthcoming from the commissioners, and he couldn't quite believe they wanted to act in the absence of one. L'Enfant felt that a city could not be built on scrawny, unpredictable infusions of capital. With hundreds of laborers already on site and ready to perform the task, stopping and starting meant not moving forward at all.

L'Enfant's memorandum covered twelve tightly spaced ledger pages divided into one section of explanation and two of lists. The premise: time was the enemy, and time was running out.

> The season already far advanced, the demand for such hands as might be procured will increase in proportion as the winter passing will afford them employment at home. Materials will be dearer when an indispensable necessity for them is known and provisions more difficult to obtain.

The major aimed for a good start, sensing that what was begun well would be finished well, while what was begun poorly would wither and die. When he had planned to stretch the city across six thousand acres, he had never been so sanguine as to assume that it could be paid for solely by the selling of lots. He now passed along to Washington what he viewed as the truth, regardless of what those arrayed against him might make of it. He continued by expressing his frustration that the commissioners had not attended to the matter of adequate funding, and he contended again that those selfsame commissioners were more concerned with opposing his outsize expectations for the city: "Their inattention to this doubtless proceeded from a misconception of the magnitude of the objects to pursue or as I observed on a former occasion from a depreciation of the improvements being carried on the grand scale I propose."

Over the past few weeks L'Enfant had huddled with foreign ministers, and those talks led him to suggest that the federal government should grant friendly nations free ground in the city for their embassies. This would encourage quick development of important properties, since these men would need places in the capital to live and do business. L'Enfant argued for the creation of a mechanism by which foreign ministries could formally apply to the American government for grants of space. Publishing such an application would bring international prestige to the city of Washington, but only if the commissioners, as the major wrote in a very Hamiltonian phrase, "put the whole machine in motion" at once. In great works, L'Enfant added, the "judicious use of time and application of objects" was more important than a few dollars saved here or there.

L'Enfant's preamble closed with a statement so fundamental to urban planning as to seem self-evident. "It will be necessary to comprehend the magnitude of the work intended," he wrote, and to "consider that the objects intended have such relation with each other that they cannot be singly effected without great inconvenience and loss." His justification established, L'Enfant put forward a list, seventy-seven items long, of the men and materials necessary to commence proper work on the city. This list, more than any other document drawn or written by the major, reveals his vision of a great city rising from the land day by day, month by month, year by year, far into the future.

Such a scheme cannot be simply desired into being. But if it had been implemented fully and carefully, his plan would have animated many thousands of hands moving across the site like a great living machine. It would have been something to behold.

L'Enfant's proposed orchestration began with 150 men shaping the western slope of Jenkins Hill into a gradual ascent to the Federal Square, that great open space five hundred yards on each side designed as a forecourt to the Congress House, to which twelve main avenues—including the Grand

Avenue itself, running to and from the Potomac—converged. Goods and building materials had to be able to flow unhindered to this location, and so 300 men would be committed to wharfing the eastern bank of the Potomac at the canal entrance and to digging the water passage all the way from the river to the Federal Square. Having reached Jenkins Hill, those same 300 men would proceed to bend and push the canal southward as they completed the link to the Eastern Branch. Once this work was complete, materials would not stall at any point of the trip into the city, and no foolish reliance on wagons would be necessary; all the marble and stone and wood they could possibly need would float serenely into the center of the activity.

In the meantime, near Georgetown, at the other end of the great connecting avenue that was now named Pennsylvania, thirty men working in ten teams of three each would level the streets adjacent to the President's Park, the executive analogue to the Federal Square. Such work would ensure the simultaneous progress of the two great public squares that would link to the mile-long greensward and create the public core of the plan. The earth dug up in the process of leveling those streets adjacent to the President's House would be moved just a few hundred yards to the southwest to assist in wharfing operations. Every step in L'Enfant's chronology of construction was designed to reduce waste and conserve time, materials, and money.

Water could not serve to transport everything, so ten teams of twenty men each would busy themselves leveling the principal streets to at least "the state of turnpike roads," making travel and supply safer, quicker, and easier. Fifty more men would be charged with building three "good stone bridges, one over Rock Creek and two over the canal, the one over Rock Creek being immediately necessary" to create a connection with the newly leveled post road so that work on the public buildings could begin without delay.

L'Enfant's vision also encompassed the lands outside the district and focused on connecting outskirts to city. Sixty men would build a set of aqueducts in order to supply the workers with water for drinking, bathing, and cooking. Twenty-five would be stationed at the three overland entry points of the city in shifting, adaptable teams, ready to bring building and other materials to where they were needed most at that moment. Thirty-five would devote themselves solely to making bricks, supported by fifty-two who would erect two mills to grind and pound plaster of Paris, cement, and clay.

Ten sawyers would go to work cutting planks, while twenty boatmen would be constantly employed aboard four scows to transport stone northward from the Acquia quarries. To work the stone and assist in loading the boats, fifty men; to cut the stone, twenty more, supported by ten attendants. Proper facilities for mixing and tempering mortar and for storing lime would be needed at all building locations, along with shade for carpenters, stonecutters, and brick makers and their planks and boards, their blocks of stone, their piled bricks. These structures were crucial stays against the summer heat and had to be built in the winter, before the materials began arriving in the spring.

All these men needed supervision, requiring the employment of seventeen overseers. Feeding the hands would require two wagon men and three commissaries as well. The major laid out a weekly menu that echoed the seasoned micromanagerial hand of Alexander Hamilton: one pound of beef or pork, one pound of flour, and a half pound of cornmeal per day; one pound of rice and two ounces each of chocolate, sugar, and butter per week. According to L'Enfant's rations, each man would receive a half-pint of spirits each evening, courtesy of the federal government.

All this activity, a dedication of four hundred men for six unbroken months, was essentially preliminary. Though the work would require urgency and long hours, it would merely prepare the ground and stockpile materials. The Fourth of July 1792 would represent the true beginning of work on the federal city. On that symbolic day, complete with patriotic ceremonies—planned by L'Enfant himself, presumably—and much national fanfare, the full investment of men and resources would be dramatically unveiled. Twenty masons would on that day increase to forty. Two specially fitted ships would arrive in the Eastern Branch, or even in the canal, lit with undying fires and all proper tools and stock for a master smith and his four assistants. Hundreds of additional hands would descend on the site to pick up axes and shovels and bricks; then and only then would the city truly begin to take shape.

L'Enfant's summation did not hide from the question of cost. His proposal had 1,070 men working the site by the late summer of 1792 and for four years afterward at a total outlay of $1.2 million. Subtracting $200,000 promised but not yet delivered from the states of Virginia and Maryland created the incontrovertible need, he explained, for a loan in the amount of $1 million. He included details about sponsors, mortgages, bonds, and interest, information likely provided by Hamilton or Theophile Cazenove or someone else familiar with the economics of land ownership and development. Meeting such a fiscal obligation, wrote L'Enfant, would not be difficult. Four years hence the city's aspect—resplendent with completed squares, public walks, key streets, and federal buildings—would be such that the inevitable appreciation of remaining lots would easily raise the rest of the necessary funds.

These numerical projections in place, L'Enfant concluded his long letter to Washington with a statement of his deepest, most closely held desire.

> It is necessary to place under the authority of one single director all those employed in the execution, to leave him the appointment or removal of them as he being answerable for the propriety of execution must be judge of their capacity and is the only one to whom they can with any propriety be subordinate—the exercise of any prepondering authority being in this respect to be restrained by the consideration that the good of the object to accomplish is only to be procured by trusting to the attention of one head who having a constant pursuit and the connection of those objects with the whole of the plan to effect.

Here L'Enfant was asking Washington to altogether eliminate the commissioners and grant him sole directorship of the project. The document was a close cousin to the memorandum the major wrote for his first successful meeting with Washington ten months earlier, but at that time his mood had seemed to closely mirror the political zeitgeist and the president's own confidence. In light of what had passed since, this document—populated with a million-dollar outlay, a thousand-man workforce, and a request for an all-powerful personal position—is so jarring and quixotic as to seem delusional. But L'Enfant's scheme was also worth considering. And as time would show, it was essentially sound. One million dollars procured and used at this time for these purposes, according to these methods, might very well have saved tens or even hundreds of millions later.

Setting aside the obvious difficulty of procuring such a large sum, this professional report—six thousand words prepared over many weeks by the only man with a true grasp of the demands or scale of the project and the only one doing this kind of analysis—might well have been looked upon as a valuable document by parties genuinely interested in the development of the federal city. But the fate of the memorandum speaks volumes about the jeopardy that now stalked L'Enfant.

Apparently no one involved in the project—the very people responsible for laying such plans—recognized its potential. Even though Washington and Jefferson were on record as eager to get the project under way, it stalled. Washington, on receipt of L'Enfant's memorandum, immediately turned it over to Jefferson for review, following which the secretary waited another *eight weeks* to hand it over to the commissioners. By that time L'Enfant was off the job. The greatest service it provided was its assessment of the sheer magnitude of the undertaking. One would think that such an assessment would have been considered worthwhile.

At the end of January 1792, after sending Roberdeau to jail, the commissioners shut down all the winter work on the capital and dismissed all the hands. Not until after the Civil War would the investment of money and manpower reach the levels suggested by L'Enfant in his memorandum. But the one thousand workmen of his four-year plan are still visible in our collective imagination. They emerge out of the dust of their inaction to become the first ghosts of the city of Washington. Major L'Enfant, we begin to understand, would soon become another.

CHAPTER 10

An Implicit Conformity to His Will

During the first week of February 1792 the post arrived on Second Street bearing all of Roberdeau's letters in a single bundle. Roberdeau had been remarkably thorough, transcribing many of the commissioners' messages into his own so that not only the outcome but the day-by-day progress of the affair would be made plain to L'Enfant. As Roberdeau sprang surprise after surprise, sometimes deep inside his letters, the major finally understood: he was involved not in a power struggle between equals but rather in the exercise of a great deal of leverage directly upon himself.

L'Enfant's first reaction was to send off a long letter to George Washington, insisting that the president absolve Roberdeau of all personal responsibility and pay the debts incurred in his name, since Roberdeau had merely acted under the only set of instructions he considered germane. The major also declared his disbelief in the necessity of dismissing the hands and complained that his orders to Roberdeau could not possibly have interfered with the commissioners' mission, which was, after all, to see to the building of the city. "The directions I gave to him," wrote L'Enfant, "were in every point consistent with the respect due to the authority vested by laws in the commissioners."

L'Enfant had left the federal district on Christmas Day under the impression that he had come to amicable terms with the commissioners, but that *esprit d'accord,* real or imaginary, had not lasted. The dispute had become a clash of willful and self-certain personalities who could no longer coexist in the same endeavor. Having now been rebuffed so decisively that he could no longer pretend not to recognize his peril, L'Enfant repeated his threat of resignation.

> Feeling myself doubly interested in the success from regard to reputation, and an ardent desire fully to answer your expectations, the confidence which from the beginning of the business you have placed in me enjoins me to renounce the pursuit unless the power of effecting the work with advantage to the public, and credit to myself, is left me.

L'Enfant's appeal to the "advantage to the public" may smack of sanctimony, but he doubtless meant it literally. He was motivated not by altruism but by the same determined concern for posterity that drove George Washington and so many of the American founders. History would watch them carefully. "And credit to myself, is left me": L'Enfant was seeking acknowledgment not only for the work he'd already done but for the progress of the entire project, for the creation of the city itself.

L'Enfant did not yet know that the commissioners hoped to tie him to the leash of a salary—all the more reason to marvel at his perspicacity. He had spent a professional lifetime in America refusing payment for his work, and here, finally, was the reason writ large: reputation was the most valuable coin of L'Enfant's personal realm, and any other recompense offered in substitution would only diminish his honor. The closing words of L'Enfant's threat made it clear that while the land of the federal city might be for sale, his design for that city was not.

Nothing suggests that L'Enfant truly wanted to leave the project. He may even have expected in his naïveté that Washington would not *allow* him to leave. But if on arriving in Georgetown the previous March the major had found himself wedged between rival landowners, only to step nimbly out of that conflict with a plan so grand that it sidelined their concerns, now he found himself in an untenable position between the president and some of the president's most trusted advisers, without understanding that Washington might take a stand on the other side of the divide.

Even more troubling, L'Enfant would soon find that it was not only credit that was slipping away. His very design, the plan he'd brought to life and ushered through so many potential perils, was in jeopardy as well.

After finishing his elaboration of the lot lines, Benjamin Ellicott, Andrew's brother and assistant, was to forward the plan directly to Philadelphia, where L'Enfant would draw the final version at a large scale so that Andrew Ellicott could prepare it for engraving. It would be a beautiful document: nuanced, detailed, all-encompassing, *final.* This accomplishment would not only move affairs forward; it would teach the commissioners and show the president once again how indispensable their planner really was. It was a simple goal, advantageous for all of the parties involved. As long as L'Enfant could get Benjamin Ellicott's delineations into his hands and get the engraving under way, little, he thought, could go wrong. The prospects of the federal city had been threatened, even wounded, but the finished plan would soon put things on steady footing.

On February 16 he learned otherwise. His business that day was to call on William Young, publisher and printer of the *Universal Asylum and Columbian Magazine,* who sometime earlier had asked for a smaller copy of the plan to publish, along with a description of the city and the elaborate textual "references" that some newspapers had already printed. Young greeted him and then gave him a most curious report: L'Enfant's assistance was no longer necessary, because Andrew Ellicott was going ahead with an engraving of the plan that would be available as soon as March.

L'Enfant did not take Young's meaning at first, thinking that two different iterations of the same plan must have been involved. The plan Ellicott was engraving for Young surely must have been an oft-proposed miniature version for inclusion in national publications, showing only the general arrangement of elements. He had no problem with anyone else putting together such a schematic drawing, but still he made his way to Andrew Ellicott's house, if only to put his mind at ease.

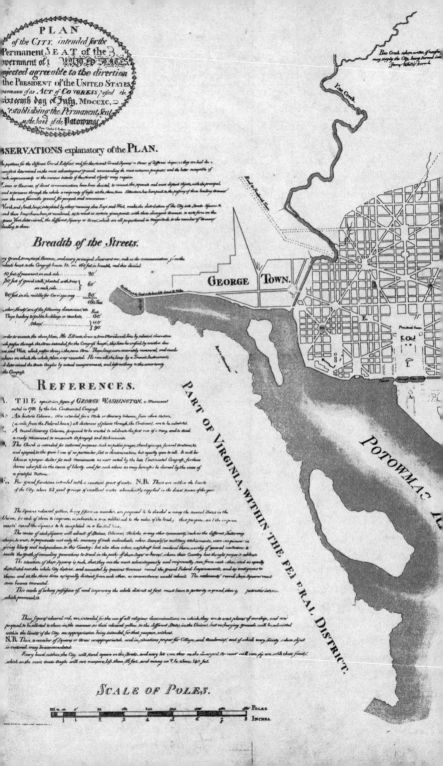

Be an tender height of the 70 even of Tiber Creek
is on the level of the tide as ft at Creek ... } E. I. F. 236. 7 4/8

The water of ship Creek is intended to be conveyed on the high ground where the Congress house stands, and after serving it is part of the City. Its water to will fall from under the bope of that hill to... and in a Cascade of 28 feet in height, and 80 in len. th into the reservoir below, thence it meandering falls down the garden into the grand Canal

The perpendicular height of the ground where the Congress house stands is between the tide of Tiber Creek, 78 feet

Perpendicular height of the 70 the branch above the tide in Tiber Creek .... } E. I. F. 145. 7 4/8

New Bridge to Bladensburg

LIVER Creek

Lat. Congress House,   38. 53. N.
Long. .... 0. 0.

EASTERN BRANCH.

PART OF MARYLAND, WITHIN THE FEDERAL DISTRICT.

Bridge

H.

E.

K.

From the outer arm of this River up to his several Bridge, the depth of water is from 53 to 4 fathom. The deepest is along the shore, where Wharfs are marked.

References.

F.   Grand Cascade, formed of the water from the survey of the Tiber

G.   Public walk, being a square of 1200 feet, through which carriages the upper Square of the Federal house.

H.   Grand avenue, 400 feet in breadth, and about a mile in length, bor Gardens, ending in a slope, from the house on each side. This same Monument A, and connects the Congress Garden, with the

I.   Presidents park, and the

K.   All th improved field, being a part of the walk from the Presidents ho 1800 feet in breadth, and ½ of a mile in length. Every lot deep o green ploy, designates some of the situations which command the prospects, and which are the best calculated for spacious houses an as may accommodate foreign Minister, &c.

L.   Around this square, and all along the

M.   Avenue from the two bridges to the Federal house, the pavemen will pass under an arched way, under which even Shops will end agreeably situated. This Street is 160 feet in breadth, and a m

N.1.

Plan of the City of Washington in the Territory of Columbia, by Andrew Ellicott, 1792

Lat. Capitol.....38: 53. N.
Long.........0: 0.

GEORGE TOWN

PART OF VIRGINIA WITHIN THE TERRITORY OF COLUMBIA.

POTOMAK RIVER

OBSERVATIONS
explanatory of the
Plan.

I. *THE positions for the different Edifices, and for the several Squares or Areas of different shapes, as they are laid down. were first determined on the most advantageous ground, commanding the most extensive prospects, and the better susceptible of such improvements, as either use or ornament may hereafter call for.*

II. *LINES or Avenues of direct communication have been devised, to connect the separate and most distant objects with the principal, and to preserve through the whole a reciprocity of sight at the same time. Attention has been paid to the passing of these leading Avenues over the most favorable ground for prospect and convenience.*

III. *NORTH and South lines intersected by others running due East and West, make the distribution of the City into Streets, Squares, &c. and those lines have been so combined as to meet at certain given points with those divergent Avenues, so as to form on the Spaces "first determined," the different Squares or Areas.*

SCALE OF POLES.

0   100   200   300   400   500   600 Poles.
0   1   2   3   4   5   6 Inches.

Perpendicular height of the source of Tiber Creek above the level of the tide in said Creek .... F. I.ᵖˢ 236, 7, ½

The water of this Creek may be conveyed on the high ground where the Capitol stands & after watering that part of the City, may be diverted to other useful purposes.

Perpendicular height of the where the Capitol is to above the tide of Tiber Creek 78 Feet.

Perpendicular height of the West branch above the tide in Tiber Creek. F. I.ᵖˢ 40, 7, ½

PLAN
of the CITY of
Washington
in the Territory of Columbia,
ceded by the States of
VIRGINIA and MARYLAND
to the
United States of America,
and by them established as the
SEAT of their GOVERNMENT,
after the Year
MDCCC.

Engrav'd by Thackara & Vallance Philadᵗ 1792.

Capitol

N

EASTERN BRANCH

PART OF MARYLAND WITHIN THE TERRITORY OF COLUMBIA.

Breadth of the Streets.

THE grand Avenues, and such Streets as lead immediately to public places, are from 130 to 160 feet wide, and may be conveniently divided into foot ways, walks of trees, and a carriage way. The other Streets are from 90 to 110 feet wide.

IN order to execute this plan, MR ELLICOTT drew a true Meridional line by celestial observation, which passes through the Area intended for the Capitol, this line he crossed by another due East and West, which passes through the same Area. These lines were accurately measured, and made the basis on which the whole plan was executed. He ran all the lines by a Transit Instrument, and determined the Acute Angles by actual measurement, and left nothing to the uncertainty of the Compass.

Once inside, the major must have needed a moment to register that something wasn't right. Ellicott was indeed preparing a plan of the city for engraving, but this was no miniature. Probably two plans of nearly equal size were present. One was, astonishingly, the most important piece of work L'Enfant had done in his entire life, the full-scale drawing he'd brought to Philadelphia to show Washington, Jefferson, and Madison in August. The other, the plan being prepared for the engraver, was not L'Enfant's but a strangely different version bearing Andrew Ellicott's calligraphy and the tell-tale lines of the surveyor's straightedge.

L'Enfant recognized his plan of the city of Washington in a glance—he knew it better than he knew any three-dimensional city. As he realized what he was seeing, a landslide of distress and confusion began to come down around him. Every bit of mistreatment he'd suffered in the aftermath of the lot sale and during the Duddington affair—even Roberdeau's arrest and the dismissal of the hands—had been nothing compared to this.

The next morning he described the encounter and his reaction in a long message to Tobias Lear, Washington's personal secretary. It was a letter written to a friend, but presumably he knew it would make its way into the president's hands with little delay.

> This draft to my great surprise I found in the state in which it is now is, most unmercifully spoiled and altered from the original plan to a degree indeed evidently tending to disgrace me and ridicule the very undertaking. Inclined as I am to persuade myself this could not be the intention, and strange as it may appear that a gentleman, to whom in every instance I have conducted myself with the greatest candor and in whom I have confided as a friend, should harbor a design so inconsistent as to endeavor to destroy the reputation of one whose contempt for the little machinations of envy has left unguarded against the treachery of false friends.

"Unguarded," he had written of himself, after rethinking in one evening six months of conversations, meetings, instructions, and agreements. What L'Enfant had thought he had understood, he had not.

The first and most obvious of L'Enfant's "false friends" was Ellicott. The surveyor had ridden beside him with the president following L'Enfant's visit to Mount Vernon. They had shared a common purpose as well as the occasional dinner. They had always spoken complimentarily of each other, and no evidence exists that Major L'Enfant ever did anything to demean or undermine Ellicott's work. In fact, the major's version of the plan presented and accepted in August, the one Ellicott was now altering, had borne only three names: Peter Charles L'Enfant, George Washington, and Andrew Ellicott, who was given pride of place in the upper left of the drawing and credit for his plotting of a set of true cardinal lines running north, south, east, and west through the center of the future Congress House.

By the time L'Enfant walked into the surveyor's workplace and into the shock of his life, though, the seeds of distrust had already been sown. The major had surely heard rumors or reports of Ellicott's role in the Duddington affair, when the surveyor had promised Duddington that the plan was only a rough draft and could be altered indiscriminately. Perhaps he had even heard of Ellicott's description of the plan as "mere fancy work." In any event, L'Enfant made it clear to Lear that whatever friendship he had felt for Ellicott was now abandoned.

> Whether this inclination to originate or improve my plan can be attributed to inattention, to the difficulty to be encountered in endeavoring to correct errors which such innovations would necessarily create, or whether drawn by the allurement of party, certain it is that he has been induced to hazard opinions and to engage himself more forward to effect objects, which, besides the impossibility to accomplish, he ought less to have done.

The major had several sudden suspicions to sort out. He undoubtedly recalled Thomas Jefferson's comment intimating that Andrew Ellicott had an equal right to the engraving of the plan. Had the idea that Ellicott might be entitled to the proceeds from the sale of an engraving been less Jefferson's mistake than the surveyor's own suggestion? Did the betrayal run along bloodlines—had Benjamin Ellicott's agreement to prepare the more precise version been nothing more than a smoke screen? Where and between whom did these nefarious connections run? Not seeing them in plain sight, L'Enfant began to see them everywhere.

The only known copy of a plan for the federal city in L'Enfant's own hand to survive into the twenty-first century rests in a refrigerated chamber in the

Geography and Map Division of the Library of Congress, where it is off-limits to the public because of its brittle condition and the extreme fading of its pencil lines. Customarily referred to as the "manuscript plan," it is the drawing L'Enfant brought to Philadelphia in August 1791, the same one Ellicott consulted as he prepared his own version for engraving.

The plan was drawn on two large sheets of handmade paper joined together to measure a little more than two feet high and three feet wide. L'Enfant used pencil for the street lines and daubs of watercolor to indicate important public features: green for grass, yellow for the fifteen state squares, red for a series of lots adjoining his Grand Avenue, and blue for water, including the Tiber canal. Stylized shadowing of the various riverbanks in blue watercolor highlighted the basic shape of the city, a lopsided and meandering V balanced on the junction of the Potomac and the Eastern Branch. Bracketing the plan on either side of the rivers were the same "references," the lists of the city's various squares and public attractions, that earlier in the month had been published verbatim in newspapers around the country. A cartouche in the far upper left contained the fifty-seven words of the title using no fewer than fifteen different calligraphic styles.

The manuscript plan in the Library of Congress bears one more noteworthy, though virtually invisible, feature. These are textual edits, made in the hand of Thomas Jefferson, for the clear purpose of guiding Andrew Ellicott as he prepared the plan for an engraver. The secretary had at some point, and without notifying L'Enfant, spent several hours on the plan making a number of semantic changes—most notably "Capitol" for "Congress House"—and eliminating all of L'Enfant's "references" with a succession of authoritative diagonal slashes.

Jefferson altered no marks on the streets themselves, and so changes in the pencil lines of the plan must be attributed to Ellicott, who later indicated that his alterations of L'Enfant's drawing were made with the *approval* of his superiors without mentioning any specific *direction* to do so. And just as a painter can instantly discern a quick and less expert copy of his own work, L'Enfant saw at once that his design—the result of months spent in thought and on the field and over the drawing—had been changed by Ellicott in collaboration with whoever had put him up to the task.

In L'Enfant's view, Ellicott's drawing not merely ignored the plan's subtle geometries; it destroyed them, along with his core strategy for the settling of the city. L'Enfant's twenty squares were reduced to eleven in Ellicott's

version. Ellicott would later defend himself by claiming Washington's approbation, but the surveyor was very likely talking about the recommendations
he'd heard the president make in June, recommendations L'Enfant had
already fully accommodated into the August plan now in Ellicott's possession. To reduce the number of squares to fewer than fifteen was to dismantle
the major's scheme to develop the city as a series of nodes spurred to growth
by state pride and economic interest. In the process, Ellicott also undid L'Enfant's careful spacing of the squares at equal distances from the core of the
plan and from one another, designed so that they would be "most advantageously and reciprocally seen from each other, and as equally distributed
over the whole city district, and connected by spacious avenues round the
grand federal improvements, and as contiguous to them, and at the same time
as equally distant from each other, as circumstances would admit."

The change most obvious to later generations occurred at the site of the
Capitol, where Ellicott's drawing summarily turned the building around so
that its front facade faced east and then moved the entire structure westward
into the middle of the square. All of L'Enfant's plans and language had
heretofore imagined an ascent from his Grand Avenue to a "federal square"
that would collect the kinetic energy from twelve radiating avenues in a great
public space, not blunt that energy at the sides and back of the Capitol. Far
from better fitting the topography, Ellicott's change also pushed the Capitol
to the very crest of Jenkins Hill, where the building would hang in space as
though it were about to tumble downward into the wet ground below—what
L'Enfant referred to as its "ill-judged stand." A similar alteration had been
made at the site of the President's House, so that again the views down Ellicott's avenues terminated in the building, whereas L'Enfant's visual destination had been a spacious public square. All of Ellicott's changes seemed to
L'Enfant *solely* mathematical and geometrical, stripped of any true sense of
the topography. If something this mechanical had been the president's
desire, he could have created it in a few weeks without spending all those
hours on the site itself and saved himself and his legs plenty of grief.

But no change made to lines of the drawing angered and dismayed the
major half as much as the simple fact that his name was missing.

One of the commissioners or perhaps Thomas Jefferson might have
been the one to suggest keeping the words "Peter Charles L'Enfant" off of
the most important document of the planner's life. But we know of one decision that Ellicott did make on his own. L'Enfant's caption referring to the

surveyor's work in plotting the meridian, one of the only pieces of text that Jefferson did not cross out in pencil, had been moved from the upper left to the lower right of the drawing. The words "Mr. Ellicott" in the midst of the first sentence had then been considerably enlarged to leave an unmistakable impression of authorship.

Andrew Ellicott's role in this story may have been that of a malicious actor, a pawn, or, probably most likely, simply a hard worker caught in a difficult position. But there was no excuse for this choice to leave the impression that the plan was his own. It was a breach of an implicit contract between professionals that negated eleven months of one man's most concentrated work and reverberated for many decades in the future.

On the evening of February 21, 1792, one week after L'Enfant made his disturbing discovery, the City Dancing Assembly of Philadelphia gave a ball at the New Rooms on Chestnut Street, in the fashionable western end of the city. The occasion was the eve of George Washington's sixtieth birthday, and social Philadelphia turned out in its most sophisticated finery. There was no pretending at republican modesty: this was an unabashedly aristocratic affair, all the more so since 1792 was America's second presidential election year and rumors were flying that Washington was serious in his contemplation of retirement. Were he to run, continuity and some sort of order would be assured in the tenuous infancy of the country. Were he not to run . . .

"I fear more from the election of another President, whenever our present great and good one quits his political or natural career," wrote Tobias Lear, "than from any other event." Lear was not alone. Many of the guests looked at the party as a chance not only to fete the man but to send him a message: *Please stay.*

The top of the guest list included George and Martha Washington, John and Abigail Adams, Thomas Jefferson, Alexander and Eliza Hamilton, Henry and Lucy Knox, and most other officers of the federal government, as well as judges and other civil officers from Pennsylvania, Governor Thomas Mifflin included. Also present were members of the diplomatic corps of a dozen nations, including the French minister Jean Baptiste Ternant. The press of people—150 "ladies" and 300 "citizens" strong—was rounded out by a number of congressmen and various others of name and influence. A social gathering of such brilliance had not taken place in Philadelphia in a decade, not since L'Enfant had been given the special permission of General

Washington to plan a party and build pavilions to commemorate the birth of the dauphin to Louis XVI.

The *Federal Gazette and Philadelphia Daily Advertiser* reported sights and sounds of epicurean delight.

> Joy and satisfaction were strongly marked in every countenance. Many of the Ladies had in their headdresses, wrought in gold letters, sentiments expressive of the general sensations of the evening; and in the front of the building, above, were transparent paintings of Vive le President, illuminated so as to have a pleasing effect to eye from the street. During supper the music was brought out of the ball room, and kept up with proper interludes.

Five toasts were made and drunk in the president's presence: to the day, to the United States, to the nations in friendship with the United States, to the rights of man, and to the Fourth of July 1776. Washington offered his own salutes to the state of Pennsylvania, to "the memory of those illustrious heroes and patriots who died in defense of American liberty," and to "the flame of liberty which hath been lighted up in the Western world to blaze and spread till it shall have illuminated every part of the globe." The president finished by drinking to the health of the company and to the Dancing Assembly.

The next morning the entire city celebrated. Philip Freneau, who by this time was in his glory as Jefferson's anti-Hamilton amanuensis and who would after the November election loose his rhetorical hounds even on Washington himself, took a paragraph to describe the festivities:

> Yesterday was celebrated, in this city, the birth-day of the PRESIDENT of the UNITED STATES, (when he entered his 61st year) with every demonstration of joy suitable to the occasion. At eleven o'clock, the volunteer corps of artillery, cavalry and infantry paraded at the state-house, and took orders for the firing and exercises of the day. At half past two, the officers of the militia battalions of the city, the northern liberties, and southern districts of Philadelphia assembled at the same place, together with the members of the Pennsylvania state society of the Cincinnati, from whence they went in procession to the home of the President of the United States. A variety of salutes

were fired, and the day concluded with every mark of harmony, good order, and undissembled joy. In the evening was exhibited an elegant display of fireworks.

Washington had skipped most of the revelry surrounding his inauguration in 1789, and he did not change his practice on this occasion. The Philadelphia newspapers made no mention of the federal city, but still the president was thinking about his namesake and its designer and trying to make sense of the report given by Lear of L'Enfant's ire at finding his name removed from the plan. Washington's collected papers include only one letter composed on his sixtieth birthday, a single short paragraph written to Thomas Jefferson concerning the credit he felt was due Major L'Enfant.

The plan I think ought to appear as the work of L'Enfant. The one prepared for engraving not doing so is, I presume, one cause of his dissatisfaction. If he consents to act upon the conditions proposed and can point out any radical defects to amend which will be a gratification to him not improper in themselves, or productive of unnecessary or too much delay, had he not better be gratified in the alteration?

All Jefferson had to do, then, was write a note to Ellicott insisting that credit for the plan go to Major L'Enfant. But the secretary's response to the president's first suggestion was, apparently, no. As for allowing L'Enfant a look at the changes, well, Jefferson himself had once issued a legal judgment stating that the exact form of the plan didn't mean much until all of the lots were sold and measured. He seems not to have wavered in that conviction.

Here it becomes tempting to go back to L'Enfant's comment the previous March regarding the "cool imagination" that would seek an unostentatious town, such as the one expressed in the secretary's own sketch plan, where a magnificent city should rightfully rise. But any theory holding that Jefferson was using Ellicott to take artistic control of the plan has a problem: Ellicott's changes hardly made the city smaller, more Jeffersonian. In fact, by straightening major avenues and casting aside L'Enfant's plan to give the states a real stake in the capital by creating small republican hamlets of their own within the larger diagram, they helped to seal the overwhelmingly centralized, Federalist character of the city design.

A much more likely reason for Jefferson's failure to accede to Washington's request is that he simply couldn't stand L'Enfant and looked forward to the day when he wouldn't have to work around the planner's mercurial and self-indulgent temperament. It was probably, in the end, a matter of personality more than politics. Civility and cultivated discourse, no matter what passions roiled beneath, were religions to Jefferson, and he found little to care for or trust in L'Enfant's hotheadedness, his overwrought manner of speech, or his tortured prose. The coolness and rigidity of the secretary's judgment in the Duddington case provides the best testimony to Jefferson's total lack of affection for L'Enfant's ostentatiously emotional and unrestrained manner.

Whoever had pulled the strings, and whatever unrecorded instructions had been spoken, the plan was finally published as Ellicott had drawn it, with the tacit approval of George Washington and to the textual specifications of Thomas Jefferson. James Thackara and John Vallance of Philadelphia were given the commission to produce the initial engraving, but Jefferson, worried about possible delays, directed that another copy be given to Samuel Hill of Boston. And indeed Hill's engraving was the first published, in August, followed by the Thackara and Vallance version in November. Two eminent engravers took six and nine months to finish the job, in other words, when many had faulted L'Enfant for failing to do so in three. The thousands of copies that the commissioners had in December requested of L'Enfant—copies in which the planner had always assumed he would have a financial stake—now issued instead from these two sources and began to disperse all over the country. For most of America and even parts of Europe, these engravings of the Ellicott alterations provided a first look at the size and shape of the capital.

The plan was published in newspapers and magazines, displayed in statehouses, and printed onto handkerchiefs, but not a single copy bore the name of Peter Charles L'Enfant. No printing of the plan in the next ninety-five years ever would.

As Jefferson read Washington's request to credit L'Enfant for his work, L'Enfant was in receipt of a separate letter from the secretary that began by not so subtly encouraging his resignation.

> The advance of the season begins to require that the plans for the
> buildings and other public works at the Federal city, should be in

readiness, and the persons engaged who are to carry them into execution, the circumstances which have lately happened have produced an uncertainty whether you may be disposed to continue your services there.

L'Enfant responded to Jefferson on February 26, 1792, with a laundry list of complaints he had made a half-dozen times before. The season was wasting. He had outlined four years' worth of work in his memorandum to Washington, a document that no one else could have successfully created, yet everyone was ignoring it. The major professed loyalty to the president in the form of "an implicit conformity to his will" but, notably, not to anyone else in view. No good had come of all the work he'd done to ingratiate himself with the commissioners and help all of the other parties involved understand the workings of his design. The commissioners should have understood that he was the only man fit for the job and relied on him to see the city complete. Instead, he wrote, they were concerned with "that pride of office which, I am mortified to be obliged to say it, has been their chief object."

With this missive, the fraying of Major L'Enfant was nearly complete. He stated once again his belief that the commissioners had shortsightedly resisted the scale of the plan from the beginning. He accused them once again of partiality to the wealthiest landowners, meaning Duddington and Notley Young, and he again bemoaned the "allurement of parties" that had brought things to such a pass, a theme he would build on over the years as the clashes between Hamilton's Federalists and Jefferson's Republicans turned into all-out political war. L'Enfant added another reference to "the determination I have taken no longer to act in subjection to their will and caprice" and ended by writing a sentence as hard and as firm in its finality as Acquia freestone.

> If therefore the law absolutely requires without any equivocation that my continuance shall depend upon an appointment from the commissioners—I cannot nor would I upon any consideration submit myself to it.

Since Major L'Enfant had been told so many times before that that was indeed the condition of his continued employment, this message became his prima facie resignation.

L'Enfant's emphasis on an "appointment" from the commissioners makes it clear that the final insult was not that he had to take their orders, as untenable as that might have been, but that they, instead of the president, had become his patrons. His life's benefactors so far had included his father, Beaumarchais, Baron von Steuben, Louis Duportail, Alexander Hamilton, and George Washington. Such a trio of men as Stuart, Carroll, and especially Johnson would not be allowed to place one toe inside that circle.

The messengers of Philadelphia were kept busy this day, February 26, 1792. Jefferson sent the major's final note directly across town to Washington, who at four in the afternoon replied with a message of his own that he would like to meet with the secretary and James Madison at eight-thirty the following morning, at which time, wrote the president, "A final decision thereupon must be had."

But in the meantime, even as he was calling this meeting, the president was trying to find a way to keep L'Enfant on the project. It seems amazing that Washington was still willing to make an overture to his malcontented planner. But late that evening he sent Tobias Lear out on a last-ditch mission. The president knew that Lear and L'Enfant were on good terms, and he hoped that a hand extended from Lear would be construed as a hand extended from Washington himself.

Lear walked four blocks from the president's residence to L'Enfant's rented rooms, where he made a final attempt to dilute the planner's venom against the commissioners. Lear was a Harvard graduate and for the moment a loyal Federalist, meticulous in his work habits and his physical appearance, a detail-oriented and cultured man who was used to life in the shadow of George Washington and had adjusted to that secondary status in a way L'Enfant had not and never would. Lear was also a true believer in L'Enfant's city and L'Enfant's talents, and he dreamed of establishing a mercantile proposition in the capital so as to increase his personal stake in its success.

L'Enfant admitted Lear, who spent no time on niceties but moved directly to the point—it was getting late, after all, and events were rushing toward the next morning's meeting. He explained that he had been asked by the president to have a private word with L'Enfant about the controversy surrounding the federal city. L'Enfant responded by peremptorily demanding total freedom from the commissioners; barring that, he would agree to stay on the project and consider himself subordinate only if there were a change of commissioners. Lear replied that he was sure neither was possible. The major cut him off. "I have heard enough of this matter," he said.

Nothing in Lear's description indicates that these words were uttered sadly, angrily, dismissively, or matter-of-factly. If the major still considered himself in charge of the federal city project, his tone was likely haughty, arrogant, delusional—all the things he had always been accused of being. But if he considered himself already resigned via his letter to Jefferson—as he seems to have done—he may have delivered his comment with much less affect. In any case, this response was his true and final resignation, delivered to Lear and therefore to Washington himself.

All that was left was the official exchange of notes. On the next day, February 27, Jefferson announced to L'Enfant that his services were no longer required:

> I am instructed by the President to inform you that notwithstanding the desire he has entertained to preserve your agency in this business, the condition upon which it is done is inadmissible and your services must be at an end.

L'Enfant sent back a provocative flourish, issuing a defense of his integrity and sounding his final warning for the future of the capital. Describing himself as "a man of capacity" with only "disinterested views" regarding the success of the city, he promised that "should this business fall into the hands of one devoid of these impressions, and of course insensible to the real benefit of this public, how great soever his power may be, self-interest immediately becomes his only view, and deception and dishonor are the issue."

L'Enfant's vision might have allowed him to see great distances, but he often missed obstacles right in front of him. He never understood that he had finally pitted himself not only against Washington's trusted associates and his secretary of state but also against Washington himself. No other reading is honest. L'Enfant was truly loyal to only one man, the president, but a good number of the sins of the previous eleven months had been committed by L'Enfant, and Washington was angry.

The matter of the exchange with Lear weighed heavily. Washington viewed his personal secretary very much as a stand-in for himself, and so for L'Enfant to summarily dismiss Lear—whatever the tone—was a personal insult such as he had never heard L'Enfant deliver. But perhaps the president was most angered by L'Enfant's umpteenth evocation of the "benefit of this public," because now, as never before, the major appeared to be acting contrary to the public interest, as his behavior and manner of departure could have put the project in immediate peril.

The day after he severed ties with the major was a tiring one for the president. That morning he and Jefferson took breakfast together and spent more than an hour talking over the prospect of retirement from public life. It is too much to suggest that Peter Charles L'Enfant had worn them out—Jefferson's discontents had mostly to do with his mounting distrust of Alexander Hamilton, while Washington expressed a more general longing for the tranquillity of Mount Vernon and an escape from the public eye—but the timing does seem curious.

L'Enfant would for the rest of his life increasingly blame Jefferson for his troubles while entirely absolving the president, but at this moment the sentiments of both his superiors were probably fairly represented in Washington's message to his former planner.

> The continuance of your services (as I have often assured you) would have been pleasing to me, could they have been retained on terms compatible with the law. Every mode has been tried to accommodate your wishes on this principle, except changing the commissioners (for commissioners there *must* be, and under their directions the public buildings *must* be carried on, or *the law will be violated;* this is the opinion of the Attorney General of the United States and other competent judges). To change the commissioners *cannot* be done on ground of propriety, justice or policy.
>
> Many weeks have been lost since you came to Philadelphia in obtaining a plan for engraving, notwithstanding the earnestness with which I requested it might be prepared on your first arrival. Further delay in this business is inadmissible. In like manner five months have elapsed and are lost by the compliment which was intended to be paid you in depending *alone* on your plans for the public buildings instead of advertising a premium to the person who should present the best (which would equally have included yourself). These are unpleasant things to the friends of the measure, and are very much regretted.

This was, as far as we know, the last letter Washington ever sent to L'Enfant. It opened L'Enfant's deepest and most lasting wound, all the more so because it had been inflicted by himself as much as by any other person.

The major would have taken cold comfort had he known that another of the president's helping hands had gone unclasped just the day before. In a note to Jefferson, Washington had asked, "Should Mr. Ellicott be asked in strong and explicit terms if the plan exhibited by him is conformable to the actual state of things on the ground and agreeable to the design of Major L'Enfant?" It is unlikely that Andrew Ellicott, based on his encounter with L'Enfant over the engraving, could have responded affirmatively to either question.

In any case, Ellicott was never asked the questions and proceeded with the two simultaneous sets of engravings. Once again, Jefferson either responded in the negative or set Washington's letter aside.

The controversy that Washington and the commissioners had feared seemed imminent. Their greatest worry was that the details of the planner's exit would make the papers in Philadelphia, where, as Washington had recently written, "the current in this city sets so strongly against the Federal City, that I believe nothing that can be avoided will ever be accomplished in it." Rumblings for repeal of the Residence Act had always been felt in Philadelphia, and they were likely to grow louder as little evidence of a federal city appeared on the ground.

The commissioners had another, more immediate worry. A thoroughly disaffected planner could, they knew, do plenty of sabotage. The first thing, then, that Johnson, Stuart, and Carroll did in the aftermath of L'Enfant's termination—and from their point of view, at least, he had been fired—was to discuss the question of proper payment. They'd already tried to put the major on a salary, and now, with Washington's approval, they put in an order to a Philadelphia bank for $2,000 and prepared to offer a second lot in the federal city. But in his usual way L'Enfant refused, offering the commissioners a stinging parting shot in return: "Without enquiring of the principle upon which you rest this offer, I shall only here testify my surprise thereupon as also my intention to decline accepting of it."

"The principle upon which" the commissioners rested their offer was clearly, to L'Enfant's mind, that of hush money, to prevent the planner from going public with his complaints. The major chose not to tell them that he had no intention of going public as long as George Washington remained alive. They would learn this fact about their planner in due time; for now, he would let them dangle.

Meanwhile, as L'Enfant's orders were remanded and his assistants released or reassigned to Andrew Ellicott, the proprietors, upon hearing the news of the major's departure, came howling back. Isaac Roberdeau kept writing to L'Enfant throughout the spring and into the summer, his letters full of barely controlled spite at a situation little short of chaotic in the wake of L'Enfant's removal. "You hardly can imagine the vexations and inconveniences into which the Honorable Gentlemen are now subjected," he wrote, "by that mismanagement which ever has been their grand characteristic as commissioners." The proprietors, led by George Walker, sent their regards to L'Enfant even as they quarreled with the commissioners over the surveying and lot sales. In one such letter to Johnson, Stuart, and Carroll, merchant Samuel Davidson referred to L'Enfant as "a gentleman who I once considered your equal in authority, and now your superior in judgment."

On June 4, amid all this upheaval, Attorney General Edmund Randolph announced the result of his extended consideration of the matter of the home of Daniel Carroll of Duddington. Duddington would in the end be forced to abide by neither of Washington's options. Rather, he would simply receive a lump sum of £1,679, about $5,000, for the value of his half-built house along the future New Jersey Avenue. This decision outraged the proprietors, whose tributes to L'Enfant became stronger and more vocal. Finally, all the proprietors—except Duddington and Notley Young, the two accused of receiving special attention from the commissioners—signed a letter to L'Enfant, probably written by Walker, that was equal parts tribute and readily acknowledged self-interest.

> We find by communications from Philadelphia that there is too much reason to apprehend that the City of Washington will lose the benefit of your future services, a circumstance which we lament extremely, not only from regard to our own interest, which we believe no other man so well qualified to promote . . . for we well know that your time, and the whole powers of your mind, have been for months entirely devoted to the arrangements in the city, which reflect so much honor on your taste and your judgment.

We still hope that some mode of accommodations may be devised, to admit of your return, on principles not derogatory to your own feelings, nor injurious to the city.

The letter offered a way to imagine the major coming back, or at least fighting to do so, but he was too proud. Walker's letter was a bittersweet vindication, and years later L'Enfant would use it as an important pillar in the case for his rightful recognition, but for now he was conspicuously ignoring the federal city. He had no intention of returning to the district and asked Roberdeau to collect the trunk he'd left behind full of nearly a year's intensive work: books, surveying instruments, collections of engravings, sketch plans for the Congress House and the President's House, preparatory designs for the city canal, bridges, and market houses, detailed plans of the Grand Avenue, and monetary vouchers for supplies and wages. L'Enfant had metaphorically folded his arms across his chest, raised his chin, and turned away. He had other connections, friends with large projects of their own.

One of those connections was Alexander Hamilton. Three years earlier, in January 1789, as L'Enfant had been working on his renovations of Federal Hall, Hamilton had met with a group of moneyed men in Rawson's Tavern near his home on Wall Street to create the New York Manufacturing Society, designed to promote American manufacturing in a direct challenge to Britain's monopoly on tools for making cotton, wool, and silk, as well as nails, steel, and gunpowder.

By the autumn of 1791 the organization had evolved into the Society for Establishing Useful Manufactures (SEUM) and was going forward with a scheme to found a company town on a dramatic scale, a model metropolis that would represent Hamilton's ultimate expression of American mercantile independence. It was intended to make concrete the proposals he was putting forth in his *Report on Manufactures*. The idea was to build not a few factories or mills or warehouses but an entire city dedicated to the production of vital goods: paper, cloth, sewing materials, coal, copper, firearms, beer, and more. The city would serve as a kind of national, even international, exposition; those interested in learning the kind of manufacturing secrets Great Britain held close could see them in operation here. The SEUM board planned to fund this city with half a million dollars in government bonds, helping to buttress the public debt and public credit that

Hamilton felt so necessary to national strength and to which Jefferson and the federal city commissioners so strenuously objected.

Alexander Hamilton was the only character in L'Enfant's life who matched him vision for vision in painting his desires onto truly immense canvases. Hamilton chose a spot by the Great Falls of the Passaic River in northern New Jersey, a picturesque bend in the river graced with a seventy-foot waterfall full of vital horsepower. The town was named Paterson in honor of New Jersey governor William Paterson, or, in a less sanguine reading, so that the governor might take the not-so-subtle hint and roll out the legislative red carpet. The society bought seven hundred acres—not the hundred square miles of the federal district or the six thousand acres of L'Enfant's plan for the capital, but not paltry. Finally, in December 1791, with Washington's official approval and undeterred by Jefferson's vehemently contrary opinion, Hamilton's ambitions were given the blessing of the federal government.

Hamilton may have been aware of L'Enfant's increasing suspicion of Jefferson, which would have made the major an all the more attractive candidate for employment once his work on the federal city came to an end. And Hamilton, who knew far better than Johnson, Stuart, and Carroll how to generate public capital on a large scale, was an attractive prospective employer to L'Enfant as well. The program needed an urban designer, someone to think big, to embody certain important philosophical and political ideas about America in the form of a city plan.

There was only one man in the country whose experience fit such a description. And that man was suddenly available.

CHAPTER 11

The Disappointment of Absolute Dues

First Lady and resolute New Englander Abigail Adams rode into the City of Washington in the District of Columbia on the afternoon of November 16, 1800, to join her husband, John, in residence at the partially completed President's House. The deadline set by the Residence Act for the transfer of federal power from Philadelphia had been met—barely. Congress was due to convene for the first time in the new capital the next day, but the frigid northern winds and falling snow were tamping down any sense of exuberance, and a majority of the legislators had yet to arrive from their homes. Mrs. Adams entered the city limits amid a light snowfall that had ushered her along roads of packed red earth as she tried to grasp the provisional aura surrounding her new place of residence.

The journey of more than five hundred miles had been full of anxieties and unknowns. She had left the Adams family home in Quincy, Massachusetts, nearly a month earlier. She stopped first in New York, where she found her thirty-year-old alcoholic son, Charles, "laid upon a bed of sickness, destitute of a home," estranged from his father, and suddenly advancing in a dropsy that made her apprehensive she'd see him alive again. In Philadelphia Mrs. Adams added her four-year-old granddaughter, Susanna, to the traveling party, which then got lost in the woods of Maryland before arriving in Baltimore on November 11. There she felt a keen distress at the sight of so many slaves, a sight she realized with foreboding would also be a common one in the new seat of government. The last leg of the journey was a race against the drop in temperature and the darkening clouds, but she was finally here and elated to reunite with her beloved John after yet another separation of too many months.

Mrs. Adams arrived to a skeleton of a city that she expected, official optimism aside, would be her home for a few months at most. Enfranchised Americans had finished casting their ballots in the nation's fourth presidential election, and few believed that the incumbent had defeated Thomas Jefferson after an election season marked by egregious and unceasing party-driven viciousness. Mrs. Adams's tenuous relationship to the federal city gives her comments a certain useful objectivity: she was neither upset to be losing her everyday connection to Philadelphia nor personally invested in making Washington a better place to live. Eleven years earlier, in New York City following George Washington's inauguration, she had carefully followed the debates on the location of the seat of government as reported in the newspapers, and she may very well have witnessed some of them from the House balcony of L'Enfant's Federal Hall. She was now able to bookend that experience with firsthand observations of the infant city.

> As I expected to find it a new country, with houses scattered over a space of ten miles, and trees and stumps in plenty with, a castle of a house—so I found it—The President's House is in a beautiful situation in front of which is the Potomac with a view of Alexandria. The country around is romantic but wild, a wilderness at present.

The "situation" of the President's House may have been beautiful, but Mrs. Adams was none too pleased with the state of the building itself. Its walls were almost entirely devoid of plaster, most of its rooms were bare of furnishings, and its many fireplaces were short on the firewood necessary, in her words, "to secure us from daily agues." Its ground floor uninhabitable, the massive edifice was cold and damp and vacant to the point of being surreal. Still, she was careful to warn her daughter back in Massachusetts to "keep all this to yourself, and, when asked how I like it, say that I write you the situation is beautiful, which is true." With a flourish of her customary provincialism, Mrs. Adams reported the woeful lack of development in the rest of the city: "If the twelve years, in which this place has been considered as the future seat of government, had been improved, as they would have been if in New England, very many of the present inconveniences would have been removed."

Many in Philadelphia even now refused to believe that the federal government would ever settle for good along the Potomac, and events offered little reason for them to think otherwise. The first session of the federal legislature in the city of Washington was postponed for four days until a sufficient number of congressmen arrived. A ceremonial procession intended to mark the event was called off because of the thick covering of snow and was never rescheduled.

As they reacquainted themselves with each other and tried to make peace with their cavernous dwelling, Abigail and John had plenty of terminology to absorb. The few streets cleared so far were named North Capitol and South Capitol, F, Seventh, Pennsylvania, New Jersey, and Maryland. "The Mall" was hesitantly gaining currency as the name for the swath of land indicated on the plan as L'Enfant's "Grand Avenue," but that land had barely been touched except for the clearing of foliage for the crossing of Seventh Street. Nor was the Tiber canal under way, and though the idea of an equestrian statue to honor George Washington had been introduced seventeen years earlier, no such memorial had been commissioned.

The Eastern Branch had acquired a nickname of sorts: the "Anacostia"—like "L'Enfant" and "Potomac," in an impressive variety of spellings—because in late 1792 Thomas Jefferson had asked Andrew Ellicott to find out the name of the original inhabitants of the river's banks. "Jenkins Hill," a sobriquet dear only to L'Enfant, had become the more stately "Capitol Hill," and this place, the "pedestal waiting for a superstructure," was the only truly vibrant spot in the city. The northern wing of the Capitol was almost complete, a two-story Italian Renaissance box of brick and Acquia stone designed by a Quaker physician named William Thornton and only recently given a roof and walled into legislative chambers. Occupying less than a

third of the outline dug for the entire building's foundation, it was designated the Senate wing, but at the moment it held by necessity most of the
federal government outside the executive branch, including 32 senators, 106
representatives, the Circuit Court, and a Library of Congress still bereft of
books, with the expectation that the Supreme Court would soon arrive as
well. According to one contemporary report, Thornton's structure was surrounded by "seven or eight boarding houses, one tailor, one shoemaker, one
printer, a washing-woman, a grocery shop, a pamphlet and stationery shop,
a small dry-goods shop, and an oyster house," while off to the south sat Duddington Manor, its site moved to conform with the line of New Jersey
Avenue and its construction completed with the settlement money authorized eight years earlier by then attorney general Edmund Randolph.

A bird's-eye view of the city of Washington in 1800 would not have
revealed L'Enfant's gridiron arrangement of streets crisscrossed by dramatic
diagonal avenues but rather a stubbornly rural region of forests, pastures,
open fields, and produce gardens interrupted here and there by brick kilns
and barracks, the entire picture dominated by two gargantuan construction
projects. In the absence of any progress on the Mall, Pennsylvania Avenue
was the city's only true axis, replacing the old ferry road with a stump-
ridden carpet of reddish earth 160 feet wide and 4 miles long running southeast from Georgetown, jogging clumsily at the President's House, then
continuing around the infant Capitol and on to the Eastern Branch, whose
banks bore no resemblance to the thriving commercial center L'Enfant and
George Washington had imagined during their original conversations about
the plan in March 1791. The river was dotted, now as on the day of L'Enfant's first arrival, with two wharfs, two ferry landings, and a few houses,
most owned and leased by Daniel Carroll of Duddington. No new bridges
were under way either here or in Georgetown because no new bridges were
yet necessary.

L'Enfant's squares, except those enveloping the Capitol and the President's House, were nearly empty and in some cases nearly impossible to
find; many of the stone markers delimiting their boundaries had been stolen
and were forever entombed in the foundation work of nearby construction
projects. The city was developing at a crawl, exactly as L'Enfant had predicted it would in the absence of a significant influx of public cash. The raw
tally of buildings spread across six thousand acres spoke loudly of the
emptiness: 109 made of brick, 263 of wood, and 2—the President's House

View of the Capitol, by William Russell Birch, ca. 1800

and the Capitol—of sandstone. Many of the district's new residents lived like country squires in freestanding town-house mansions set away from the public edifices and surrounded by flower and vegetable gardens or wild grasses and personal forests. These self-styled estates, oases of seclusion close to the presumptive halls of power, were usually oriented more or less true to the lines of the Ellicott version of L'Enfant's plan; but with neighbors mostly uninterested in building, adhering to those lines seemed a purely academic exercise.

Oliver Wolcott, Jr., of Connecticut, Alexander Hamilton's successor as secretary of the treasury, articulated the impression of many of the new arrivals.

No stranger can be here a day and converse with the proprietors, without conceiving himself in the company of crazy people. Their ignorance of the rest of the world, and their delusions with respect to their own prospects, are without parallel. Immense sums have been squandered in buildings which are but partly finished, in situations which are not, and never will be the scenes of business.

Wolcott was correct: unchecked speculation had indeed become the rule, and the results had been disastrous. A series of disappointing lot sales in 1792 and 1793—notwithstanding the detailed and full-scale engraving of the Ellicott plan on prominent display at each—had finally driven George Washington and the federal city commissioners to gamble the immediate fortunes of the capital on the remarkable charisma and considerable cupidity of an unmarried twenty-eight-year-old tycoon named James Greenleaf.

Greenleaf, the son of a well-to-do Boston merchant of French Huguenot descent, had left America in his early twenties for a consulship in The Hague, and while overseas he'd proven himself spectacularly good at making money in the manipulation of American promissory notes. That talent had brought him back to the United States in 1793 a paper millionaire, ready to speculate with the cash and credit he'd built up in Amsterdam. Greenleaf's political instincts had at first been razor sharp. He knew that the twin executive forces of the city were George Washington and the commissioners, and with this in mind he'd ingratiated himself with two of the men closest to the president, providing seed money for T. Lear & Co., Tobias Lear's ambitious but still mostly speculative mercantile proposition, and buying $14,000 worth of Thomas Johnson's Maryland property. The commissioners and Washington responded by giving Greenleaf an extraordinary bulk discount. With the average price of a lot during the summer of 1793 hovering between $200 and $300, their offer of three thousand parcels at $66 apiece was an outright gift; at the going rates, he would have to dispose of only half his property to individual buyers to make a considerable profit. By December Greenleaf had brought Robert Morris and fellow financier John Nicholson into the deal and procured another three thousand lots under conditions L'Enfant would have found outrageous: the three investors were assigned fifteen hundred specific lots in the northeast quarter of the city and told to choose the rest wherever they wished.

The commissioners imposed some stipulations. Greenleaf had to loan them $2,660 each month to help finance the work on the public buildings. And he would not be permitted to let all of his land sit undeveloped; Johnson, Stuart, and Carroll had finally seen the wisdom of L'Enfant's proposed requirement that buyers be required by contract to build on a percentage of their newly acquired property. What "required" and "build" meant, though, was a matter for the lawyers to decide, with the result that the city was filled with dozens of houses begun by Greenleaf, Morris, and Nicholson but finished only up to the attic story. Few of these houses or their lots found buyers, and by 1797, in the wake of the second economic depression in five years, Greenleaf had defaulted on his payments and was living off family charity after spending time in a Philadelphia debtor's prison. A year later Morris found himself behind those same bars, and Nicholson followed after another two years. The insolvency and incarceration of the district's most active speculators helped to push property values so low in the months before the scheduled arrival of Congress that the board of commissioners had summarily cut the plummeting price tags in half in a desperate attempt to get them moving in the other direction.

Still, the newly arriving members of the government did not find the city entirely vacant or urban life completely stagnant. A professional class was sputtering to life in the form of a handful of doctors and a few more lawyers and clergymen. Well-to-do mothers were ready to guide their marriageable daughters into the ambit of powerful young men of rising influence. Plans for a permanent theater were under way, and in the meantime Mrs. Adams and other arrivals could attend regular outdoor concerts, dancing assemblies, lectures on subjects ranging from botany to Masonic astronomy, and even one-night-only performances by the occasional trained animal. The coming of Congress also encouraged the birth of several new newspapers: the daily *National Intelligencer* and its weekly partner, the *Universal Gazette*, in the city; the *Advertiser* in Alexandria; and the *Washington Federalist*, the *Museum*, and the *Cabinet* in Georgetown.

In the spring census takers had combed the city—not an exhausting task—recording 3,210 free residents and about half that many slaves, numbers that made the seat of government larger than Georgetown, at least, but still considerably smaller than Alexandria. These two towns, envisioned by L'Enfant as a pair of synergistic suburbs buttressing a commercial juggernaut, had instead become outright rivals. In Georgetown especially, a residue of confusion and bitterness lingered for the proprietors who in 1791 had made what they'd thought was an ironclad bargain, only to see much of their land unsold and work on the city slowed to a crawl.

Those in the capital with mercantile dreams had been forced to down an equally bitter dose of reality, no one more so than Tobias Lear, who, after abandoning his scheme to establish a leading international trading concern in the district, was by 1800 slowly and painfully extricating himself from his business debts. Greenleaf's backing had vanished, Lear's own credit had run out, and in September 1800 he had discovered to his dismay that Virginia's stringent bankruptcy laws would do little to keep the creditors of T. Lear & Co. at bay. He still sat on the board of the Potomac Navigation Company and still ran a wharf in the channel between Rock Creek and Mason's Island, but the faith in the prospects of the city that had led him to so eagerly have L'Enfant purchase him a lot at the first sale had been quashed.

For a time L'Enfant had experienced a steady series of successes: his fete for the dauphin, his emblems for the Society of the Cincinnati, and his Constitutional ratification celebration, followed by the commission for Federal Hall and his capture of the federal city design; but by 1800 he had traveled down an equally steep slope of disappointment. Every task L'Enfant took on after his final exchange of letters with George Washington in February 1792 went wrong. He had bad luck and bad faith to blame, but he also seemed to be caught up in a pitiless cycle, as if everything he put his hand to were in one form or another a fruitless attempt to finish the business of the federal city.

Alexander Hamilton's industrial city of Paterson had quickly become less a quasi-utopian moneymaker and more a cousin to Washington's Potomac navigation schemes: truly remarkable for its aspirations but ultimately resilient only as a concept. Successful manufacturing ventures required an economy ripe for large investment, but the severe financial downturn of early 1792 that lasted well into 1793 dried up investment money. It also exacerbated the outright criminality of the Society for Establishing Useful Manufactures governor William Duer, also Hamilton's second in the treasury, who all but emptied the society's accounts through a variety of embezzlements discovered in March 1792.

Hamilton, concerned about "the public interest and my reputation"—his career, as he saw it, was riding on the success of the enterprise and the repudiation of Duer's machinations—shut himself inside his office and soon emerged with a new plan for the SEUM, one that included the aggressive pursuit of workers and loans from Europe to replace the capital his felonious associate had squandered. Hiring the well-known L'Enfant, his old Valley

Forge comrade, was presumably another way of emphasizing the solid footing of the project. But in reality it had no footing. The major's promise to Hamilton early in the proceedings that he would keep financial affairs under control went by the wayside as he found himself pushed and prodded to work at a large scale by one group of investors even while another was censuring him for making such grandiose plans.

L'Enfant's SEUM overseers turned out to be no antidote to the federal city commissioners. The SEUM board quickly exposed itself as a group of professional speculators unfamiliar with the techniques and systems of manufacturing that they would be supporting and promoting. Even worse for L'Enfant, they acted ever more distressingly like Johnson, Stuart, and Carroll in their lack of interest or expertise in the building of cities. Many of them had no way to understand, much less approve of, L'Enfant's very Washingtonesque plan; no copy of it has survived, but it was always described in terms of its large diagonal avenues and its ambitious infrastructure.

Finally, in an uncanny replay of the major's recent experience with the federal city, he had decamped to Philadelphia to prepare a more advanced version of the SEUM plan only to endure another spate of antagonistic decision making in his absence, including, most ominously, the appointment of a new superintendent named Samuel Ogden, an ironmaster with ideas of his own about the design of Paterson's canal and a low opinion of L'Enfant's engineering abilities. By March 1793 the narrative of disintegration had become oppressively familiar to L'Enfant, who wrote Hamilton in an all-too-practiced mode of complaint. "My whole labor," he said, "is likely once more to be made a means to gratify the petit interest of some men to the expulsion of me and the subversion of all my views."

By the end of the summer L'Enfant was no longer connected with the SEUM. And by 1796, the cotton mill having been sold and the other buildings abandoned, it was clear that Paterson would never approach the broad dimensions of Hamilton's dreams and L'Enfant's city plan. In the meantime, the major moved from one project to the next. During his residency at Paterson he had received a letter from Robert Morris, who had written simply and with his characteristic dryness, "I had like to have stopped work for fear of wanting money, that difficulty being removed, it will now be stopped from want of Major L'Enfant." Morris, it seems, wanted to own the grandest house in Philadelphia, and L'Enfant dedicated himself, on and off, to building it in the three years after his employ by the SEUM ended. The two men had probably first met in February 1778, when Steuben and his train had stopped at Morris's rented home in Manheim, Pennsylvania; the financier had later helped to arrange and pay for L'Enfant's foray back to France in the service of the Society of the Cincinnati. Now, in the early 1790s, Morris had a choice piece of property at the end of Chestnut Street and the wherewithal to build a formidable house. L'Enfant, whatever his travails in the interim, was still remembered as the designer of that memorable expression of nationalist ideals, Federal Hall, and a man who was not afraid to think big.

L'Enfant began work on Morris's mansion in 1793 but was pulled away in April 1794, when he received his first military commission in more than a decade. Secretary of War Henry Knox—presumably at the urging of Federalist friends and with the knowledge of President Washington—asked L'Enfant to supervise the replacement of an earthen defense on Mud Island, just south of Philadelphia. The major declared the existing design insufficient (it was the work a decade earlier of Louis Duportail, the man who'd been instrumental in procuring L'Enfant's promotion to major) and immediately suggested the flattening and reconstruction of the entire fort. But the Pennsylvania legislature refused to allocate the $6,000 that L'Enfant and Governor Thomas Mifflin had requested for the job, complaining about not only the price but also the navigational difficulties engendered by all the dirt being dumped into Delaware. After ten months the major was replaced.

No matter what the project, L'Enfant seemed able to work only on a grand scale, beyond the means and patience of his employers. He returned the greater part of his attention to Morris's house in 1794 and began adding to it almost maniacally, as if Morris had infinite wealth, inexhaustible patience, and taste that was open to almost any architectural exuberance. An explosion of rococo elements, "Morris's Folly" was most famous for its extravagant amount of marble and its incomplete mansard roof in a neighborhood of conservative colonials. In 1797 Morris finally put on his own temporary copper ceiling, just before his business reversals—the collapse of his speculations in the federal city prominent among them—landed him in debtor's prison.

Finally, late in the decade, less than twenty years after France and the United States had partnered in blood and glory at Yorktown, the two nations—one the land of L'Enfant's birth, the other his adopted home—came to the brink of war. Offended by Washington's negotiation of the Jay Treaty with Great Britain in the spring of 1795, the Directory (the ruling body in France) refused to host American envoys and began to seize American shipping vessels. By 1798 armed conflict had seemed all but certain, a dread exacerbated by news of General Napoleon Bonaparte's ominously bloody scythe through Italy and Austria.

The Quasi-War, as it would come to be known, quickly assumed paranoid proportions. Wild rumors spread in the newspapers and on the streets: the French fleet, led by Napoleon himself, was already headed toward Louisiana with designs on the entire American continent. In April 1798 High Federalists in Congress, orchestrated by Alexander Hamilton, armed American merchant vessels, earmarked $1 million for fortifications, and empowered the U.S. Navy, such as it was, to fire on French ships. On July 2 George Washington was nominated leader of the "New Army," with Hamilton as inspector general and second in command and Tobias Lear as a newly commissioned colonel. The entire affair, indisputably the lowest and most farcical political mark of the decade, eventually petered out thanks to President John Adams's refusal to buy into the chest beating, but in the meantime

An Unfinished House in Chestnut Street ("Morris's Folly"), by William Russell Birch, 1800

it created the spectacle of Washington leaving his farm once more, Hamilton making plans to march his army through the southern states to quell vocal Republican strongholds, Jefferson maintaining that blood-soaked France was soon destined to become an Arcadian democracy, and Adams reluctantly signing the heinous Alien and Sedition Acts at Abigail's enthusiastic prodding.

The farce had trickled down into the ranks as well. As George Washington and Alexander Hamilton formed a new military command and packed their officer corps with members of the Society of the Cincinnati, L'Enfant would naturally have sought to involve himself. In the same week that Washington accepted his final commission in service of his country, L'Enfant's direct application to Hamilton for an unknown post—possibly as a fortification engineer, but most likely for the reactivation of his majority within the army—was rebuffed. L'Enfant, learning through a third party that Hamilton may have called his national loyalties into question, immediately wrote his former patron to object: "I cannot hesitate nor do I delay one instant requesting your own explanation in what way has my former public employment become [a] matter for your animadversion!"

The letter sounds like any number of L'Enfant's defensive pleas over the years, with a crucial difference: this language was intended beyond doubt to initiate an affair of honor. Hamilton, no stranger to the code, simply turned L'Enfant's letter over and scratched his reply on the reverse, denying having made any such statements and concluding that "I could not wish to wound you but have uniformly desired and endeavoured to serve you." He wrote almost as if he were dealing with a deranged man, and in some ways he may have been.

Though L'Enfant would continue to elicit Hamilton's aid in his various claims on his federal city and Federal Hall work, any residual fellow feeling had been all but extinguished. The patron had become patronizing. The jocular sansculotte party at Valley Forge—that roomful of young officers in service to George Washington, forming lasting nationalist bonds beneath the ironic bonhomie—was a distant memory. Baron von Steuben perished in November 1794, and L'Enfant's other protectors fell by the wayside too. Robert Morris was in jail and no longer a person of consequence. In June 1799, one year after L'Enfant's challenge to Hamilton, news reached America of the death of Beaumarchais. But nothing, not even the letter twelve years earlier that had told him of his father's demise, could match the impact of the announcement in December 1799 that George Washington had died in his bed at Mount Vernon.

A week before his death the irrevocably re-retired general had written a famous description of the federal city to Capitol architect William Thornton, demonstrating that the seat of government was still very much on his mind: "By the obstructions continually thrown in its way, by friends or enemies, this city has had to pass through a fiery trial. Yet, I trust it will, ultimately, escape the ordeal with éclat." L'Enfant, who'd been the most expansive of optimists upon his arrival in Georgetown in 1791, now believed that the city's "escape" was impossible in the short run and dubious in the long. But the major had never openly second-guessed Washington and was not about to start now.

L'Enfant would write, often and in many different formulations, that the death of Washington deprived him of a "friend and principal dependency" in his "cause." This was equal parts wistfulness and self-delusion, as the president had barely, if ever, lifted a finger on L'Enfant's behalf after their parting of ways. Most likely L'Enfant was clinging to this consoling belief because he felt himself more alone than ever. Besides, though Washington's death may have denied L'Enfant his "friend," it also meant that he could now invoke the late president's name without shame or fear of correction.

Ironically, Washington's death was the best thing that could have happened for the capital, as Federalist and Republican ruptures temporarily closed, at least on the surface, in the genuine outpouring of grief for the passing of the country's first indisputable military and political hero. For a few crucial months, those in Philadelphia or anywhere could no longer so brazenly resist the transfer of government to Washington. William Thornton wasted no time in proposing that his design for the rotunda of the Capitol now include a mausoleum containing the president's remains at the very center of the great circular chamber. The proposition was put forth in genuine tribute but also to generate funds for an acceleration of work on the structure.

The death of Washington had many other ripples beyond the predictable outpourings of grief and the instant readjustment of the political landscape. One of those ripples was the return of Peter Charles L'Enfant to the city of his design, ready to make a case for proper acknowledgment and redress now that the one man to whom he felt silence was owed was no longer alive.

L'Enfant's lodging in Pontius Stelle's hotel, near the Capitol, was sublet from the official consul from Sweden, a man named Richard Soderstrom. A singularly mysterious character in the major's story, Soderstrom, despite his early and apparently easy camaraderie with L'Enfant, was to cause him more grief and less good than any other man he met in the United States, his antagonists in the federal city affair not excepted.

The spheres of Alexander Hamilton and Baron von Steuben in which L'Enfant moved, both in Philadelphia and New York, regularly intersected the international community. Most consuls were decidedly Federalist in their sympathies, banking on the advantages of dealing with a United States fully free of its cumbersome confederate origins, able to pay its debts, borrow money, and set up large-scale systems of trade. Soderstrom arrived in America in 1784 and easily made friends in the higher reaches of mercantile society, but he also seems to have been dogged by accusations of financial misconduct. He was recognized as consul from Sweden by Massachusetts in 1785 only after a threat of debtor's prison was blunted by a parade of wealthy and reputable Bostonians testifying to his character. L'Enfant was introduced to Soderstrom in New York at some point soon thereafter, writing later that "I lent him money the day we met, or rather the morning after the day we met." Their second recorded financial connection occurred in 1790, when the major, fresh off his renovation of Federal Hall, was able to help extract Soderstrom from yet another series of troublesome debts.

In 1794, immediately following L'Enfant's dispiriting sojourn in Paterson and two years after his exit from the federal city project, the major became Soderstrom's boarder in Philadelphia. L'Enfant spent much of this time at the home of Robert Morris, the rest living in Soderstrom's residence at the corner of Filbert and Eighth streets, near where Isaac Roberdeau resided with his new wife, the former Miss Blair, to whom the major had passed endearments during the winter of 1792. Owing to the legal documents that his financial relationship with Soderstrom eventually produced, more is known about the particulars of L'Enfant's daily existence in the middle 1790s than at any other time of his life. He was clearly in great pecuniary distress and living an almost ascetic life, sharing the rent for half of the house in return for "two unfurnished rooms." So as not to incur the expense of servants, he cleaned his own boots and shoes and lit his own fire. His wardrobe consisted of three shirts that were regularly sent out to a washerwoman.

Thirty dollars sufficed to furnish his rented bedroom with a small pine table and a pine bedstead covered with a simple mattress, coarse cotton sheets, and a small blanket. In his other room, his "study room," he placed two old chairs and an "old broken table" belonging to Soderstrom. The house seems to have been a fairly rowdy place, as Soderstrom often entertained "masters of trading vessels" with liquor, expensive meals, and apparently more than occasional prostitutes.

By 1799 L'Enfant had run out of work, had made his challenge of honor to Alexander Hamilton—based in large part on gossip passed along by Soderstrom himself—and seems to have found himself unable or unwilling to leave what had become little more than a cage. In 1800, finally, the two men moved their arrangement to the city of Washington, Soderstrom in the natural course of his consular duties and L'Enfant because George Washington was dead and the Congress would be meeting for the first time in the new capital.

While still in Philadelphia the major had sent two "memorials" to the federal city commissioners, asking for monetary compensation for his services as designer of the federal city. The commissioners had not obliged. Now at "so auspicious a juncture as that of the first seating" of Congress in the city of Washington, L'Enfant turned to the assembled federal legislators to seek relief from what he felt was a most unjust penury. This, then, is what he was doing in Richard Soderstrom's austere rooms in Stelle's Hotel, a building owned, in a discouraging irony, by Daniel Carroll of Duddington: he was penning a plea for recognition. The man who had so often refused payment for his services was asking for money, writing like a man possessed.

Over the next two decades L'Enfant would submit a new petition to nearly every new seating of Congress. He would recycle text, insert new information, revise or emphasize particular claims, but never would he waver far from the argument or the bitterness embedded in his first one, submitted in December 1800. The pages unfurled over the years, tens becoming hundreds, his contentions simple in outline but enormously complex in their details—too complex, certainly, for the forbearance of his audience. The memorials were effusions of outrage and frustration and confusion and sadness in a language that quickly unraveled when he was roused and unable to rely on sympathetic editors. More than one acquaintance, Soderstrom included, warned L'Enfant not to write so many words—his original memorial to the commissioners had run thirty-nine barely coherent pages—but he rarely showed any evidence of listening.

L'Enfant began his first memorial to Congress with a rambling summary sentence of nearly three hundred words, then described the terms of his engagement as he understood them when he came to Georgetown: George Washington and George Washington alone had been "the high authority by whom I acted." Supremacy over all the hands employed in the city had been conceded to himself, he wrote, as evidenced by the fact that workmen, surveyors included, had for months been sent to him without prior instructions. Only this arrangement, the possession of total authority for the delegation of work, could have produced a plan and system so particularly and masterfully adapted to Washington's desires.

His orders, as he had understood them, were to come directly from the president through the secretary of state, and for six months that was exactly how he had received them. From L'Enfant's perspective, the chronology was perfectly clear. First, Washington had approved his elevation to designer and announced it to the commission; second, he—L'Enfant—had made a beginning at all points; third, he'd brought the fully delineated plan to Philadelphia, where it had received rave reviews; finally, and suddenly, his authority had been removed and handed over to a body inimical to the health and future of the project. "The enemies of enterprise," L'Enfant called the commissioners, and he put at their feet the desire to rid themselves of the architect and the resulting "evil of injury to my fame and . . . the destruction of my fortune." Now, ten years later, L'Enfant had come to blame an unnamed mastermind, "an inimical envious genius," Washington's "primary consulted" who "precluded the president's own judgment." Interestingly, both Thomas Jefferson and Thomas Johnson were candidates for this villain's role, and by 1800 their crime was, to L'Enfant, obvious.

> The dearest interest of the City of Washington was sacrificed through the passion and weakness of its most esteemed supporters and the infatuation of some whom, wishing the seat of government stand a mere contemptible hamlet, had rested better satisfied with giving great name to small things than with having in reality those things done which were to have reflected an immortal honor on the nation.

An immense inconsistency lay at the core of L'Enfant's argument. If the interest of the city had been "sacrificed," as he said—and the evidence laid before the newly arriving Congress in 1800 seemed to support that conclusion—part of the responsibility simply had to fall on George Washington. The more L'Enfant wrote, the more convoluted became his detour around this reality. His method was to make Washington into a kind of oblivious covictim—precisely the same tactic perfected over the past decade by Jefferson, ironically, in his rhetorical assaults on Alexander Hamilton. Wherever logic indicated that Washington might have played a role in the reversal of his fortunes, L'Enfant called him "misled" or "innocent." In this formulation his patron had always been curiously passive wherever L'Enfant's detriment was concerned and curiously active where L'Enfant's interests lay. Always supporting his plans unconditionally, Washington was, apparently, equally and totally ignorant of their subversion or alteration. The truth lay somewhere in between, but for L'Enfant there was not and had never been any middle ground.

As claims for specific monies, his petitions made little sense. L'Enfant sometimes seemed unsure, in fact, just what he was asking for, other than some kind of large and just award. But as cries of pain, they are exquisitely clear. L'Enfant now began to refer to the "injuries" done him, and his tally of them were lengthy and comprehensive: injuries done to his fame and fortune in the disposal of his plan; injuries respecting the choice of architects for the Capitol and the President's House, "the design of which had been a primary condition of my engagement"; injuries caused by the theft of the sketches of these buildings as well as his plans for aqueducts, bridges, a "grand dock," and the Tiber canal; injuries resulting from the diminishment of his professional prospects in New York; and injuries related to his loss of salary and recognition. L'Enfant was congenitally unable to restrain himself from romantic exaggeration and suspect similes, but in this case the metaphor of a wound seems entirely apt.

> The cases offered here for consideration are not cases merely of a missing of gain or of deprivation, the causes of trivial embarrassment momently felt—but cases of real loss, of disappointment of absolute dues, of right dependency and of abuses altogether—the cause, the active cause, of my total ruin.

His return blow at those who had harmed him was simply put and deeply felt: whatever scars he bore, the city shared. All of L'Enfant's points—about speculation, altered plans, neglect of public areas, design of public buildings—circled back on themselves, leading to his most bitter and prophetic statement, his prediction that "the work of a century" would now be required to finish the work he could have accomplished in less than twenty years.

Here was his most powerful assertion hurled at the commissioners and Jefferson. Not only had they ruined L'Enfant; far worse, they had failed in their public trust—and the city had suffered because of them. Why this should lead the House of Representatives to award L'Enfant back pay for his services he never made clear; in fact, about all that was clear was the astonishing depth of his disappointment and anger.

As L'Enfant continued to compose his memorials, Mrs. Adams did indeed get her equivocal wish to go back home to New England when Thomas Jefferson was sworn in as president in March 1801. For many years now, in private conversations with friends of various Federalist shadings, L'Enfant would have heard Jefferson disparaged, derided, and denounced, and he must have had plenty to add. But in the end the Federalists had lost. Jefferson's individualistic vision had routed the nationalist energies generated during the era dominated by George Washington and Alexander Hamilton, and now the country was settling into what would be a quarter century dominated by the man from Monticello and his political disciples.

On November 22, 1800, with Abigail in New York tending to their fading son, John Adams had delivered his State of the Union address, exhorting the members of Congress to think of the city of Washington "as the capital of a great nation advancing with unexampled rapidity in arts, in commerce, in wealth, and in population, and possessing within itself those energies and resources which, if not thrown away or lamentably misdirected, will secure to it a long course of prosperity and self-government." Jefferson's first inaugural address five months later, in unsubtle contrast, did not mention the city at all. In fact, the subject seems to have been out of his field of vision for a long while. Between 1796 and 1800—as he'd mounted total political warfare against the Federalist administration to which, as vice president, he ostensibly belonged—Jefferson's mountain of correspondence related to the seat of government had dwindled to one reasonably spirited defense of a charge laid against him that he wished it to remain in Philadelphia.

The stewardship of the city of Washington was not entirely absent from the new president's mind. But in Jefferson's definition the capital consisted of the two public buildings, the avenue connecting them, and very little else. It was a point he made explicitly to the city commissioners just a few months after his inauguration, a statement that became a manifesto of sorts, a clear set of limits on the city's scope as well as a philosophy about the proper function of the seat of government.

> I consider the erection of the Representative's chamber and making a good gravel road from the new bridge on Rock Creek along the Pennsylvania and Jersey avenues to the Eastern Branch as the most important objects for ensuring the destinies of the city which can be undertaken. All others appear to me entirely subordinate and to rest on considerations quite distinct from these.

By 1802 these projects were under way. The first step was the graveling of Pennsylvania and New Jersey avenues to finish the connection between Georgetown and the Eastern Branch that L'Enfant had made a central part of his very first memorandum to Washington in March 1791. Next came the beautification of Pennsylvania Avenue between the President's House and the Capitol. To this end Jefferson rather proprietarily made his own section drawing for a guide, almost as if he were sketching out a new idea for the approach road at Monticello. He illustrated a set of footpaths, gutters, and four rows of Lombardy poplars that were to provide relief from constant soreness of foot and the oppressive summer sun.

Jefferson followed this initiative by hiring English expatriate Benjamin Henry Latrobe for the newly created position of surveyor of public buildings to oversee "public construction." This meant, most immediately, that Latrobe would design and erect the south wing of the Capitol for the House of Representatives and oversee the renovation of the Senate chambers. Latrobe—who had been privately trained in architecture and engineering in Britain and had the design of only a few country houses to his name when he emigrated to America in 1796—showed contempt for nearly everything about L'Enfant's plan, including its scale, and he followed the president's lead in focusing closely on a small but highly symbolic portion of the overall ground.

Jefferson's silence on the precincts outside the city's center can, in fact, be viewed as his third major contribution, part of a series of counterpropositions to L'Enfant's work that set the stage for decades of presidential indifference to the larger plan for Washington, D.C. A man who at his death would leave behind far more personal debt than any other founder was, perhaps understandably, violently allergic to incurring public obligations, and so Jefferson categorically refused to reopen the question of obtaining a large loan for the development of the seat of government. He also denied the legal right of the federal government to build its own wharves on the Eastern Branch, and most notably he worked behind the scenes in Congress to ensure that no mausoleum in honor of George Washington would ever grace the Capitol rotunda. This was no personal feud; it was a matter of Jefferson's deep-seated belief in the rule of law over the glorification of any one man. The seat of government must remain an administrative center and never become a shrine to a single dead hero. Naming the city "Washington" had, to his mind, been more than enough.

The federal city to Jefferson and the Jeffersonians was only one place, not *the* place. Without executive enthusiasm of the kind that Washington had tried to provide and that John Adams had at least nominally continued, a truly national character and scale for the city was abandoned. It was as if Jefferson had made a binding decision for successive generations of politicians not to think about most of the federal district. The stance was not unpopular, and indeed such a laissez-faire attitude would reign for seven more decades and seventeen more presidential administrations.

L'Enfant would not have found any of this indifference surprising. But in one way, at least, he had reason to appreciate the inauguration of the new president: Jefferson's arrival meant that Adams, a man L'Enfant knew not the slightest bit, was replaced by a man who had personally experienced the federal city project in 1791 and 1792. For two years the major's petitions to the city commissioners and to Congress had brought him no satisfaction, and now, in November 1801, he appealed directly to Jefferson, in a memorial reduced to an almost unbelievably brief four pages.

Nearly five months later he had still heard nothing. With Congress coming up for adjournment in March 1802, L'Enfant sent a tortuously apologetic reminder to the president. "Under the apprehension of impropriety in the liberty I took of addressing you," he began, "you will excuse where the intention was purely to prove my respect and esteem." A direct appeal to the highest authority in the land was the way Major L'Enfant had received his commission as a major in the Continental Army and secured his position as planner of the federal city, and he must have hoped that one more use of the method might prove the charm.

But Jefferson was not Washington, and upon receiving this second importunity he responded promptly, mostly because what he had to say required little mental effort. After an interval of just two days he replied to L'Enfant with their final recorded communication.

> Your letter of the 12th is at hand. Immediately on the receipt of the former one I referred it to the board of commissioners, the authority instituted by law for originating whatever proceedings regarding this city have been confided by the legislature to the executive. Their opinion, which I approved, was that they could only repeat you the offer formerly made with the approbation of General Washington, and they undertook to do this. For any thing else, the powers of the legislature are alone competent, and therefore your application to them was the only measure by which it could be obtained.

Again, it was a typically implacable Jeffersonian recourse to the letter of the law. At the end of his services on the federal city, L'Enfant had been offered a lump sum of $666 (which he had declined), and now Jefferson was telling him that this amount would have to suffice. Though L'Enfant was hardly finished appealing his case to the United States government, Jefferson's message seems from the long vantage of history to be the real closing of the major's hope for a satisfactory resolution, if by "satisfactory" we mean one that included official recognition of his services from a person in a position to gratify L'Enfant's desire for proper credit.

CHAPTER 12

Getting the Go By

By the second decade of the nineteenth century, a succession of cash-strapped heirs had left the main house at Mount Vernon in a sadly dilapidated state, nearly a ruin. Its roof was falling in, and its portico was standing thanks only to a row of wooden beams wedged beneath. The view of the Potomac from the once immaculately foursquare porch was overgrown, the lawn full of untended foliage. But to follow L'Enfant's life to its end, we need to work through this bramble and bracken and down to the banks of the river, where the view was still picturesque and unbroken. About a mile to the north on the opposite shore rose an estate called Warburton Manor, just visible from the late president's decaying docks, where a man named Thomas Attwood Digges was finishing out the last two decades of one of the truly astonishing lives of his time or any other.

Scion of a wealthy family with an aristocratic lineage stretching back centuries, Thomas Digges was born in 1742 at Warburton Manor to William and Ann Digges and was connected through blood and marriage to most of the dominant Catholic clans in the tidewater Potomac, including the Carrolls, the Notleys, the Youngs, the Roziers, the Brents, the Waltons, and the Attwoods. But famous kin hadn't kept Digges in Maryland, from which he'd fled in 1767 at the age of twenty-five for mysterious legal reasons, perhaps a consequence of his unfortunate tendency to make off with the personal property of others. He first made his way to Lisbon, where he got involved in the shipping trade, then left after a few years for London. There he wrote and anonymously published *The Adventures of Alonso,* a woolly picaresque featuring a Portuguese businessman and stuffed full of adultery, elopement, South American wanderings, enslavement, dramatic nautical escapes, smuggling, and assassination. "A political romance," one British literary magazine called it, but whatever it was, scholars would eventually credit Digges as its author and accept it as the first novel written by an eventual American citizen.

In London, when he wasn't writing, Digges ingratiated himself with pro-Whig members of Parliament and others who sympathized with American grievances, a group that may have briefly included Pierre-Augustin Caron de Beaumarchais. Digges was certainly present in the British capital and involved in intercontinental intrigues between 1775 and 1777, the period when the fantastically wealthy French playwright was also in town finishing an exile from Paris and forming the fictional export firm of Hortalez and Company to cover the shipping of arms and men to America—cargo that would soon include an art student named Pierre Charles L'Enfant.

While on a short visit to Paris in 1777, Digges swore his allegiance to the newly declared United States of America, an oath personally administered by Benjamin Franklin. During the latter part of the war, Digges was instrumental in providing news of two men imprisoned in Great Britain. One was L'Enfant's fellow artist John Trumbull; the other, held in the Tower of London, was Henry Laurens, first president of the Continental Congress and father of John Laurens. In his spare time Digges published pro-American propaganda and helped to convey secret overtures of peace to John Adams from British prime minister William North.

After the War for Independence, Digges moved to Ireland to spur immigration to Virginia as a way of augmenting the crews of the Potomac Navigation Company. In Belfast he befriended Wolfe Tone and may have aided the legendary rebel in his effort to foment revolution against the Crown. In the early 1790s, just as L'Enfant's federal city turmoil was coming to a full boil, Digges was in communication with Alexander Hamilton as an "industrial spy," looking to recruit talented mechanics and inventors for the Society for Establishing Useful Manufactures. While in Ireland, Digges also fought off an effort to deny him his lawful inheritance as the family's oldest surviving male after learning that his name did not appear in his father's will. In this effort he was aided by Trumbull, now free, and by a character reference from George Washington. With allies such as these, Digges won that battle in 1795 or 1796, and in 1798, after more than thirty years abroad, he returned to Maryland at the age of fifty-six to at last take possession of Warburton Manor.

Digges's efforts on behalf of American independence, the Potomac Navigation Company, and the SEUM earned him at least four invitations to dine at Mount Vernon in the year preceding George Washington's death. Digges extended a final hand of friendship to Washington, his Masonic brother, by serving as an informal host and assistant during the solemn funeral held at Mount Vernon on December 18, 1799. He then ferried across the Potomac and back to Warburton, where the years unwound until 1816, by which time Digges was no longer alone in his manor. He had taken in a very peculiar boarder, a permanent charge whose path across the American firmament had been as unique and transfixing as his own.

This information first appears in the postscript to a letter written in 1816 by Digges to his friend James Monroe, who was doubling as secretary of state and war under President James Madison. Digges made special mention of his charge to Monroe because the boarder was a person they both happened to know and whom they had clearly discussed on some previous occasion.

> The old major is still an inmate with me, quiet, harmless, and unoffending as usual. I fear from symptoms of broken shoes, rent pantaloons, out at the elbows etc. etc. etc. etc. that he is not well off—manifestly disturbed at his getting the go by.

The "old major" was Peter Charles L'Enfant, removed once and for all from the onrushing current of American history. The final leg of his journey had turned the accomplished orchestrator of grand public spaces into the forlorn ward of a private family. But he had found his way out of the avaricious clutches of Richard Soderstrom. Thomas Digges was perhaps the first patron, in a career filled with exceptional patrons, who was able to give L'Enfant what he needed when it was needed.

Shortly after receiving President Jefferson's perfunctory final letter in 1802, L'Enfant, the haunted, scribbling figure in an upstairs bedroom, had become the victim of an outright swindle. Richard Soderstrom seems to have known—and would have been in a position to know—that L'Enfant would one day receive a favorable decision in response to one of his memorials. Soderstrom's advice to keep the petitions short and simple, and therefore more likely to succeed, may have originated in conversations with members of the House Committee on Claims. These same legislators may also have given Soderstrom reason to believe that the time was ripe to file a lawsuit seeking to garnishee a portion of L'Enfant's future earnings, an action that otherwise makes little sense given that its target was a man who had no job and could not afford more than three shirts. L'Enfant, in his response to the lawsuit, made no doubt of his astonished subscription to such an interpretation: "Upon what principle, but that of the most villainous speculation can he presume to charge me for those expenses?"

Soderstrom's suit reached back a decade to charge L'Enfant not only for rent money but also for play tickets, newspapers shipped to Sweden and Denmark, pay and meals for Soderstrom's servants, parties for Dutch and Swedish ship captains, and firewood for half of the house. "With respect to his charge for the wages and victuals of his servants," L'Enfant wrote in his defense, "with as much propriety I think he could have charged me with his horse food and for the expenses of the number of harlots of his friends who he had in care to provide for.

"I was merely a lodger," he continued, "one who Mr. Soderstrom had the audacity to tell everybody he had taken in charitably, when at the same time for two unfurnished rooms I agree to share half the rent of the whole house." L'Enfant also referred to his "negligence of particular documents to prove legally" his side of the story, a tragic recurrence of one of the major's central flaws: his failure to take care of his own finances in the expectation that someone else would. In 1808, four years after dissolving his living arrangement with Soderstrom and two years after predictably losing the lawsuit, L'Enfant finally received from Congress a settlement of $4,600. Most of that sum went in lien to the Swede, the rest to various attorneys and to the owner of Rhodes Tavern, where L'Enfant had lived on credit for a time after quitting Soderstrom. His claim nominally successful but his distress unrelieved, L'Enfant continued to produce his petitions and was awarded another $1,300 two years later. All of it, apparently, went to an additional round of creditors, and so he kept writing.

L'Enfant's repeated pleas for money had whittled away the elegance and self-assurance of his younger self. He had become very much a beggar, even a living ghost, perhaps the capital's very first. Benjamin Henry Latrobe had written of L'Enfant in such a vein in an 1806 journal entry.

> Daily through the city stalks the picture of famine, L'Enfant and his dog. The plan of the city is probably his, though others claim it. He had the courage to undertake any public work whatever that was offered to him. He has not succeeded in any, but was always honest and is now miserably poor. He is too proud to receive any assistance, and it is very doubtful in what manner he subsists.

L'Enfant had managed to become itinerant within the bounds of a city of no more than fifteen thousand people, moving from tavern to tavern and running up debts under the intermittent threat of eviction. He seems to have aged two years for every one in the decades following his departure from the federal city project. A man who was once the picture of impetuousness and self-assured animation now seemed old and tired beyond recovery.

In this context an old revolutionary acquaintance reached out with an unexpected offer of startling generosity. In July 1812, as the drums of war against Great Britain were beating in Congress, L'Enfant received a letter containing a most surprising instruction: he was to proceed to West Point to begin his tenure as a professor in "the Art of Engineering." The letter was signed by Secretary of War William Eustis, but there was no doubt that the proposal was in some part the work of L'Enfant's old Valley Forge companion Secretary of State James Monroe.

It might have been just the thing to draw L'Enfant out of his cocoon, but characteristically he refused the appointment. He provided a lengthy and apologetic set of reasons for leaving the teaching post "unaccepted but not rejected," perhaps because it was a government position and not just an offer of recompense, or because he sensed the hand of Monroe and did not want to seem ungrateful. L'Enfant explained to Eustis that he preferred an appointment as an engineer of fortifications, outlining his worry that an instructor's position at West Point would foreclose that option. Perhaps in his paranoid way he assumed that this was the intent of the offer, but if so he exercised a rare judiciousness by not including the accusation in his response. L'Enfant's reply of July 17, 1812, was a remarkable show of self-awareness for a man who so often seemed blind to his own psychological excesses.

> I have not the rigidity of manner, the tongue, nor the patience, nor indeed any of the inclinations peculiar to instructors. I am not fond of youth. I am adverse to the society of those self important talkative temperaments whose vanity for what little they remember from the reading of works makes them talk at random about every subject and on matters and things which they often do not understand and which so frequently makes fools be mistaken for genius.

He also protested, tellingly, that as an instructor he "would have to encounter the difficulties of language."

Monroe now wrote him a quick and personal note "in the spirit and feelings of an old revolutionary fellow soldier and friend," as he put it, trying to talk the major out of his decision.

> The appointment offered to you is an honorable one. It is a comfortable asylum and independence for life. It was, I am satisfied, intended for you as such. You have been so long out of the public service, in the civil engineer department, and other proper obtained place, that it was impossible to do better for you. Indeed you are the only foreigner in the country for whom as much could have been done.

L'Enfant, who would not have been happy to see himself referred to as a "foreigner," remained unswayed and continued to prepare his petitions for delivery to Congress. Still Monroe, one of the few members of Washington's early military family to become a staunch political Jeffersonian, did not abandon him. L'Enfant had expressed a preference for work as an engineer, and that was what he soon received. As the Napoleonic Wars raging across

Europe threatened to spill over into a naval conflict in American waters, Monroe engaged the major in May 1813 to report on the condition of the fortifications along the Potomac that had been deployed to protect the federal city from attack. Specifically, Monroe wanted him to head for a walled battery of artillery named Fort Warburton.

This commission brought the major to Warburton Manor, though perhaps not for the first time, as some of Thomas Digges's own letters refer to previous surveys of his property by "a French engineer officer of some celebrity," which could have meant L'Enfant. But those surveys had occurred in 1794, when Digges was still in Europe, and so the two men probably met for the first time when L'Enfant arrived to inspect the fort standing watch over the Potomac a few hundred yards west of the Digges family mansion. L'Enfant made his tour of the defenses and suggested, predictably, that they be totally demolished and replaced with a larger and more elaborate fortification of his own design. This report was filed, no such action was taken, and the major seems not to have returned to the site until 1814, after the British navy came calling.

John Armstrong, William Eustis's short-lived successor as Madison's war secretary, had been firmly convinced that the redcoats would never attack Washington. "What the devil will they do here?" he had reportedly said, only to realize far too late that the federal city was indeed a British target, part of a purely symbolic campaign to exact revenge for the destruction of government buildings in Canada and to divert American attention from more tactical objectives on the shores of Lake Ontario and Lake Erie. No strike was more symbolic than the torching of Washington on August 24, 1814, which was inaugurated by the spectacle of British soldiers holding a mock session of Congress in the Senate chamber. As the ashes of the capital cooled, the British sent seven warships up the Potomac, and on August 27 they stopped at Fort Warburton in readiness for a fight.

The battle never happened. At seven in the evening the British hurled a few shells at the fort, following which, much to their commander's surprise, the Americans ran. The garrison, mistakenly fearing that British troops fresh from burning Washington were heading south to occupy the high ground and make themselves at home in Thomas Digges's house, spiked the cannons, abandoned the post, and set off explosive charges to finish the job the British warships had barely begun. Samuel Dyson, the fort's commander, was eventually court-martialed for dereliction of duty; meanwhile, the enemy fleet spent three days looting Alexandria of tobacco, cotton, and sugar before heading back out to sea unmolested.

This self-inflicted destruction finally united L'Enfant, Digges, and Monroe as they walked together amid the ruins of Fort Warburton, stepping among Acquia blocks, bricks, small timber, and several hundred barrels of lime, and discussed the sorry state of the Potomac defenses. L'Enfant took one look and repeated the suggestion he'd made a year earlier to tear down and rebuild, his case bolstered now by the sight of so much blasted rubble. This time Monroe agreed. By September 15 L'Enfant was answering to "sir" again and enthusiastically receiving men, wheelbarrows, spades, and axes. As Digges noted just two weeks into the work, "The engineer major, as usual, is ardently at it Sundays not excepted. Seems well pleased at what he is about."

L'Enfant had told Monroe the truth: his greatest desire was simply to take charge of a building project. But all of the temperamental flaws he'd described to Eustis could not be submerged simply because the assignment was more to his liking. Rebuilding Fort Warburton should have been a routine charge, more or less, but L'Enfant would not let go of his insistence that anything he did be done *en grand* and exclusively on his terms. By May 1815 he had stopped providing updates to Eustis, and in response to Monroe's insistence on a progress report, L'Enfant snapped in spectacular fashion. His reply to Monroe's letter of May 19 went further in its paranoia and hypersensitivity than any of his memorials to the commissioners or Congress. As if justifying every prior wariness shown toward him, L'Enfant complained of being asked to work too quickly and then leaped past any concrete discontents to write of "the evil genius who seems bent to my destruction," some sort of metaphysical entity sapping his strength and will and making him prey to flu and toothaches and severe headaches "caused no doubt by the perplexity of my mind and the afflicting contemplation of late events."

The letter became less and less comprehensible until it is difficult to make sense of individual sentences. One inconclusive but hardly improbable line of thought holds that the pain in L'Enfant's wounded leg had by this time caused him to develop an opium habit, and such an addiction would help to explain some of the pronounced emotional and mental bewilder-ment he now exhibited. But whatever its confusions, the letter ended on a painfully clear note of despair.

> The retrospect review of the cause of my misery truly dispirits me and makes me pray for an end to my existence. I now truly find myself as a robbed castaway individual on a strange shore without home without friend without resources whatsoever at my command and deprived of all relations on whom I could call for assistance, and a debtor of several thousand dollars besides for the bitter bread I have eaten and this in a country too in whose cause I engaged in the early time of life for whose service I bled and spent a good fortune.

It is not certain that L'Enfant ever sent this letter. Its date is difficult to specify, thanks to a tear in the upper corner of the first page, and there is no record that Monroe ever received it. In September 1815 the War Department terminated L'Enfant's contract on a technicality, the British threat having been extinguished and wartime commissions at an end, but from the point of view of history, this message to Monroe, probably written and perhaps sent in June, was very much the major's goodbye. He had thrown tantrums before, but none like this one, which reveals not his usual vigor in promoting his cause but rather an irreversible weariness at his core.

The old major might well have returned to one of his rented rooms at this point and perished there, forgotten. But if L'Enfant always alienated people, he also attracted solicitude and found someone willing to take him in or shelter his ambitions. His work on the fortification behind him—it was to be his last public employment—the major stayed put at Warburton Manor, taken in by Thomas Attwood Digges.

In 1816 Digges was well into his seventies and had become, as far as we can tell, a man satisfied to care for his estate and his odd collection of charges. His return to America and his advancing age seemed to have made him quieter, more sanguine, no longer the rake. The continuing work on Fort Warburton—now renamed Fort Washington—and his willingness to shelter peregrine acquaintances made the manor a lively and unpredictable place. "I call it a hotel," wrote Digges, "myself little less troubled than the bar keeper of a tavern, all however pro bono publico." The Latin ("free and in the interest of the public") was obviously meant ironically, but in the case of the old major, it seems to have been true.

In a more positive echo of his time with Soderstrom, L'Enfant became a kind of permanent houseguest, continuing his petitions to Congress with the same aggrieved sense and mangled English but with less underlying intensity. Digges's solicitousness is palpable—in one letter he described L'Enfant to Monroe as "a harmless honorable minded man and though a great oddity I believe as good an engineer as any one we have," and in another added an empathetic note about the old major's routine: "Never facing toward the fort, though frequently dipping into the eastern ravines and hills of the plantation, picking up fossils and periwinkles. Early to bed and rising, working hard with his instruments on paper eight or ten hours every day as if to give full and complete surveys of his works, etc., but [I] neither ever see or know his plans."

Reading this note, one might rather romantically imagine the major in his rooms with compass and pencil creating a portfolio for posterity: a refined plan of the city of Washington, a finished drawing of Alexander Hamilton's manufacturing center at Paterson, new and better designs for the charred Capitol and President's House. But none of the work L'Enfant was doing at Warburton with his "instruments" seems to have survived. Digges, meanwhile, had his own suits to settle resulting from the work on Fort Washington as completed by Colonel Walker Armistead, L'Enfant's successor. For this purpose Digges began to spend considerable time in the city of Washington, leaving L'Enfant at Warburton Manor, the two men sending small notes and news up and down the Potomac. L'Enfant's health continued to deteriorate, his once indomitable energy sapped by fevers, headaches, and the ague. In one late letter to Digges he describes being "quiet sick of rheumatism"—the misspelling adding a soft touch of pathos—and adds a melancholy and yet somehow comforting botanical note.

> The snowstorm of the day before . . . has done . . . injury to every vegetable thing than could be imagined. All our peas and other things which began to appear above ground are lost and the peach tree and grape vines I fear destroyed.

These are the last words that survive from L'Enfant as a resident at Warburton Manor. They seem to stand as their own kind of eulogy, and the end of his tale must surely have seemed near. But his time there was not to be the final turn in the strange story of L'Enfant's life.

Thomas Attwood Digges died in Washington on December 6, 1821, at the age of seventy-nine. He was eulogized five days later in the *National Intelligencer,* the capital's most prominent paper, as "an undeviating republican and patriot." The comically reductive notice also made note of those "numerous acquaintances of the deceased" who had "partaken of the pleasures of his hospitable mansion."

L'Enfant continued to reside at Warburton for another three years, keeping watch over the estate during a time of uncertainty, until the property passed into the possession of Digges's sister Elizabeth, a daughter-in-law of former commissioner Daniel Carroll. She had little interest in keeping old lodgers on, which threw L'Enfant into such acute fear and distress that he prefaced a January 1824 petition to Congress—the last he'd ever deliver—by saying "such is the gloom of my situation as indeed I feel at time inclined to hasten the doom which seems to await me." The old major might even have made good on his threat of suicide had he not received an unexpected letter from Thomas Digges's nephew less than a month later.

> I have to inform you that it would give me pleasure if you would come up and take your residence here. You may rest assured, Dear Sir, that I have considered your situation and know that it has been an unpleasant one; if a hearty welcome to Greenhill will make it more pleasant, I can assure you have it from all my family.

A mule would be sent for his things. With this move of about twenty miles, to a homestead just outside the federal district on its northeast angle, close by the Eastern Branch, L'Enfant's list of major patrons was complete: his father, Beaumarchais, Baron von Steuben, Alexander Hamilton, George Washington, James Monroe, Thomas Attwood Digges, and, finally, William Dudley Digges.

Green Hill was less dramatically situated than Warburton, but it was still a sizable plantation. Slave quarters surrounded a twenty-five-year-old two-story frame house, perched on a grass terrace above a small garden embraced by peach and plum trees. Here L'Enfant lived less as the resident of a makeshift inn, as he had at Warburton, than as a kind of eccentric elderly relative living out his days amid an active family estate. By one report L'Enfant spent much of his time tending flowers and looking at the sky, planning to go into the city of Washington to continue his pursuit of his aging claims but somehow never making the trip.

All this time, and into all of his temporary residences, he'd carried with him a sizable selection of his life's correspondence. He'd kept statements of account, letters of appointment to the ranks of captain and major in the Continental Army, his invitation to become professor of engineering at West Point, his parole certificates, various congressional petitions and affidavits, and letters to and from Tobias Lear, Baron von Steuben, Robert Morris, the Marquis de Lafayette, Thomas Jefferson, James Monroe, Alexander Hamilton, and George Washington, among others. Taken as a whole, the collection was and is a record of his remarkable service, and of the wrongs visited upon him, but also an account of the epic times he saw and the luminous folks with whom he had been associated: great artists, movers of great events, and four of the first five presidents of the United States. The correspondence forms the core of the documentary record of his life and tells a bitter tale: here was an artist in retirement just a few miles away from the city he'd designed, an accomplishment for which he'd never been given proper recognition.

But L'Enfant's stay at Green Hill was also a sweet tale, for he had finally found shelter among people who seem to have genuinely cared about his well-being. Nor was his past entirely finished with him. For in the parlors and gardens of Green Hill we arrive at a narrative coincidence that seems to belong to nineteenth-century fiction, to the kind of overdetermined incidents that the late Thomas Attwood Digges had written into *The Adventures of Alonso.* L'Enfant's final place of residence was to link him to a time so far in the past that it must have seemed to belong to another person's life.

It is November 1791, thirty-three years earlier. L'Enfant is riding his horse out of the federal district, heading for the quarries at Acquia Creek after peremptorily ordering the destruction of a half-finished mansion belonging to the wealthiest man in the region. He is not worried; he is sure of his right to do so and believes in his heart that he has the goodwill and approbation of President Washington. He has given the rising mansion walls much thought, but perhaps not so much to their owner. Daniel Carroll of Duddington is no less headstrong than L'Enfant; he is a young man with deep local roots and the means to provide a large and comfortable house for his family. His wife is the former Ann Brent, sister to the Brents who own the sandstone quarries toward which L'Enfant is traveling. The latest addition to the Carroll family is little Eleanor, not yet age one. This is to be her place of growing up—at least until the major's assistants arrive to take it down brick by brick.

After a few years and some legal maneuvering, the house is rebuilt a few hundred feet away at the expense of the federal government. Eleanor Carroll grows up in Duddington Manor, a spacious Federal-era Georgian with a stolid four-columned front porch built on lot 93 along the unfinished avenue called New Jersey. She watches the federal city slowly emerge from the land-scape—she grows faster than it does—and then goes on to meet and, after a time, marry a man named William Dudley Digges. Eleanor Digges moves to Green Hill, just across the northeastern boundary of the federal district, and settles into a life typical of the wealthier sort at this time and place, having many children and running with her husband a small plantation with nu-merous slaves and other resources.

In 1821 her husband's fabled uncle Thomas dies. After an interval of three years, when it becomes clear that William will not gain title to the War-burton mansion down the Potomac, Eleanor agrees to take in the harmless old architect with the French accent and the hickory cane and the trunk full of drawing materials and letters who, she cannot help but understand, will make Green Hill the last home of his life.

She seems to take in the old major without hesitation. As a girl, Eleanor had heard the story of how the house in which she was to spend her child-hood had been torn down by George Washington's impatient and imperious designer. Given her good fortune and happy marriage, given the passage of time and the dilatory progress of the city, the demise of that house may have become nothing more than a curiosity, a tale for the amusement of the next generation.

If Major L'Enfant and Eleanor Digges ever share a smile of bewilder-ment over the vagaries of fate, though, it is never recorded.

L'Enfant was not the last man to exit his employment on the federal city in a state of antagonism or disillusionment. In fact, nearly everyone who followed in his footsteps came to equal grief, and in 1824, the year of his move to Green Hill, the entire proposition was still shadowed by the dark clouds of its original troubles.

During the first slow lot sale in October 1791, Andrew Ellicott had expressed his pique that buyers weren't asking him, the surveyor, about the division of lots. His complaints had only grown louder after L'Enfant's departure. Ellicott returned to the city of Washington from Philadelphia on March 31, 1792, taking charge of the design in the midst of the proprietors' agitation for the major's return. His surveys had not been completed quickly enough to please the commissioners, and Ellicott, a skilled, meticulous professional tired of being rushed, soon began to write letters that sounded like barely paraphrased versions of L'Enfant's. "In the execution of the plan of the city of Washington," he summarized, "I have met with innumerable difficulties." Ellicott's tenure as official planner of the city would exceed L'Enfant's by only a month, his imminent exit signaled in an ultimatum to President Washington on March 16, 1793: "I do require an examination into the general execution of the plan by men of known professional abilities in that way otherwise I shall consider myself a sacrifice at the shrine of ignorance."

In the complete absence of such men of "known professional abilities," the sacrifice was made, and Ellicott left for Pennsylvania and less chaotic responsibilities there. The role of chief surveyor and planner of the federal city then passed to a rapid succession of men: Isaac Briggs, Benjamin and Joseph Ellicott, Thomas Freeman, Nicholas King, Robert King, Sr., and Nicholas King again, until in 1802 Thomas Jefferson took the sensible though long-overdue step of abolishing the board of commissioners, against whom all these men had struggled, and replacing it with a quartet of professionals, each responsible for a different facet of the work on the city and reporting directly to the president. In June 1802, ten weeks after referring L'Enfant's final personal appeal back to the commissioners—a body Jefferson probably had already decided to dissolve—the president appointed Robert Brent, former owner of the Acquia quarries and Duddington's brother-in-law, as the federal city's first mayor. A few months later the commission was dissolved, and Thomas Munroe was named superintendent, Nicholas King surveyor of the city, and Benjamin Henry Latrobe surveyor of public buildings.

In Latrobe the federal city encountered a man whose architectural expertise and self-regard began to match L'Enfant's. He was also a friend and artistic sibling to Jefferson, and his derision for L'Enfant and George Washington and the city the two men had planned reached vituperative levels.

It has been said that the idea of creating a new city, better arranged in its local distribution of houses and streets, more magnificent in its public buildings, and superior in the advantages of its site to any other in the world, was the favorite folly of General Washington. After the law had been established, that there should be a city, General Washington seems to have thought that enough had been done towards making it. Everything else was badly planned and conducted. L'Enfant's plan has in its contrivance every thing that could prevent the growth of the city.

Latrobe blamed L'Enfant, whom he called "this singular man, of whom it is not known whether he was ever educated to the profession, and who indubitably has neither good taste nor the slightest practical knowledge," for the rash of disastrous financial speculation and the city's lack of progress, without the slightest knowledge of everything the major had done to try to avoid the dangers of speculation and put the project on a sound footing. L'Enfant had, of course, been "educated to the profession" at a school, the Royal Academy of Painting and Sculpture, that in the early nineteenth century an Englishman such as Latrobe would still have recognized as one of the best in the world.

The major turned seventy on August 2, 1824. Latrobe had called the capital a "gigantic abortion," and though L'Enfant's physical afflictions prevented his traveling to Washington after his move to Green Hill, he had no reason to disagree. Many connected with the city were pretending otherwise, publishing maps and illustrations that did not remotely reflect the reality on the site, maps full of completed neighborhoods, paved and graded streets, and gleaming federal buildings. The view from the President's House and Capitol Hill was the same as it had been at the turn of the century: full of the bucolic waters of the Potomac, dominated by halfhearted construction work closer at hand. Jefferson had passed down his small-scale priorities through the Republican administrations of Madison and Monroe, and to think of the seat of government as a city with an expansive future took a great deal of imagination. If visitors didn't use their imaginations, they saw nothing but the calamity described by Latrobe.

The President's House and Capitol were still recovering from the conflagrations of the previous decade. Charles Bulfinch came to Washington from his practice of architecture and urban planning in Boston in 1818 to complete the Capitol by building a circular chamber linking the House and Senate chambers (the rotunda from which Jefferson had spirited a Washington mausoleum), topping it with a low copper-covered wooden dome that was now near completion. The Tiber canal was also fitfully under way, a shallow and pungent ditch carrying flatboats to and from Capitol Hill and providing a convenient home for millions of malarial mosquitoes. Brick buildings for the departments of Treasury and State had risen on either side of the rebuilt President's House, and a majestic City Hall was slated for the plot that L'Enfant had once entitled Judiciary Square and earmarked for the Supreme Court, given prominence thanks to its placement on a forty-foot elevation and three separate approach vistas from Pennsylvania Avenue and the Mall.

A real estate depression in 1819 had dropped lot values yet again, but the city had managed to gain a navy yard and harbor, a fort, a post office, a city hall, a theater, a penitentiary, a circus, a Masonic hall, four banks, and fourteen churches. It was a start. In 1820 the federal census counted 13,247 whites, 1,696 free blacks, and 1,945 slaves. This added up to only 10,000 more souls than in 1800, spanning an era when Philadelphia had gained four times that amount. L'Enfant had once predicted that the city of Washington would someday house half a million people. He would be right, eventually, but during his lifetime the estimate made him look like a dreamer, a madman, or a charlatan.

The major was clearly a more realistic man in his old age—fatigue and affliction had seen to that—but that realism was not doing him much good. He had to have understood from the evidence that no designer would have lasted thirty-five years on this project, given the people and politics that had given it birth. But L'Enfant had the kind of imagination that could see things that weren't there and erase things that were, and surely at some point in his walks around Green Hill he reenvisioned the past thirty-five years of his life. Was he thinking of lost opportunities and alternative futures? L'Enfant's desires, while grandiose, were never outright fantasies, and under the shelter of William and Eleanor Digges, he retreated into a mind-set that is impossible to penetrate, his invective silenced and nearly all of his thoughts unrecorded. He may have once eagerly, anxiously, frenetically looked forward to having a place in history, but now that his life had entered its twilight, one hopes that he wasn't dwelling too much on his losses.

As the summer of 1824 reached its height and L'Enfant settled into the rhythms of his life at Green Hill, Thomas Jefferson, now in his eighties, was perched on his mountaintop in central Virginia, living a life devoted to the pleasures of the mind, writing four or five substantial letters nearly every day and describing himself as a man who had "given up newspapers in exchange for Tacitus and Thucydides, for Newton and Euclid." All but finished with four decades of work on Monticello, Jefferson had now turned his attention to the estate's extensive flower and vegetable gardens and was giving little scrutiny to the output of his farms, the great agrarian becoming in his own word "indifferent" to the pursuit of agriculture. Twelve grandchildren and their families, more than two hundred slaves, and a never-ending stream of visitors animated the property nearly every day of the year.

Jefferson still served as a kind of Republican flag bearer, but the fullest evidence that the political storms of his career had finally subsided was that he had renewed his friendship with John and Abigail Adams, an intimate connection that had been lost in years of bitter, near total silence between 1800 and 1812. Jefferson's political life was now expressed not in party subterfuges but in a wide-ranging correspondence with John Adams. Their discourse tended to flow in parallel streams, as Adams held forth on history, politics, and religion while Jefferson preferred to expound on science and law, but the two men also engaged in head-on, spirited exchanges on the subject of Adams's perceived weakness for the concept of aristocracy, Jefferson's naïve view of the French Revolution, and the ever more difficult question of slavery. By the 1820s the pattern had become decidedly elegiac, their passions finally cooled and their pens more often reflective than argumentative.

The correspondence is a treasure of staggering value to historians, but during its creation it was clearly of greater importance to Adams, who produced a substantial majority of the pages, than to Jefferson. This was partly because Jefferson was busy being a Renaissance man—he still took a complete set of meteorological measurements every morning and evening—but also because he was actively involved in leaving another substantive legacy. Four miles to the northwest of Monticello, on land once owned by James Monroe, the institution that would become known as the University of Virginia was finally taking shape on the ground after many years of planning.

The Thomas Jefferson whom L'Enfant had encountered in 1791 had one completed piece of architecture under his wing—the state capitol building in Richmond, a nearly exact copy of the Maison Carrée at Nîmes, in southern France—and he had proposed to L'Enfant that the designs of the President's House and Capitol mimic those of the Garde-Meubles and the Galerie du Louvre in Paris. In the intervening years Jefferson had devoted so much time to Monticello that it had become an end in and of itself, an American improvisation on Palladian ideals that was as much an ongoing aesthetic and intellectual hobby as a project with a beginning and a conclusion. The work on his residence had not been subject to governmental budgets and boards, leaving him free to act as his sole overseer and to rack up his own monumental debts.

Jefferson's progression from working on Monticello to working on the University of Virginia was, in the end, not so different from L'Enfant's own leap from renovating Federal Hall (another important American improvisation on classical forms) to creating his all-encompassing vision for the city of Washington. The federal city was far more complex than the university, and its plan was produced under much more intense scrutiny and time pressure, but the two are without question unacknowledged artistic kin. Jefferson the respectful and respected amateur architect became, with Monticello, Jefferson the unparalleled American innovator. But it was the University of Virginia that gained Jefferson his standing as a consummate planner.

In 1824, after many years of preparation and five of building, construction of the university was nearing completion. Jefferson, like L'Enfant, had purposely begun his design without a historical model in mind, though it has some formal similarities to Louis XIV's château at Marly, a set of pavilions arranged around a green, which Jefferson had visited in the fall of 1786. He wanted to make something unique, an "academic village" that would be a particularly American architectural gloss on the particularly American commitment to public education. To this end he'd enlisted Latrobe's help in establishing three principles to guide his work, principles that would not have been out of place in L'Enfant's earliest memorandums to George Washington.

> 1. That the creation was, not to be a single grand edifice, but was to consist of distinct yet blended, separate yet united, independent yet affiliated units; that it should be an architectural democracy.

2. That these units, despite the use of modest materials which the extent of his funds might prescribe, should in their lines and in their proportions conform with the law of the art.

3. That in the arrangement of this artistic democracy—this academic village—there should be a central "square," an open court, a commons for both teacher and taught, professor, proctor, and student, who, having discarded their robes of rank in the environing pavilion and dormitory, as mere men might mingle there together.

An idealism regarding public education as fervent as L'Enfant's belief in the inevitable triumph of American nationalism armed Jefferson with a similar bravado in the face of financial constraints. When the commonwealth provided only $15,000 a year to support construction, the hiring of teachers from Europe, and the beginning of classes, Jefferson simply proposed spending more than twice that amount, writing a memorandum listing personnel, expenses, and materials. The General Assembly of Virginia, reenacting the obstructive role of the federal city commissioners to the hilt, complained that Jefferson was placing undue emphasis on the value of public education, that the university's buildings were too grandiose, its plan too extravagant and impractical, and that taking out ever larger loans to finance the school (Jefferson had in this sole instance become a convert to Alexander Hamilton's cause of public debt) was impracticable. In a close replay of L'Enfant's travails, Virginia legislators even complained at one stage that Jefferson had failed to produce a sufficiently exact drawing of the university for engraving, leaving them to rely on a rough sketch and verbal descriptions as they deliberated ways to fund the project.

In the end $50,000 appeared, money owed Virginia by the federal government for funds borrowed during the War of 1812, and by 1824 all ten of the pavilions facing the central lawn had been built, graced with their alternating Doric, Ionic, and Corinthian columns and their flanking dormitories, while the central rotunda awaited only the final touches on its domed roof. An agent had been sent to London and Edinburgh to seek professors in modern languages, classics, natural philosophy, natural history, and anatomy and medicine. Jefferson as recently as two years earlier had been able to make the trip to and from the site nearly every week—he'd surveyed the

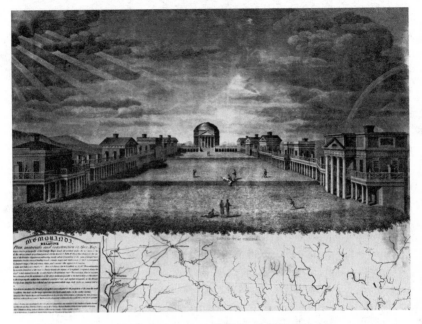

University of Virginia Campus in Charlottesville, by B. Tanner, 1827

grounds himself at the age of seventy-five—but now such rides wore him out and afterward kept him in bed for days on end. Instead of making these visits, he now spent hours at home cataloging the second seven-thousand-book library of his life (the first had gone to the Library of Congress) to form a stock pond for the school library. The university seemed likely to open in early 1825, in a race against Jefferson's own mortality, which he was beginning to fear he'd lose.

If Jefferson's face was to the university, his back, literally and figuratively, was to the American capital. His friendship with George Washington had been finally and completely ruptured by the end of 1798, and now, in 1824, his relationship to Washington the city was equally moribund. Jefferson is often painted as the city's champion, and certainly he was present at its creation; the dinner-table bargain of 1790 probably did play a decisive role in bringing it to the Potomac; and he did welcome L'Enfant in March 1791 with kind words and a roll of his prized city plans. He never explicitly objected to the major's design or expressed any public displeasure over twice seeing others chosen to design the public buildings. He might have retained a kind of pride even now for his work to beautify Pennsylvania Avenue and for his considerable efforts to move the Capitol toward its completion. But the best evidence of Jefferson's feelings toward the place are illustrated by his actions. After leaving the presidency in 1809 at the completion of his second term, even though his longtime protégé James Madison followed him as president and served in that office for eight years, Jefferson never again took the three days' ride to set foot in the District of Columbia.

If Jefferson saw his work as part of an architectural continuum, he would never have included the major's designs in that company. But he should have. Though Jefferson was genuinely if excessively modest about his skills, the campus of the University of Virginia was a meaningful and lasting American creation—as L'Enfant had said in reference to his own work on Washington, "a plan wholly new." In fact, it was L'Enfant, and not Jefferson's old friend Latrobe, who would have been the American best equipped to fully absorb and understand the achievement on display in Charlottesville.

Peter Charles L'Enfant died at Green Hill on June 15, 1825, two months shy of his seventy-first birthday, and was buried at the base of a newly planted cedar sapling near the graves of the Digges family servants and slaves. No public funeral brought old friends back to him; he had no old friends. The record of his passing amounted to a single obituary in the *National Intelligencer*. It was a paper to which Jefferson subscribed—it had been created in 1800 at Jefferson's urging to provide the federal city with a Republican party organ—but one he rarely read.

The paper devoted just over four hundred words to the architect's passing. It reported the date inaccurately, but it got plenty right. No more eloquent tribute was paid to the major during his life, no more succinct explanation of why he initially refused payment then later went after it so doggedly.

> On the 14th inst. at Green Hill, the Seat of WM. DUDLEY DIGGES, Esq. in Prince George's county, Md. Major PIERRE CHARLES L'ENFANT. Of the age of this interesting but eccentric gentleman, we have no accurate knowledge; but it could not have fallen short of seventy years. We should be glad to have possessed materials for a complete biography of the deceased. In the absence of these, we can state, from general knowledge of him, that he was a native of France, of good

family. During our Revolutionary war, he was an officer of engineers, and in that capacity was severely wounded at the attack upon Savannah, and was the last of the wounded taken out of the ditch. After the present government was organized, he was employed as an Engineer in making the plan of this City, of which he is the author, and with which his name ought to be gratefully associated. He thought himself ill remunerated for this service, and, because full justice was not, as he thought, measured to him, he refused to receive what was tendered, and lived a life of sequestration from society, and austere privation, which attracted respect, whilst it excited compassion. Compassion, however, was not what he wanted: his mind was of a cast to be gratified only by receiving that sort of consideration which his talents and high and delicate sense of honor entitled him to.

It was such an assured and empathetic piece of writing that William Dudley Digges, loyal nephew of the first American novelist, might well have had a hand in it himself. The obituary was not, however, the final contemporary account of L'Enfant's life. A more prosaic record of his fall from grace is written in a ledger that appears toward the end of his papers now held by the Library of Congress. Labeled simply as "Inventory," it has been grouped with other financial documents, undated letter fragments, and a set of notes regarding the "National church building" and the "Location and improvement of state squares."

An inventory of the personal good and chattels of Peter Charles L'Enfant:

Three watches one silver and two gold,	$30.00
1. compass,	$10.00
two pocket compasses,	$2.00
one lot of surveyor's instruments and books,	$2.00
one lot of maps,	$1.00

This list seems such an unfortunately fitting end to the tale of L'Enfant's life that more than one journalist and biographer has been unable to resist the lure of such obvious symbolism and has concluded that the architect was worth $45 at the end of his life.

But this tally did not represent the whole of L'Enfant's financial worth on the date of his demise. Though his claims for his work on Federal Hall and on the federal city had been foreclosed or partially paid, he still retained an interest in some New York land that he had originally bought with Robert Morris. And the federal government still owed him for his services at Fort Warburton, the major's final employment as an architect and planner. When the time came to settle that account, an unidentified clerk in the office of the secretary of war reported to William Dudley Digges a balance of $92.80 in L'Enfant's favor.

Sixteen years after his last public service for the United States of America, money was still owed the dead man whom the clerk knew no better than to call "Major La-Fon."

CHAPTER 13

A Share in the Undertaking

WEDNESDAY, DECEMBER 12, 1900

THE CAPITAL IN 1800, cried the front page of the *Washington Post:* BIRTH OF WILDERNESS CITY WAS WITHOUT A PRECEDENT—ALL THE WORLD JEERED OR CARPED. One hundred years had passed since Abigail Adams rode into Washington to join her husband, John, for their abbreviated stay at the President's House, and it was a day for reflection, perhaps the first such opportunity in the city's history. The mode of the writing was epic, the history revisionist, the end point inevitable: the turn of the previous century, the newspaper continued, had been "a time when old customs, old modes of thought, old institutions, and old ideals were falling shattered on every side, and it was taken as a matter of course, when no existing city seemed suitable for a capital, that the young republic should build a city to its liking."

Official observation of the centennial began at eleven o'clock in the East Room of the White House, where President William McKinley played host to the members of his cabinet, the nine justices of the Supreme Court, and twenty-one governors. They listened to orations on the history of the capital and applauded a set of atrocious and ultimately unrealized plans for enlarging the White House; then, initial encomiums complete, the collection of dignitaries paused for a military procession down Pennsylvania Avenue before entering the Capitol, where a long slate of congressmen battled to deliver the airiest speech exulting in the move from Philadelphia a century earlier. Perhaps the most oleaginous tribute came from Senator Louis McComas of neighboring Maryland.

> One hundred years ago President Adams first visited Capitol Hill. From this eminence how different then the scene. Around him stood the primeval forest. Here and there were naked fields. Through the thick oak woods had been cleared the streets and avenues. On this hill stood the north wing of the Capitol. On the Eastern Branch of the Potomac, then navigable, and near the Arsenal was the hamlet of Carrollsburg . . . About the new President's house clustered a few buildings; behind these, wide marshes stretched away to the river. Across Rock Creek lay the Maryland village of Georgetown. At these four points widely separated, were about 600 houses. All else was marsh, and field, and forest. Such was—

> > The young city round whose virgin zone
> > The rivers like two mighty arms were thrown.

Reporters didn't record where McComas did his research or in what possible way the forests of the federal district in 1800 could have been described as "primeval." Neither did they reveal what poet had wrought the mighty sexual metaphor of his rhyming couplet. Perhaps it was the senator himself, who concluded his address by calling the centennial the city's "day of fulfillment."

The melodramatic rhetoric fairly reflected the mood. It was an era in which politicians in Washington, D.C., publicly promoted an unswerving belief in the country's destiny and heartily believed it in private. Progress was the theme of the era. America was enjoying an overall standard of living higher than the world had ever known, and its capital was flush and growing rapidly, home to a quarter-million residents, up from sixty thousand at the start of the Civil War. At long last none of these residents were slaves. The surge in Washington's fortunes seemed a synergistic expression of unfettered national energy, and the sound of self-congratulation was thick in the air.

The next day, as the centennial guests departed and the weather continued cold, seventy-five members of the American Institute of Architects (AIA) gathered in Washington to begin their biannual convention. They arrived at odds with the official line on Washington: to these professional descendants of Major L'Enfant, the praise for the capital was only so much braying. The theme of the meeting, "The Unified and Artistic Development of the City," had been carefully worded to communicate a conviction that the city's development had so far been neither. In their own ways and for their own reasons they were as wary of the pronouncements of public servants as L'Enfant had ever been—or perhaps should have been.

The city of Washington seemed to them a haphazard place, striving and failing to make a whole out of potentially magnificent parts. And no problem was as pressing to them as the Mall, where the architects saw little unity of design, little common vocabulary of form or style, little relationship among monumental points of reference. A half-dozen entities—among them the Army Corps of Engineers, the Department of Agriculture, and the nascent Smithsonian Institution—laid claim to different sections of the ground, each one building and planting as it saw fit: a formal arrangement here, a small plot left to nature there, a high fence surrounding a botanical garden at the western foot of Capitol Hill, a train depot slicing the Mall in two at Sixth Street. The result of this uncoordinated patchwork was that Washington, after more than a century of fitful growth, still seemed to be made mostly of two absurdly proportioned sandstone buildings rising out of an apathetic fabric of streets, buildings, and landscape elements. The literal and symbolic core of the city—and therefore of the nation—had never become a single thing unto itself. As much as any aesthetic displeasure, it was this lack of profundity, of *meaning*, that the members of the AIA had come to address.

Their convention began on the morning of December 13 in the banquet hall of the Arlington Hotel on Lafayette Square, across from the White House, then reconvened for the evening session at the Columbian University, two blocks east at Fifteenth and H. Here, beginning at eight-forty-five and going well into the night, the substantive work commenced. One by one well-known architects stood in a lecture hall to present drawings that dramatically reorganized the Mall and surrounding streets, each hoping that his plan would send off the brightest sparks. The audience—august and successful colleagues—listened with interest, but many felt that this opening set of talks only danced around the edges of the problem. If the lion architects of America had come to link arms behind a new vision for the seat of government, they were not yet fulfilling their aim.

That feeling began to change with the last scheduled speaker of the evening. At thirty, Frederick Law Olmsted, Jr., was probably the youngest man in the room. Some in the audience knew of his work as a landscape architect, many more didn't, but every one of them recognized his name. In fact, some of the assembled architects may have thought they were about to hear a talk from the legendary Frederick Law Olmsted, Sr., who forty years earlier had saved New York City from the uncompromising relentlessness of its gridiron street plan with his design for Central Park. Now his son and namesake had come to Washington to perform a no less important mission of urban redemption.

Rick had just finished his first semester as a professor at Harvard and was an accomplished designer in his own right, but he also remained the kind of voracious learner who listened and read and sketched and photographed before reaching conclusions or offering opinions. On this occasion he found a group of designers who were too eagerly putting forth solutions before carefully pondering the problem. All of their proposed redesigns of the city had a patina of self-aggrandizement, an air of game playing. Rick Olmsted was no cynic, and he believed that all the work had been done in earnest, but he could also see the temptation. By laying a sheet of tracing paper over the current plan of the city and sketching away, talented architects named Smith, Cobb, Gilbert, Pelz, Seeler, Totten, and Brown could indulge in an image of themselves as the prime movers of a resurrected Washington, D.C. Their plans, full of "wiggling roads and confused informal planning," as Olmsted Jr. later put it, were at the core essentially academic exercises, a set of overly fussy schematics useful for creating discussion but not as the kindling of real change.

Few of the members of the AIA knew what Rick Olmsted was about to say, and fewer if any knew of the weighty emotional and professional burden the young man was carrying as he spoke. It was a closely guarded family secret that the elder Olmsted was at this moment sequestered in a Massachusetts asylum and disappearing down a dark tunnel of dementia. If there was still to be a Frederick Law Olmsted at the vanguard of landscape architecture in America, he would have to be Rick, and he would have to claim that inheritance now.

He would somehow manage to meet the demand. Not only would he help to redeem the promise of a world capital and justify the professional expectations placed on his shoulders in the bargain; he would also help to set in motion a chain of events that would figuratively and literally raise Peter Charles L'Enfant from the dead.

In 1842, just seventeen years after L'Enfant's death, Charles Dickens had scathingly memorialized the federal city in his best-selling travelogue *American Notes*. The British author was an international celebrity following three smash hits in quick succession: *The Posthumous Papers of the Pickwick Club* in 1836, *Oliver Twist* in 1837, and *Nicholas Nickleby* in 1838. Riding the transatlantic wave of this popularity, Dickens made his first trip to America to lecture, perform dramatic readings, and gather observations for his next book. Possessed of a famous knack for immortalizing locales, he had already, in his novels, made London into a world whose safe and sunlit dressing rooms stood in riveting contrast to sinister and shadowed alleyways. His Washington, D.C., though, was neither light nor dark. It was barely even a city.

> It is sometimes called the City of Magnificent Distances, but it might with greater propriety be termed the City of Magnificent Intentions. Spacious avenues, that begin in nothing, and lead nowhere; streets, mile-long that only want houses, roads, and inhabitants; public buildings that need but a public to be complete; and ornaments of great thoroughfares, which only lack great thoroughfares to ornament—are its leading features. To the admirers of cities it is a pleasant field for the imagination to rove in; a monument raised to a deceased project, with not even a legible inscription to record its departed greatness.
>
> Such as it is, it is likely to remain.

This description reached readers all over the English-speaking world and became so emblematic of Washington that both nicknames, the honorific and the sarcastic, would still be in wide use in 1900, when the architects of the AIA arrived to share their speculative transformations.

During the nineteenth century the city's progress had taken the form of undistinguished stutter steps until the Civil War, when millions of men from North and South took up arms against one another with the national capital caught on the border between them. Threatened by a southern invasion, the sleepy federal town had awakened with a jolt to find itself overcrowded and in danger of devolving into chaos. Much of the land in the federal district, even patches within the much smaller boundaries of L'Enfant's plan, was still given over to pastures, fields, and forests. Twenty-four hours a day military and governmental traffic coursed along its unpaved roads, churning them into rivers of mud and then, during dry spells, cutting them full of ruts and raising so much dirt and dust that women of the more refined sort—who were fast outnumbered by their more entrepreneurial counterparts—tended to restrict themselves to certain stretches of Pennsylvania Avenue.

Bearing an uncanny resemblance to the country it purported to represent, Washington during the Civil War was full of half-realized evidence of the highest of aspirations. Begun eleven years earlier, the Washington Monument was only partially finished, a truncated obelisk that was nonetheless the tallest and most visible structure in the city. In his description of the forlorn stump in *The Gilded Age,* Mark Twain would go Dickens one better.

> It has the aspect of a factory chimney with the top broken off. The skeleton of a decaying scaffolding lingers about its summit, and tradition says that the spirit of Washington often comes down and sits on those rafters to enjoy this tribute of respect which the nation has reared as the symbol of its unappeasable gratitude. The Monument is to be finished, some day, and at that time our Washington will have risen still higher in the nation's venerations, and will be known as the Great-Great-Grandfather of his Country.

Work on a higher and more ornate dome over the Capitol rotunda was suspended in 1862, its structure still visible like the exposed ribs of a gruesome battlefield casualty. The one project that *was* fast being completed was a gargantuan neoclassical extension to the Treasury Building, just east of the

White House. The design had been approved by Andrew Jackson during his first term three decades earlier, but the arrogance of the decision was only now evident, as the building's monumental front blocked the view westward along Pennsylvania Avenue and destroyed forever L'Enfant's reciprocal line of sight between the President's House and the Capitol.

In the aftermath of the Civil War several things had happened in Washington to shake the federal city loose from seventy-five years of diffidence and distraction. The first was the election of Ulysses S. Grant as president in 1868. The war had provided an unimaginably bloody lesson in the human and political costs of an infirm Union, and Grant arrived in 1869 for his inauguration determined to establish Washington, D.C., as the physical manifestation of a powerful and unified nationalism once and for all.

He began with a change of language, officially abandoning "seat of government" and "federal city" for the more allusive and substantial "capital," which had been used since the eighteenth century only as a nickname. But changing names would do only so much. Meanwhile, influential newsmen and politicians in Chicago and St. Louis had begun organized campaigns to move the seat of government well to the west. Such a move was hardly inconceivable, and one of the upstarts' effective arguments—in addition to an appeal to geographic centrality, the same appeal that James Madison had long ago used so adroitly to bolster the case for the Potomac location—was that while western cities were rapidly advancing in size and wealth, the capital seemed gripped by a permanent torpor.

In 1871 Grant made one of his most far-reaching decisions as chief executive, appointing Alexander Shepherd vice president of the newly created Board of Public Works in order to manage the long-overdue modernization of the city of Washington. Shepherd, the most important figure in the development of the federal city since L'Enfant himself, was a native of the capital, and at thirty-seven he was already a veteran of the city's Common Council and a successful land developer. A politician with an iron hand and multitudinous connections, he avoided direct personal implication in a host of prosecutions only by the skin of his teeth. Like L'Enfant he committed himself to grueling hours and insane deadlines. Shepherd and his board took only four weeks to create a proposal outlining a host of immediate and noticeable improvements: grading and paving and curbing the streets, creating median strips on the diagonal avenues, extending water mains throughout the city, adding and improving bridges and culverts, and planting sixty thousand trees. His enemies included those who disapproved of the original proposal's price tag of $6 million, a tally that would balloon to almost $30 million before the project was completed. They also included thousands who found their houses and businesses in or beside the path of progress, their peace and in many cases their property sacrificed unceremoniously to the civic good à la Duddington Manor.

For a time the prestige of Grant overrode most of these objections, so for three years squadrons of engineers and contractors worked around the city with tornadic energy. It was as if the Civil War had held all else in abeyance, not only for the country but also for its capital, and now that the war was over, the fortunes of Washington could be addressed. The upheaval wrought by Shepherd's crews created a sizable political and legal backlash, but it also filled residents with a sense of accomplishment and even, for a change, of destiny. Shepherd's successes were bolstered by a separate program of government construction that included the mammoth State, War, and Navy Building (later known as the Old Executive Office Building) west of the White House and the Thomas Jefferson Building of the Library of Congress facing the east front of the Capitol. Most significant, perhaps, the pestilential eyesore that was the Tiber canal was finally abandoned and replaced by a trunk sewer designed to flow beneath a new east-west thoroughfare named Constitution Avenue.

Shepherd's reign lasted little longer than L'Enfant's, ending in 1873 when a national depression stanched the flow of construction money and emboldened a growing rebellion against the planner's totalitarian bent. But he left behind a momentum that could not be easily checked. In just three years' time, Shepherd had in many ways carried out the work outlined in L'Enfant's memorandum of January 1792 to George Washington, and for that—and for his larger-than-life personality—he deserves better notice. But Shepherd, for all his influence, was not L'Enfant. The American capital had found someone to pave its streets, but it still needed artists of vision to reclaim the greatness of its original conception.

In 1874, one year after Boss Shepherd resigned his public works position to become the first governor of the District of Columbia, Frederick Law Olmsted, Sr., arrived to accept an invitation from President Grant to redesign the Capitol grounds. The need was long-standing and obvious. Andrew Ellicott, perhaps at the instruction of Thomas Jefferson, had pivoted the Congress House away from the symbolic core of the city and moved it far enough westward that it forever seemed to be slipping backward off of the crest of L'Enfant's great "pedestal." New York's Central Park, for all its struggles, was revealing itself as a popular and political success, and Grant's hope was that the world's most famous landscape architect could perform the same magic for the capital.

Asked to create a new setting for the Capitol, Olmsted had taken the word "setting" to mean the entire central zone of the city. Leaping far beyond the boundaries of Grant's commission, he submitted a proposal to remake *all* the public lands between the Capitol and the White House. His vision—some of it borrowing from an unrealized plan created by gardener Andrew Jackson Downing two decades earlier—argued strongly against aesthetic "disunion," a shrewd analogy appropriate for the times. To Olmsted Sr. it was a matter of history: the city had passed through a horrifying crucible, and then it had been sanctified by the blood of Abraham Lincoln. A capital carrying such symbolic weight had to finish off this transformative trial by presenting a unified face to the world.

Shepherd had left the Mall untouched except for his important decision to make the Tiber canal into a sewer beneath Constitution Avenue, but that one dramatic move gave Olmsted his wedge. The "canal district" was land owned and controlled by the federal government, and that was where the work could begin. His next suggestion was to bring together the nation's best landscape architects—he named H. W. S. Cleveland, William Hammond Hall, and himself—to form Washington's very first commission made up solely of artists. Together the three men would create a single public park stretching from Capitol Hill to the Potomac along the east-west line of the old water route, revealing a dramatic symbolic space to which both the Capitol and the White House could relate.

As Olmsted must have expected, Congress agreed to fund no part of his expanded scheme; a plan limited to the Capitol landscaping would have to suffice. Olmsted went to work without sulking and did not disappoint, gracing the grounds on the building's eastern side with a circular drive, tulip trees, and two ceremonial fountains before turning his attention to the more problematic western elevation. Here he produced his master stroke: a grand terrace with broad steps designed to embrace the fact that the building stood on the crest of a hill. The plan was accepted eagerly, but the $200,000 appropriated for the project soon ran out, and Olmsted would face a decade-long struggle to complete the terrace, referring to it as his "most important active work" during that time.

But for all the considerable reputation they earned Olmsted, neither the Capitol renovation nor the continuing work on Central Park was the project foremost in his mind. In the very same year that he accepted Grant's offer to come to Washington, he took the extraordinary step of changing the name of his four-year-old son, Henry Perkins Olmsted, to Frederick Law Olmsted, Jr., with the express purpose of creating a blank slate on which he could write the future of landscape architecture. Even from this early date, he sought nothing less than to remake the boy in his own personal and professional image.

One of Olmsted's many Whitmanesque precepts was the supreme advantage of the pedestrian point of view. At some point, as he and Rick walked from the banks of the Potomac to the base of Capitol Hill, if not before, Olmsted must have spoken of Pierre Charles L'Enfant. Anyone who presumed to understand the history of the capital could relate how L'Enfant had been removed from the project after less than a year for the sin of "insubordination," but the lessons at hand for young Rick involved not only L'Enfant's departure but also the hows and whats and whys of his presence.

That presence had been ripe with allegiance to a core Olmstedian belief: think a very long way ahead and imagine "distant effects." And even L'Enfant's ignominious fall perhaps contained another lesson. The education of Rick Olmsted would extend beyond the art of landscape design and into the capricious realms of boards and commissioners and committees and bureaucrats, none of whom were ever quite as farsighted or amenable as planners would like. Olmsted would require Rick to cultivate an articulate, socially at ease persona, to make himself comfortable amid the kind of men who commanded the resources and land necessary for the proper exercise of landscape architecture.

After the completion of the Capitol terrace in 1881, Olmsted was able to immerse himself in the professional completion of his son. His letters to Rick, even when the boy was barely a teenager, exhorted him to work to become a "leader of the van," a standard-bearer in the field. Year after year Rick absorbed his father's long extracurricular reading lists and followed his rules of behavior without complaint, except for one small but intense uprising at Christmas 1894, when Rick, just graduated from Harvard magna cum laude, threatened to abandon the entire enterprise for zoology. "It is too late to turn back," his father summarily replied. "There is not another man in the world who, at your age, has been as well-prepared as you are for the practical study of our profession." Rick retracted his threat at once, stepping into the persona he'd been groomed to inhabit so completely that his father dropped the distinctions "Jr." and "Sr." from much of his correspondence.

During the final six years of the century, then, Rick had trained according to his father's strict directions. He spent his first postgraduate summer as an apprentice surveyor in Colorado, then entered into a most unusual internship on the six-thousand-acre North Carolina mountain estate of George Washington Vanderbilt, who had inherited $10 million from his father, William, and was using it to create Biltmore, a lavish retreat graced with a grand formal garden in the symmetrical French style. Here, on Lone Pine Mountain, Rick learned his "scientific forestry" while at the same time practicing his father's rules of comportment: exercise, be pious, become a good sportsman and dancer, and always cultivate the finest manners.

Rick demonstrated a startling willingness to assume this responsibility, especially because he had much more on his mind now than learning names of plants and trees and practicing an aristocratic ease. Just as he was making his entrance into the field of landscape architecture, he learned that his father and professional mentor was sick—and getting sicker fast.

The elder Olmsted had long been given to bouts of "melancholia" that interrupted his sleep and sometimes kept him away from important work. As he became more depressed, he had written to Rick more frequently, penning desperate variations on a theme he had introduced into the correspondence years earlier: "You must make . . . good my failings." It was a strange thing to hear from such a successful man, but Olmsted Sr. truly believed that the field of landscape architecture was embodied in his own person. Any flaw in himself flawed the whole pursuit. He increasingly saw himself as an old and fading man passing on not only a family legacy but the letter and spirit of an entire profession.

In early 1896 the correspondence had stopped. A year later Rick was taken into the firm of Olmsted Brothers as an equal partner, but despite this new demand on his time, he spent most of his weekends commuting to and from Felsted, the retreat built in Maine for his father's "retirement." By August 1897 Olmsted needed more care than the family could provide, so Rick moved him to McLean Asylum in Waverly, Massachusetts, whose grounds the older man had designed two decades earlier. Only twenty-seven then, he began a vigil that would last for several years, sleeping in his father's cottage whenever he could, their conversations unrecorded and ranging who knows where.

At the turn of the century Rick took an office at Harvard to form the country's first curriculum in landscape architecture. All the while his father's illness, turning now into total dementia, was kept secret. For all many of his colleagues knew, Frederick Law Olmsted, Sr., was enjoying a comfortable and well-earned retirement. Rick had just started teaching in the fall of 1900 when Glenn Brown, secretary of the AIA, contacted him about speaking at its biannual convention as a nonmember guest of the organization. It was a gratifying recognition of his position as leader of the landscape architecture "van," but he knew too that he had been selected only because his father was no longer available.

If, when he arrived in Washington in December 1900, Rick Olmsted was known only as the son of the world's most famous landscape architect, by the time he finished his talk, many of those in the room viewed him as a very real and viable successor to his father. In fact, this talk was probably the moment when Rick began to realize his father's dearest goal: not only to ensure the success of his namesake but also to raise their field to the same professional status enjoyed by architecture and engineering.

The title of Rick Olmsted's talk was "Landscape in Connection with Public Buildings in Washington." To his way of thinking, the failure to articulate a set of first principles was the central problem of his colleagues' presentations. Where were the discussions of the precepts by which a new design for the capital's public spaces could even be attempted? Where was the statement of boundaries? A few drawings hung in front of a room full of architects would accomplish nothing, not at this stage. A framework was needed, and that was what he was here to propose.

Olmstead Jr.'s presentation did not include the display or discussion of a single piece of his own work. The metallic *chunk* of the lantern slides being changed at the rear of the room accompanied his voice as he showed image after image: Lafayette Square and the White House from the Washington Monument, the Capitol from Pennsylvania Avenue, the south end of the Capitol terrace, the Capitol from the Botanic Garden, the Kew Gardens, the "long walk" at Windsor, the Champs-Élysées, the Tapis Vert at Versailles.

Perhaps his summer spent developing the landscape architecture curriculum of Harvard, sui generis, had provided the photographs and suggested ready points of discussion. Perhaps Professor Olmsted's inaugural set of students had scribbled notes as he exhibited slides titled "Building, Landscape, and Foliage," "Water with Low Banks and Trees," "Picturesque Building and Surroundings," "Open Park Way with Buildings," "Bad Effect of Extreme Formality," and "A Vista of Informal Outline." But this was no audience of twenty-year-olds, and like L'Enfant in 1791 and his father in 1874, Rick Olmsted ranged far beyond the prescribed limits of his assignment.

He began by seeking to expand the meaning of "landscape." He spoke not about trees and lawns but rather called for "a discussion of the location of public buildings and the arrangement of land about them, whether in a formal or informal fashion." This was an adroit way of saying that the business of the design and placement of buildings was every bit his business. To prepare for his talk, Rick had studied L'Enfant's maps, not in an effort to produce a scheme of his own but to understand the original designer's modes of thought. He praised the scale of the streets and public reservations that allowed a monumental facade to be seen from an appropriate distance, and then he did a little communing with the major's spirit.

The Mall was not laid out on the main axis of the Capitol without a reason, and it did not happen to come there because the land was cheap, or for any such temporary cause. It was laid out there because it was meant to relate directly and visibly to the Capitol; while it has been planned and planted for the most part in utter disregard of this primary purpose.

The purpose of the Mall was, and ought to be, to emphasize, support, and extend the effect of the Capitol as the dominant feature of the city and the most important building in the whole United States, to strike a chord in the magnificent chorus of which the keynote is the great white dome.

Throughout the early years of its life, Washington, D.C., had been filled with property owners appealing to L'Enfant's design in order to establish the value of one piece of land or another. But Rick Olmsted's use of "ought to be" and "meant" a century later was the first time an artist of comparable talent and vision had posed the question of original intent—of L'Enfant's hopes and purposes as a designer. By showing slides of the Champs-Élysées and the Tapis Vert at Versailles, Olmsted Jr. was also bringing in pieces of the context out of which L'Enfant had done his work, another first in the history of Washington.

Had Rick Olmsted pondered the day of L'Enfant's arrival in Georgetown in March 1791, when the territory was a tabula rasa? If any man in the world had an imagination prepared to inhabit that scene, it was the younger Olmsted. It is very doubtful that he had read much, if any, of L'Enfant's writing, which makes it all the more extraordinary that he could produce such a recognizable echo of the planner's tone, voice, and vision.

> In any great plan time must develop features which seem under the conditions of the present moment capable of improvement, but unless the plan appears upon thoughtful and conservative judgment distinctly bad the one safe course is to adhere steadfastly to its fundamental features. Once open the plan to a radical change, once establish the precedent of seriously altering it to meet the ideas of the moment, and the bars are thrown down for caprice and confusion.
>
> Here is a plan not hastily sketched, nor by a man of narrow views and little foresight. It is the plan with the authority of a century behind it, to which we can all demand undeviating adherence in the future; a plan prepared by the hand of L'Enfant, but under the constant, direct, personal guidance of one whose technical knowledge of surveying placed the problem completely within his grasp, and who brought to its solution the same clear insight, deep wisdom, and forethought that gave preeminence in the broader fields of war and statesmanship to the name of George Washington.

Major L'Enfant had known artistic peers, people such as his classmates at the Royal Academy and John Trumbull. For a short time he may have considered Thomas Jefferson part of that group. But most of the people whose paths the major had crossed had had plenty of time for the generation of argument, oratory, ideology, and money but very little time for art. Not only did Rick Olmsted establish himself as L'Enfant's kindred soul— another artist emerging from under the close tutelage of his father to take his own place on a national stage—but he also knew enough to tie the city's original designer tightly to George Washington in a one-on-one relationship, the collaboration that L'Enfant had hoped so fervently to see recorded for posterity.

Olmsted Jr.'s talk did not once mention the commissioners or the men given charge of the design of Washington after L'Enfant. Nor did it mention those, such as Ulysses S. Grant or Alexander Shepherd or even his own ailing father, who had finally paid the city the kind of attention its originators had assumed necessary for its success. Rick Olmsted wanted only to begin once more at the beginning. It was one of the greatest favors ever done by one artist for another, an homage and collaboration across a span of more than one hundred years. And it was, in the end, a true and lasting cause of the redemption of Peter Charles L'Enfant.

CHAPTER 14

The Assurance of Things Hoped For

On the morning of January 15, 1902, little more than a year after Rick Olmsted's talk, President Theodore Roosevelt and a train of cabinet members arrived at the newly built Corcoran Gallery of Art on Seventeenth Street and New York Avenue to take the first look at a display of architectural ideals unlike any in the country's history. The assassination of William McKinley in September by the anarchist Leon Czolgosz had lifted Roosevelt into power, and the new president had from his first day in office been filled with a belief in American empire to match that of George Washington. He was here to witness the future of the capital of that empire, and his mischievous eyes were bright.

Each room was a revelation, beginning with the gallery just to the right of the Corcoran's entry hall. The first and most arresting image on display was a rendering of proposed changes to the core of the city of Washington,

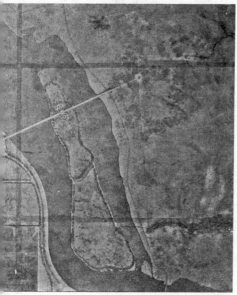

Above: *Bird's-Eye View of General Plan, from Point Taken 4,000 Feet Above Arlington,* by Francis L. V. Hoppin, 1902

Below: *General Plan of the Mall System,* 1902

a watercolor measuring three feet in height and six in width and given the misleadingly prosaic name *Bird's-Eye View of General Plan, from Point Taken 4,000 Feet Above Arlington.* Painted by Francis Hoppin, best known as the designer of a home for writer Edith Wharton, this dramatic perspective in rich rusts, creams, and olives was to become the iconic image of the reimagined capital.

For decades magazine and postcard illustrators, most prominently Currier and Ives, had idealized Washington, D.C., in any number of panoramic images bent with bad perspective and often containing such hypothetical treacle as a columned base for the Washington Monument and a Tiber canal full of serenely floating pleasure craft. The Hoppin painting, by contrast, was a razor-sharp reintroduction of L'Enfant's raw diagram for the Mall, reclaimed and comprehensible to all observers. Before this day, in fact, there had *never* been a national consciousness of L'Enfant's design for the core of Washington. Hoppin's majestic rendering made the point dramatically that there was a better way, a way that had been ignored for more than a century.

It was as if a giant cleansing hand had swept through the center of the city and scooped away all of the clutter and confusion wrought since L'Enfant's departure 110 years earlier. The patchwork collection of informal gardens was gone; the tracks cutting across the Mall at Sixth Street were nowhere to be seen; the Tiber canal had been covered over by Constitution Avenue; and the unsightly tidal flats of the Potomac were not only filled but capped with gleaming presidential monuments. The painting's vantage point high overhead provided the ideal perch from which to transmit a startling geometrical possibility. Suddenly the White House and Capitol had a visually obvious relationship, not as blind and indifferent bookends along Pennsylvania Avenue but rather in their common foursquare orientation to L'Enfant's open greensward. Whatever the Mall had or hadn't become since March 1791, the Hoppin painting made it seem one of the world's great inevitable spaces.

Opposite the Hoppin perspective hung a facsimile of L'Enfant's 1791 plan, recently reclaimed from the attic corners of architectural history. A third wall in the room was devoted to a set of close-up renderings of the Washington Monument, the fourth to plans and drawings of a proposed memorial to Abraham Lincoln destined for the land reclaimed from the Potomac. Intermixed with these views of Washington were images of parks in London, Paris, New York, and Boston, including several designed by

Frederick Law Olmsted, Sr., who was still alive in his New England asylum but no longer recognizing his own son.

The Hoppin perspective was the eye-opener, but the next room, a domed space decorated to invoke the Roman Pantheon and nicknamed the "Hemicycle," held the crown jewels of the exhibit: two fifteen-foot-square models of the core of Washington, D.C., at a scale of 1:100—one "The City as It Is" and the other "The City as It Is Intended to Be." These models, which had been built at breakneck speed in Brookline, Massachusetts, under the supervision of Rick Olmsted, were raised on chest-high platforms so that people would not have to crouch to put themselves and their imaginations inside the new design for the center of the city.

Both were fascinating examples of the model maker's art, but "The City as It Is Intended to Be" was the real wonder. Children were hoisted to gawk at it, while their parents pointed to the open spaces of the Mall and worked themselves into position to peer down the great axes toward the White House and the Capitol. The buildings around the Mall were faced with hundreds and hundreds of tiny modeled columns, creating long curtains of startling white in the middle of a sea of faithfully reproduced brick red. In an industrial age coated with soot and smoke, this, in pristine miniature, was a feast of neoclassical clarity. The exhibit was opened to the citizenry the following morning, and so many of them aped Roosevelt's growing enthusiasm that the reimagined city of Washington became a quantifiable sensation.

THRONGS AT ART GALLERY
SPECTATORS VIEW PLANS AND MODELS
FOR GREATER WASHINGTON

Washington was out in force yesterday afternoon to view the plans prepared for beautifying the city. For two hours and a half the rooms of the Corcoran Gallery of Art in which the models and paintings representing Greater Washington are on exhibition, were thronged with eager and interested spectators. From 1:30 until 4 o'clock there was a continual stream of humanity pouring through the large entrance. Inside the north room the visitors who came in carriages jostled against those who came in cars, the one motive of all being to get as close to the models as possible. After the first ten minutes it was practically impossible to secure a footing on the platform erected for the purpose of enabling visitors to view the model Washington as it is at present and as it is expected to be in the future.

During the next three days twenty-six thousand people crowded into the Corcoran to look at the display. The first presentation of the Senate Park Commission plan in 1902 was, in fact, a flawless example of one of L'Enfant's central tenets and the core of his argument against the debilitating influence of speculation: show people what they might have instead of asking them what they want, and you will find all eyes trained in your direction.

Chosen by Senator James McMillan of Michigan and rubber-stamped by Roosevelt, the first two seats on the Senate Park Commission had gone to Rick Olmsted and Chicago's Daniel Burnham, whose surging reputation as an urban architect rested on his firm's innovative steel-frame skyscrapers, including the Reliance Building in Chicago and the Flatiron Building in New York. Burnham had in turn recommended the appointment of Charles McKim, a fifty-three-year-old graduate of Harvard and the École des Beaux-Arts in Paris, who by 1901 had established himself as one of the standard-bearers of the American Beaux Arts style with his firm's design for the Boston Public Library. McKim recommended that the group include the sculptor Augustus Saint-Gaudens, most famous at that date for his statue of Admiral Farragut in Manhattan's Madison Square Park. All four of the commission's members had contributed in some measure to the 1893 World's Columbian Exposition at Chicago, the most dramatic social and cultural event in nineteenth-century America. The White City, as it was popularly known, had enticed three million visitors to the shores of Lake Michigan to stroll beneath its uniform neoclassical cornices and dare a breathtaking ride on the world's first Ferris wheel.

The McMillan Commission, as it was also known, began its work determined to rescue the country's capital city from a century of bad luck, bad taste, and bad advice. Its members' various contributions to the Chicago world's fair had culminated in a highly stylized theme park, not a true living city, but still that event had served to crystallize an amorphous movement in urban design that focused on the inclusion of large landscape elements and classical structures, a movement that would soon be given the name "the City Beautiful." America in the first decade of the twentieth century was obsessed with the desire to out-Europe Europe, and in that pursuit these four men had to a large degree already succeeded. The White City had accomplished something never before seen in America: it had made heroes out of architects.

Burnham, who had superintended the work in Chicago to rapturous acclaim, would years later make a statement to an urban planning conference in London that was as evocative to architects as the Declaration of Independence had been to oppressed British subjects in the American colonies. In some ways it *was* a declaration of independence, the independence L'Enfant had always demanded but never received.

> Make no little plans; they have no magic to stir men's blood and probably themselves will not be realized. Make big plans; aim high in hope and work, remembering that a noble, logical diagram once recorded will never die, but long after we are gone will be a living thing asserting itself with ever growing insistency. Remember that our sons and grandsons are going to do things that would stagger us. Let your watchword be order and your beacon beauty.

Like L'Enfant, the members of the Senate Park Commission possessed a vision of cities as entities full of potential power and grace, but they were also cognizant of their place in a long continuum of professional achievement and were not averse to learning from that history. They believed in the notion, so familiar in L'Enfant and George Washington's era but so soon to become passé, that performing a public service for the nation would be as good for their reputations as making a fortune working for private clients. To that end the commission, at Burnham's instruction, made one of its earliest orders of business a trip across the Atlantic and back in time in an attempt to better understand the antecedents of Washington, D.C.

The three men, minus Saint-Gaudens, left aboard the steamship *Deutschland* in June 1901, just seven months before Roosevelt would attend the display at the Corcoran. Rick Olmsted brought along a set of detailed plans of Washington, including a print of L'Enfant's, and gave them serious study every day of the crossing. In six weeks the architects would visit Paris, Rome, Venice, Vienna, Budapest, Paris again, Versailles, and London. While in Rome they walked along the long diagonal avenues of Pope Sixtus V, and while in Paris they viewed the Champs-Élysées and the park at Versailles, as well as the street system of Baron Haussmann and Napoleon III, dominated by the great boulevards that had not existed in L'Enfant's lifetime but that still seemed so reminiscent of the plan of Washington, D.C.

The travelers sought to obtain systematically and with considerable haste a sense of the world of L'Enfant's youth and the places he had committed to memory. If they were not going to find L'Enfant himself—not enough was known about the major's biography at the time to tell them where to begin looking—they were at least able to make meaningful contact with the origins of his design sensibility. Senator McMillan's aide Charles Moore later recorded the relationship of this European sojourn to the plan eventually illustrated by Hoppin and displayed in the Corcoran.

> The Palace of the Tuileries as the Capitol, the Tuileries Gardens as the Mall, the Obelisk in the crossing of the two Paris axes as the Washington Monument centers the Capitol and White House axes; and then a Lincoln Memorial as a national monument in location at the termination of the composition, and also as a center of distribution comparable to the Arc de Triomphe.

This connect-the-dots genealogy was not really true to the spirit of L'Enfant, who had once argued to Thomas Jefferson that he would "reprobate the idea of imitating and that contrary of having this intention it is my wish and shall be my endeavor to delineate on a new and original way the plan." But the members of the Senate Park Commission were at least aware that the capital's designer had an artistic and geographic past and that delving into that past was an important part of bettering Washington according to his design.

When Olmsted Jr., Burnham, and McKim returned to America in late July 1901, they wasted no time in getting to their drawing boards. The commission had no legal power to impose a plan on the city, but the display to the public at the Corcoran and the approbation of the president had created a kind of architectural San Juan Hill on which it was perilous to stand in opposition. Roosevelt would recognize this groundswell, without acknowledging his own special role, in a speech given to another meeting of the AIA later in the decade.

> The only way in which we can hope to have worthy artistic work done for the nation, state, or municipality is by having such a

growth of popular sentiment as will render it incumbent upon successive administrations, or successive legislative bodies, to carry out steadily a plan chosen for them, worked out for them by such a body of men as that gathered here.

Over the next several years such "popular sentiment" for the commission's plan, though not universal, was unquenchable. The Hoppin perspective and other renderings were reprinted across the country in *Century Magazine, Architectural Record, American Architect and Building News, National Geographic,* and *Life.* Newspapers from New York to San Francisco editorialized favorably on the plan. If Chicago's White City had been the wildly popular testing ground of neoclassical principles of stateliness and grandeur, the commission's work on the city of Washington would be a large-scale and real-world laboratory of those principles.

The Senate Park Commission report, modestly and disingenuously titled "The Improvement of the Park System of the District of Columbia" and released on the day the Corcoran exhibit opened, is one of the most extraordinary town-planning documents in history. "It had no legal standing, its cost was prohibitive and only idealists would think of executing such a scheme," wrote Glenn Brown. "[But] many of us believed that idealism backed by merit was a moral force that would produce practical results."

The commission had to deal with two essential conditions that had not affected L'Enfant. One was the position of the Washington Monument, finally completed in 1884 and dedicated the following year. So much larger and heavier than the proposed equestrian statue of L'Enfant's plan, it had been shifted off axis in two directions to avoid lower, less solid ground and now rested about three hundred feet southeast of the crossing point of L'Enfant's two primary vistas. The other condition was the elongated Mall. Over the past two decades the Army Corps of Engineers had filled in most of the eastern half of the silting Potomac, halving the river's width and lengthening the major's one-and-a-half-mile Mall by nearly a mile. The plot of landfill called West Potomac Park created so much new open ground, in fact, that to speak of a dramatic westward vista over the Potomac became nonsensical. From the vantage of the Capitol's terrace, the river was no longer a dominating landscape element but merely a thin ribbon of silver-blue bisected by the Washington obelisk.

The report consisted of 124 pages of text, 9 appendices, 107 illustrations (many of them photographs taken by Rick Olmsted on the *Deutschland* excursion), and 11 maps, the first of which was L'Enfant's August 1791 plan. In the report's vision, the capital was full of monumental buildings ringing the White House and the Capitol and lining the great green space of the Mall, all set off at appropriate distances to allow for the creation of clearly defined public lawns and squares.

The report may have honored L'Enfant, but it also, sometimes by necessity and sometimes by choice, ignored much of the major's original plan. No attention was paid to his scheme for the distribution of state squares; all of the lots surrounding the squares were by now in private ownership, and the number of states had ballooned to forty-five. Most of all, the major's "Grand Avenue" now ceased to be an avenue at all. Where L'Enfant had envisioned the Mall as a national boulevard, busy with pedestrians, horses, and coaches, the commission, perhaps a bit starstruck, recommended a duplication of the Tapis Vert at Versailles in the form of a greensward containing a shallow reflecting pool named, with unintended irony, the "canal." The westernmost end of this greensward, in the center of a grand circular drive, was designated as the site for a memorial to Lincoln, who was called the "one man in our history as a nation who is worthy to be named with George Washington."

The McMillan Commission's report, then, and not any one of L'Enfant's drawings, was the first statement of the plan that gave birth to today's Washington, D.C. But the core of L'Enfant's plan remains visible. Rick Olmsted and the other members of the commission had produced a blueprint of remarkable clarity and resilience. Its rehabilitation of Washington was well under way, and all that was left now was for history to turn its attention to the major himself.

A wide sea of years separated L'Enfant's obituary in the *National Intelligencer* and an article by an anonymous journalist on the second page of the June 22, 1881, edition of the *New-York Tribune.*

AN OLD-TIME ARCHITECT
THE LIFE OF PIERRE CHARLES L'ENFANT
MEMORIES OF THE MAN WHO DESIGNED
FEDERAL HALL, NEW YORK,
AND LAID OUT THE CITY OF WASHINGTON

L'Enfant's collection of letters, commendations, commissions, and receipts had finally emerged from the stone mansion of George Riggs, a retired Washington banker who now owned the estate called Green Hill where William Dudley Digges had sheltered the old major in his final years. L'Enfant's papers had caught the attention of Digges's grandson, a physician named James Dudley Morgan, who was helping the elderly Riggs organize his effects and who made it a personal mission to put the documentary stash in order. Whether Morgan called the reporter or the reporter called him, he was far enough along to provide some significant materials for the purposes of a small biography.

The anonymous journalist's sketch of "one of the most obscure characters in American annals" was based on only a small portion of the extant documents. The article was full of extrapolations and suppositions that would become received wisdom and take decades to undo, including the description of L'Enfant as "clearly a young officer in the French line" before his departure for America, rather than the art student he really was. But it also contained plenty of revelations, enough to put together a rough chronology of his life out of the details of his military service, his connection to so many of the prominent men of the time, the failed lot sale and L'Enfant's objections to it, the Duddington affair, the Roberdeau letters, and the subsequent tussles over his insubordination.

The magazine *American Architect and Building News* printed a condensed version of the *Tribune* biography in October, and thus began a slow and steady surge of interest in L'Enfant's life and work. His manuscript plan was finally traced and a facsimile made in 1887; in 1899 the recently chartered Columbia Historical Society devoted its second volume of records to the origins of the city, transcribing for the first time a selection of L'Enfant's memorials to Congress and including for good measure a lengthy defense of Andrew Ellicott, whose reputation had suddenly and perhaps unfairly been turned upside down. By the time the AIA met in Washington the following year, Rick Olmsted and his colleagues had at hand the original plan and some kind of outline of a man.

L'Enfant also had politics on his side. In the first year of his presidency Teddy Roosevelt had become fast friends with the French ambassador, a puckish and wiry diplomat named Jules Jusserand, who doubled as a scholar of medieval cultures and authors. Roosevelt had read and admired Jusserand's study of *Piers Plowman* and liked to talk Chaucer and Shakespeare over wine, but most of all he liked to partner with the agile and aggressive Frenchman on the brand-new White House tennis court. "He has taken the oath as Secretary of State," Roosevelt joked of Jusserand, and for the ambassador's part Roosevelt was a most useful tool in his quest to keep France at the center of American attention. Part of that quest involved rebuffing the efforts of German ambassador Baron Hermann Speck von Sternberg, also a friend of Roosevelt's, to raise Baron von Steuben as a revolutionary war hero on a par with the Marquis de Lafayette. Enter Major L'Enfant, now referred to exclusively as "Pierre," whom Jusserand began to champion in his mission to return attention to the role of French heroes in the American War for Independence.

The persistence and promotional energy of Jusserand acted as the final catalyst in the rehabilitation of L'Enfant. The payoff came in May 1908, when one hundred years after granting the major $4,600—not a penny of which he had been able to keep away from his creditors—Congress allocated $1,000 "to remove and render accessible to the public the grave of Major Pierre Charles L'Enfant." In December Secretary of War Luke E. Wright approved a grave site in Arlington National Cemetery, and the process of properly honoring the designer of Washington was under way. L'Enfant had left Paris in 1776, the year of the signing of the Declaration of Independence, on a voyage across the ocean and toward what he must have imagined as a rendezvous with destiny. But only now, 132 years later, was *gloire* appearing over the horizon.

The exhumation of Major L'Enfant commenced on April 22, 1909, at the old Digges family cemetery in Prince George's County, Maryland. The slender red cedar tree that had been planted at the head of L'Enfant's grave was felled, and a few spadefuls of earth were removed, but then lightning and thunder delayed the work for twenty minutes. When the digging resumed, reported the *Washington Post,* the witnesses soon discovered that "a layer of discolored mold three inches in thickness, two pieces of bones, and a tooth were all that remained of the great engineer."

These remains, such as they were, were placed in a metal casket wrapped in Old Glory and conveyed to Mount Olivet Cemetery along the nearby Bladensburg Road—the same route along which, most likely, L'Enfant had first approached Georgetown late on a wet evening in March 1791. At nine o'clock on the morning of April 28, 1909, a mild spring day, the casket arrived in Washington, escorted by a Corps of Engineers honor guard. It was brought into the Capitol rotunda and placed atop the catafalque of Abraham Lincoln. Here L'Enfant lay in state, the first foreign-born individual and only the seventh person ever to be afforded such an honor. In a fitting coincidence, the walls of the rotunda were covered with the work of John Trumbull, the artist and friend who had spoken at some length with the major about L'Enfant's never-realized plans for the very building in which he was now being honored.

President William Howard Taft arrived at ten-thirty, accompanied by First Lady Helen Taft and surrounded by members of the Society of the Cincinnati. Vice President James Sherman spoke first, followed by Ambassador Jusserand, who praised his expatriated countryman for his prescience. "For Major L'Enfant," he said, "the planning of the city of Washington was a work of love. A mere glance at that work showed the officer had decided not to work for a nation of 13 States, but one of 50. The streets were unexampled anywhere; gardens, parks, fountains, statues to famous men—all were devised in view of a great and powerful nation, the nation of today."

Around noon eight army engineers carried L'Enfant's casket out to the east front of the Capitol and set it on an artillery caisson pulled by six bay mares. Cavalry from Fort Myer led the way, followed by the Corps of Engineers band. A cortege of five hundred people, sometimes outnumbering the crowds flanking them, began its procession up Pennsylvania Avenue and across the Rock Creek bridge to M Street, reversing the direction of L'Enfant's original ride around the site. Flags flew at half-mast all along the way, while children and their teachers, freed by a decree from the District of Columbia Board of Education, edged to the curb to peer at the horse-drawn cart and its solemn cargo.

The new grave had been placed on the highest promontory in Arlington National Cemetery, under a towering oak less than twenty yards from the front steps and the fat faux-marble columns of Arlington House, built in 1808 and home to Martha Washington's dissolute grandson George Washington Parke Custis and, later and most famously, to Robert E. Lee, who had abandoned the estate to Union forces in 1862. The view of the federal city from this spot was and is magnificent, described by the Marquis de Lafayette in 1824 as the greatest vista in the world. Lafayette's hyperbole aside, it is indeed the best place from which to perceive the monumental nature of Washington.

L'Enfant's caisson on the way to Arlington National Cemetery, April 29, 1909

In 1909, years before the construction of the Lincoln Memorial and the bridge symbolically connecting the Union's leader to the home of the legendary Confederate general, the view from the top of Arlington Cemetery was dominated by the sweep of the Potomac and the Washington Monument and Capitol beyond. The trees along both shores were thick enough then, as today, that the imagination could easily retreat all the way to 1801 and the first year of Thomas Jefferson's presidency, when the city seemed made of a pair of imposing federal edifices rising from the fields and forests and little else.

The grave into which L'Enfant's presumed remains were lowered was a simple affair, awaiting the completion of the more substantial memorial authorized by Congress in 1908 and still under construction in Tennessee. Two years later the piece was completed, and in May 1911 several hundred distinguished visitors returned to congregate on the porch of the Lee Mansion and witness L'Enfant's second day of belated apotheosis. Rector William Russell of St. Patrick's Church, where L'Enfant had once been listed as a communicant, opened the ceremony with a prayer, giving way to a tribute read by President Taft: "There are not many who have to wait one hundred years to receive the reward to which they are entitled until the world shall make the progress which enables it to pay the just reward." The president spoke of L'Enfant's arrival in America as "a soldier" and referred to the major's "highly artistic temperament" along with "the defects which not infrequently accompany that temperament." He also provided an even-handed verdict in a continuing battle of professional legacies. "I would not for a moment detract from Mr. Ellicott's merits," he said, but added that "the evidence goes to show that the great originality in the plan was L'Enfant's, that where the ideas in the design were original they were L'Enfant's."

Six years later, in 1917, Jules Jusserand would win the Pulitzer Prize in history for a collection of short biographies and essays entitled *With Americans of Past and Present Days,* a misleading title in that many of the featured "Americans" were French contributors to the War for Independence. One of the book's biographies would rely on the Digges-L'Enfant-Morgan Papers and be the first serious attempt to reconstruct the life of L'Enfant from beginning to end. Jusserand had barely begun that project when he addressed the crowd of statesmen, architects, and Washington socialites with his second and final eulogy for the major.

> All of those who visit the Federal City are unanimous in their praise of its beauty, its exact adaptation to the needs of a great nation. With the mind of a poet, with the soul of a prophet, perceiving future ages as clearly as if they were the present, a man foresaw over a century ago what we now see, and that man lies under the monument which a generous vote of Congress allows us to dedicate today, Major Pierre Charles L'Enfant.

Today L'Enfant's grave offers a relatively undisturbed perch from which to view the resting place of John F. Kennedy fifty feet below. It is a beautiful site, but one full of distractions, not least of which is the panorama of Washington, D.C., from such a dramatic vantage point. Camera-happy visitors stop in front of the Robert E. Lee Mansion to line up picture after picture of the Mall, the major's monument always just to the right and just outside of the frame.

In 1846, four years after Charles Dickens made the trip he'd memorialized in *American Notes,* the residents of that portion of the original one-hundred-square-mile diamond west of the Potomac had voted to leave the federal district. In a kind of early shadow of the great secession to come, they wanted to become Virginians once again in order to regain their representation in Congress, to make their own economic way, and to fend off any effort to halt their trade in slaves. The federal government, which had paid almost no attention to that portion of its territory and had no money to do anything with it, simply let it go.

Standing next to L'Enfant's grave on land retroceded to Virginia, then, it is easy to forget that we are not inside the city of Washington, D.C. But it is probably appropriate, a true reflection of the unfulfilled aspirations that came to rule his life, that L'Enfant has been left to rest forever on the outside looking in.

Epilogue

Midway through his second petition to the government of the city of Washington, D.C., written in August 1800 just before his return to the city, L'Enfant paused to "particularize" twelve "grievances" he considered the greatest sins committed against him by Thomas Johnson, David Stuart, and Daniel Carroll. The complaints ran together pell-mell and included, as usual, the theft of his right to profit from sales of the engraved version of the map, the use of Andrew Ellicott as a "disguised personage" to betray himself and the plan, and the erasure of his credit as the city's designer. But for those following the steps of L'Enfant two hundred years later, grievance 10 was the most significant: the trunk he'd brought with him to Georgetown, the one he'd filled with early plans and draft memorandums and drawings of the President's House and Congress House, was missing—a result, he wrote, of "the forcible seizure of particular drafts and manuscripts in deposit and of other abstracts, papers, and effects likewise stealed away from my agents and out of my own quarters."

The truth, as always, was more complicated than L'Enfant was willing to admit. In the aftermath of his departure from the federal city in February 1792, he and Isaac Roberdeau had exchanged a series of letters in which the major exhorted his assistant to collect his effects, while Roberdeau exhorted his former supervisor to free him from the debts he'd taken on in L'Enfant's name. When the two men were reunited later that year in Paterson, New Jersey, to begin the survey and design of Alexander Hamilton's manufacturing city, L'Enfant seems to have all but abandoned his attempt to retrieve his things, and by the time George Washington was dead, those things were no longer available to him. As it turns out, neither are they available to us. The next time his effects are mentioned in the documentary record, in 1802, they are part of an exchange of letters between L'Enfant and landowner Samuel Davidson, in which the major described how his trunk was "laid open and the contents were then scattered amongst other effects and handed about at everybody's pleasure to ransack." He blamed Davidson for the dispersal of the objects, an accusation that the merchant took with some of the same forbearance Alexander Hamilton had displayed in 1798 upon being challenged to a duel. Davidson, who had been among the planner's most vocal supporters a decade earlier, thanked L'Enfant for his "very polite letter" and included a notarized statement of his bemusement that he was even involved in the affair.

> As to the number and magnitude of Major L'Enfant's package containing his effects, or the intrinsic value of such his effects, I know nothing of. At the same time it is presumable that if their contents were of real material value he would have enquired more particularly after them some years prior to his late call upon [me].

Just as the wholesale destructions of the French Revolution left potential biographers to sift through a depleted inventory of official records relating to his family, so too has the disappearance of L'Enfant's working papers and drawings left architectural historians with only partially informed guesswork as to his working methods, his use of precedent, his preliminary ideas for the White House and Capitol, and the changes he made in the plan of Washington, D.C., in the five months between his first and final versions.

What does remain to posterity is a single smudged and tattered drawing, the plan L'Enfant presented to Washington, Jefferson, and Madison in
August 1791. This is the drawing that the president felt was complete
enough to initiate a lot sale, the drawing displayed in Philadelphia for Congress in December of the same year, and the one on which Jefferson made
his textual additions and emendations before giving it to Andrew Ellicott in
January 1792 without L'Enfant's knowledge. Its life has not been happy or
healthy. In fact, by the time George Washington handed it over to the commissioners' office in 1796, he was already bemoaning its fading pencil lines,
the first evidence of two centuries of disintegration.

The first attempt to ensure the drawing's longevity was made early in
the nineteenth century, when an anonymous preservationist in the city's
employ mounted the cracking and curling plan on a piece of cotton cloth
and applied a transparent glue varnish to the entire surface in broad hori-
zontal brushstrokes. A common practice at the time, this care only hastened
the shortening of the paper's linen fibers and turned the cream-colored surface a muddy sepia. After the Civil War, the plan was transferred to the newly
created Office of Public Buildings and Grounds in the basement of the Capitol, where according to one report it sat loose among sundry other maps and
blueprints.

When in the 1880s the decision was made to fill in the Potomac's dangerous and unsightly tidal flats, the plan was temporarily transferred to the
U.S. Coast and Geodetic Survey so that a facsimile might be made for use in
the lawsuits sure to result from the remaking of the city's physical shape.
Two dozen expert draftsmen and cartographers assisted as a copy of the
drawing was made onto two sheets of tracing paper for use in creating a clear
photolithograph. The document was then returned to its basement room at
the Capitol, and for thirty more years its watercolor washes and pencil lines
continued to fade while its iron gall ink continued to bleed, ringing the letters of L'Enfant's text labels with dingy halos.

In 1918 Charles Moore, former secretary to Senator McMillan and
chronicler of the *Deutschland* expedition, brought the plan to the Library of
Congress, where he had recently become director of the Manuscripts Division, and here L'Enfant's handiwork finally began to receive the attention it
so badly needed. Placed in a wooden box, under a thick glass shield, the
plan was seldom viewed until 1951, when another effort at restoration was
made, replacing the cotton cloth backing with sturdier material and mend-

ing what cracks and tears could be mended. This was the last time the draw-ing was altered in any way, as an extensive study ten years later provided a determination that still obtains today: *It's been through enough. Leave it alone.*

Technology is slowly catching up to L'Enfant's plan. Less than 20 ounces of paper now sit encased in 108 pounds of polystyrene, anodized aluminum, and Plexiglas, sealed off from the outside and breathing an otherworldly atmosphere made of pressurized argon gas. Only five documents at the Library of Congress have been placed in this type of life-support apparatus: L'Enfant's plan, George Mason's Virginia Declaration of Rights, two drafts of the Gettysburg Address in Lincoln's hand, and Thomas Jefferson's draft of the Declaration of Independence.

The presence of Jefferson's very best work, encased in its own preser-vative shell and resting nearby in the same refrigerated chamber, is especially provocative, linking the two erstwhile collaborators in a way neither could ever have imagined. Born in a great rush of activity and inspiration, L'En-fant's 1791 manuscript plan is a founding document able to take a place beside its more famous written counterparts as an early and lasting expres-sion of the democratic political experiment that was the United States of America. His design echoed the designs of cities across Europe, but it was also the first great artistic achievement that could truly be called "American." He was an impatient and impolite man who refused to surrender even the smallest detail of his grand design—qualities that resulted in his failure and in his success. All Major L'Enfant wanted was to be judged by his work, and that work was all-consuming. It was also brilliant.

If he should take miff and leave the business, I have no scruple in declaring to you (though I do not want him to know it) that I know not where another is to be found who could supply his place.

—George Washington to the federal city commissioners,
DECEMBER 18, 1791

A Note on Sources

Anyone beginning a study of the life and work of Peter Charles L'Enfant quickly learns to make a touchstone of the correspondence collected in the Digges-L'Enfant-Morgan Papers in the Manuscript Division of the Library of Congress. Without this treasure, neither *Grand Avenues* nor any other book-length work about L'Enfant would be possible. Other indispensable primary sources include L'Enfant's memorials to Congress and the records of the commissioners for the District of Columbia, both found in the National Archives; *The Papers of George Washington* and its unmatched editorial apparatus; *The Diaries of George Washington; The Papers of Thomas Jefferson; The Papers of Alexander Hamilton;* "Autobiographical Letters of Peter S. Duponceau"; *The Autobiography of Colonel John Trumbull;* and *Letters of Thomas Attwood Digges*. I'm forever grateful to the editors and librarians responsible for bringing these documents to the public view and keeping them there.

Four biographies exist, each with its unique strengths: Jules Jusserand's *With Americans of Past and Present Days;* Elizabeth S. Kite's *L'Enfant and Washington;* Paul Caemmerer's *Life of Pierre Charles L'Enfant;* and Ken Bowling's *Peter Charles L'Enfant,* which uses little space to recount L'Enfant's adventure in the federal city and instead focuses on the lesser-known later stretches of his life. Taken together, these texts—all but Bowling's written before 1950—allowed me to make historical and chronological sense of L'Enfant's life story. Two collections of selected primary documents—Saul Padover's *Thomas Jefferson and the National Capital* and Paul K. Walker's *Engineers of Independence*—provided welcome assistance at many important moments, while the early twentieth-century architectural criticism of Elbert Peets and William T. Partridge was equally valuable.

James Thomas Flexner's four-volume George Washington biography and Dumas Malone's six-part *Jefferson and His Time* are still the most comprehensive lives of this pair of paramount founders. Several histories of Washington, D.C., informed nearly every chapter of *Grand Avenues*, including Wilhelmus Bryan's *History of the National Capital;* Constance Green's *Washington: Village and Capital, 1800–1878;* William Tindall's *Standard History of the City of Washington;* Frederick Gutheim's *Worthy of the Nation: The History of Planning for the National Capital;* John W. Reps's *Monumental Washington: The Planning and Development of the Capital Center* and *Washington on View: The Nation's Capital Since 1790;* and Ken Bowling's *Creation of Washington, D.C.: The Idea and Location of the American Capital* and *Creating the Federal City, 1774–1800: Potomac Fever.* I also relied heavily on the scholarship collected in *Records of the Columbia Historical Society* and in *Washington History,* the magazine of the Historical Society of Washington, D.C. Two more compilations provided invaluable assistance: the Winter 1979 issue of the now-defunct *Quarterly Journal of the Library of Congress,* devoted to L'Enfant's 1791 manuscript plan, and *The Mall in Washington, 1791–1991,* a collection of papers presented at the National Gallery of Art in 1987 and edited by Richard Longstreth, which did more than any other source to tie together the work done on Washington by L'Enfant in 1791 and by the Senate Park Commission 110 years later.

I would like to add one more person to this list of writers who made *Grand Avenues* possible: the anonymous journalist working for the *New-York Tribune* who reintroduced L'Enfant's life story to the world in 1881 by digging through the bags of letters and other documents being sorted by James Dudley Morgan and destined eventually for the Library of Congress. I do not know who you were or what happened in the rest of your life, but from one writer to another, thank you for paying attention.

My hope is that the following method of attribution will provide sufficient illumination without creating an unduly lengthy notes section. For each chapter, a brief headnote lists secondary sources of particular importance, after which citations for quoted material appear. The Digges-L'Enfant-Morgan Papers (indicated as DLM) generally take precedence and are cited whenever possible. Correspondence involving George Washington, Thomas Jefferson, and Alexander Hamilton not found in DLM can be located in their respective *Papers,* unless otherwise noted. Most newspaper citations came from research in the Newspaper and Current Periodical Reading Room at the Library of Congress or from the ProQuest Historical Newspapers databases.

Grand Avenues is a work of narrative history by a nonfiction writer and journalist who has put his trust in a collection of brilliant but often disappointingly underappreciated scholars. Still, any mistakes of fact or problems in historical interpretation are mine alone. Those wishing to do their own delving into the story of L'Enfant and the federal city are encouraged to consult the sources listed above and in the full bibliography that follows.

Spellings have been changed to conform with modern American English, with a few purposeful exceptions. Punctuation and capitalization have also been modernized for ease of reading.

The following abbreviations are used to indicate frequently quoted individuals:

AH	Alexander Hamilton
FLO	Frederick Law Olmsted, Sr.
GW	George Washington
IR	Isaac Roberdeau
PCL	Peter Charles L'Enfant
RO	Rick Olmsted (Frederick Law Olmsted, Jr.)
TAD	Thomas Attwood Digges
TJ	Thomas Jefferson

Notes

CHAPTER 1

Hawkins, "The Landscape of the Federal City: A 1792 Walking Tour," was my essential guide to the territory before it became the federal city. On Andrew Ellicott and Benjamin Banneker, I consulted Bedini, *The Life of Benjamin Banneker* and "The Survey of the Federal Territory: Andrew Ellicott and Benjamin Banneker," while Holmes, "Suter's Tavern: Birthplace of the Federal City," allowed me to locate and describe L'Enfant's first home in the federal district.

3 "A Pedestal Waiting for a Superstructure": PCL memorandum to GW, June 22, 1791, in Kite, *L'Enfant and Washington.*

8 "When the President shall have made up his mind": TJ to GW, November 29, 1790, in Padover, ed., *Jefferson and the National Capital.*

9 "so as to excite no suspicion": GW to Deakins and Stoddert, February 3, 1791.

9 "nothing further is communicated": GW to Deakins and Stoddert, March 2, 1791.

10 "drawings of the particular grounds": TJ to PCL, early March 1791, in Padover, ed., *Jefferson and the National Capital.*

11 "to obtain a knowledge of the whole": PCL to TJ, March 11, 1791, ibid.

15 "Wednesday evening arrived in this town Major Longfont": *George-Town Weekly Ledger,* March 12, 1791.

CHAPTER 2

Two books by Garrioch, *Neighbourhood and Community in Paris, 1740–1790* and *The Making of Revolutionary Paris,* provide a remarkably thorough picture of the urban fabric of Paris from the mid-eighteenth century to the beginning of the French Revolution, while the intellectual and philosophical ferment of the time is most usefully presented in Echeverria, *Mirage in the West,* and Roche, *France in the Enlightenment.* Coural, *Les Gobelins,* and Weigert, *French Tapestry,* helped me to enter the world of the royal tapestry manufacture that was L'Enfant's childhood home. Morton and Spinelli, *Beaumarchais and the American Revolution,* is without compare as an examination of the famous playwright's role in recruiting French soldiers to the American cause. For the curriculum of the Royal Academy of Painting and Sculpture, I read Perry and Cunningham, eds., *Academies, Museums, and Canons of Art,* and Pevsner, *Academies of Art, Past and Present.*

17 "An Infinity of Small Moments": Diderot, *Salons.*

23 "It is, after all, necessary to be a master colorist": Ibid.

31 "In my heart I prefer fame above all else": Louis XIV, *Mémoires.*

CHAPTER 3

Several sources combined to bring the physical environment and social structures of Valley Forge alive for me: Royster, *A Revolutionary People at War;* Bodle, *The Valley Forge Winter;* Stoudt, *Ordeal at Valley Forge;* and Bill, *Valley Forge: The Making of an Army.* My attempts to make sense of L'Enfant's ill-fated military adventures in the South were abetted by Borick, *A Gallant Defense;* Gordon, *South Carolina and the American Revolution;* Lawrence, *Storm over Savannah;* Massey, *John Laurens and the American Revolution;* and Morrill, *Southern Campaigns of the American Revolution.* To describe L'Enfant's postwar career, I consulted Myers, *Liberty Without Anarchy: A History of the Society of the Cincinnati* and *The Insignia of the Society of the Cincinnati,* as well as Stinchcombe, "Americans Celebrate the Birth of the Dauphin."

35 "A Powerful Friend Among the Princes of the Earth": GW, general orders, May 5, 1778.

37 "Thus this determination was first invented in America": Duponceau, "Autobiographical Letters."

39 "I could not keep my eyes from that imposing countenance": Ibid.

40 "creature of B"; "good for drawing figures"; "embellishing plans with cartouches": Du Coudray to Congress, July 1777, *Papers of the Continental Congress,* vol. 156.

40 "an old German baron, with a large brilliant star": Duponceau, in Palmer, *General von Steuben.*

42 "friendly European powers": GW, general orders, March 5, 1778.

42 "When you requested me to set for Monsr. Lanfang": GW to Lafayette, September 25, 1778.

43 "the conciseness of the work": GW to Steuben, February 26, 1779.

44 "marching": PCL to Steuben, May 24, 1779, in Caemmerer, *Life of L'Enfant.*

44 "period of inertia": PCL to Steuben, July 6, 1779, ibid.

45 "All I can tell you": Ibid.

46 "It is without partiality to say": PCL to GW, February 18, 1782.

47 "I attached myself wherever I could render": Ibid.

47 "my hard captivity": PCL, memorial to Congress, December 7, 1800, in Caemmerer, *Life of L'Enfant.*

47 "intentionally go within twelve miles": PCL, certificate of parole, July 1781, DLM.

49 "a rising sun surmounted by 13 stars": Jean Francois Louis Clermont-Crèvecoeur, September 1782, in Stinchcombe, "Americans Celebrate the Birth of the Dauphin."

50 "The affair at Savannah": PCL to GW, February 18, 1782.

50 "much younger Captain of Engineers": Ibid.

50 "I flatter myself Your Excellency will not oppose": Ibid.

50 "your zeal and active services are such": GW to PCL, March 4, 1782.

52 "I have found but one who is not opposed": TJ to GW, April 16, 1784.

52 "against the confederation": Ibid.

52 "charge des affaires"; "perfection": PCL to Henry Knox, September 27, 1783, Society of the Cincinnati Library.

53 "Having now finished the work assigned me": GW to Confederation Congress, December 23, 1783.

54 "The permission which this powerful monarch": PCL to GW, December 25, 1783.

54 "elegant entertainment": PCL to GW, April 29, 1784.

CHAPTER 4

Torres, "Federal Hall Revisited," and Scott, *Temple of Liberty,* provided the best descriptions of L'Enfant's work on the renovation of Federal Hall. For a more general picture of life in New York City at the time, see Burrows and Wallace, *Gotham: A History of New York City to 1898;* Pomerantz, *New York, an American City, 1783–1803: A Study of Urban Life;* and Smith, *The City of New York in the Year of Washington's Inauguration, 1789.*

57 "The Remembrance of My Former Services": PCL to GW, September 11, 1789.

58 "No building under similar circumstances": *New-York Morning Post and Daily Advertiser,* March 14, 1789.

59 "Long live George Washington": Flexner, *Washington and the New Nation,* vol. 3 of *Washington.*

60 "It was a day which will stand immutable and indelible": Tobias Lear to George Augustine Washington, May 3, 1789, in Brighton, *Checkered Career of Tobias Lear.*

62 "perfect knowledge"; "natural-philosophy": PCL, *Papers of the Continental Congress,* December 15, 1784, in Walker, *Engineers of Independence.*

62 "an engineer should be possessed of good natural parts": Ibid.

62 "immediate benefit of the United States": Ibid.

63 "I had made considerable progress in the survey": PCL, memorial, undated, National Archives (Committee Papers, 1816–1946).

63 "tavern living": PCL, undated correspondence, DLM.

65 "to be entrusted to the Assistants to take proper precautions": *New-York Morning Post and Daily Advertiser,* April 30, 1789.

66 "The whole composition": *New-York Journal and Weekly Register,* March 26, 1789, in Torres, "Federal Hall Revisited."

66 "the master piece of the whole": Ibid.

67 "We cannot close our description without observing": *Massachusetts Magazine; or Monthly Museum of Knowledge and Rational Entertainment* 1, no. 6 (June 1789), in Torres, "Federal Hall Revisited."

68 "inherit the President's virtue": Bowling, *Creation of Washington, D.C.*

68 "by pointing to a map": *New-York Morning Post and Daily Advertiser,* September 7, 1789.

68 "the late determination of Congress": PCL to GW, September 11, 1789.

69 "it will be obvious that the plan should be drawn": Ibid.

69 "I shall conclude by assuring you": Ibid.

CHAPTER 5

73 "In Every Respect Advantageously Situated": PCL to GW, memorandum, March 26, 1791.

74 "when considering the intended city on that grand scale": PCL to TJ, March 11, 1791, in Padover, ed., *Jefferson and the National Capital.*

74 "As far as I was able to judge through a thick fog": Ibid.

75 "There are certainly considerable advantages": TJ to PCL, March 17, 1791, DLM.

75 "in future": TJ to GW, March 11, 1791.

75 "mobs of great cities": TJ, *Notes on the State of Virginia.*

76 "no offer worthy of consideration": GW to PCL, April 4, 1791, DLM.

77 "Dined at Suter's Tavern": GW diary, March 28, 1791.

78 "a rough drawing in pencil": PCL to TJ, April 4, 1791, in Padover, ed., *Jefferson and the National Capital.*

79 "Such regular plans indeed": PCL to GW, memorandum, March 26, 1791.

80 "From these heights every grand building": Ibid.

81 "properly manage": GW diary, March 29, 1791.

83 "The parties to whom I addressed myself": GW diary, March 30, 1791.

83 "All the land from Rock Creek along the river": GW to TJ, March 31, 1791.

84 "The enlarged plan of this agreement": Ibid.

85 "I had the satisfaction to see": PCL to TJ, April 4, 1791, in Padover, ed., *Jefferson and the National Capital.*

86 "particular maps of any such sea ports": Ibid.

86 "I need not assure you I shall do my best": PCL to AH, April 8, 1791.

87 "If I had not already intruded too long": Ibid.

87 "the President has left the planning of the town": TJ to PCL, April 10, 1791, DLM.

88 "As they are connected with the notes": Ibid.

88 "Whenever it is proposed to prepare plans": Ibid.

92 "a thick wood": Trumbull, *Autobiography.*

CHAPTER 6

George Washington's diary covers the period between June 13 and June 27, 1791, with a single sentence: "I remained at home; and spent my time in daily rides to my several farms and in receiving many visits." This brevity, unusual even by Washington's standards, means the evidence that L'Enfant visited Mount Vernon with the second draft of his plan is circumstantial. But a strong case, built on three facts, may be made: 1) L'Enfant's memorandum describing the plan was dated June 22 and could not have been delivered earlier; 2) by the time Washington met with the commissioners and proprietors on June 27, he had clearly received not only that memorandum but a detailed verbal explanation of the plan; and 3) Washington's unusually lengthy diary entry for June 27, when he left Mount Vernon for Georgetown, does not mention a meeting with L'Enfant on that day prior to presenting the plan to the commissioners and proprietors. There seems to me to be little reasonable doubt that L'Enfant's visit occurred, a conclusion also reached by several of the scholars cited below.

Mount Vernon as an architectural composition is considered at length in Greenberg, *George Washington: Architect,* and in Dalzell and Dalzell, *George Washington's Mount Vernon,* while George Washington's complex relationship with the Potomac River is laid out vividly in Achenbach, *The Grand Idea.* Because L'Enfant declined to discuss any existing models or inspirations for his design of Washington, D.C., the urban forebears of his plan have become a hotly debated topic, second only perhaps to the thorny and equally unresolvable question of just how much of the federal city was made of "swamp" in 1791. My own sense that Rome, Paris, and the unrealized plans for London by Evelyn and Wren were three overarching influences on L'Enfant (and my deemphasis of Versailles) has come from conversations with Donald Hawkins and from Bacon, *Design of Cities;* Morris, *History of Urban Form;* Kostof, *The City Shaped;* Dougherty, "Baroque and Picturesque Motifs in L'Enfant's Design for the Federal Capital"; Jennings, "Artistry as Design: L'Enfant's Extraordinary City"; and Driskel, "L'Enfant's Suitcase: The Imprint of Paris on the Plan of Washington" (a talk presented at the 2005 Paris on the Potomac conference in Washington).

93 "A Plan Wholly New": PCL to GW, memorandum, August 19, 1791.

95 "if Washington were not a better general": Duponceau, "Autobiographical Letters."

95 "might be considered handsome and perhaps elegant": Ibid.

97 "No estate in United America is more pleasantly situated": GW to Arthur Young, December 12, 1793.

98 "There is the strongest speculative proof": GW to Thomas Johnson, July 20, 1770.

98 "I am inclined to think that, if you were to exhibit": Ibid.

98 "A more enlarged plan": Ibid.

99 "There is such an intimate connection": GW to David Stuart, April 8, 1792.

99 "The opening of the navigation": *Maryland Gazette,* December 2, 1784.

100 "Now, therefore, in pursuance of the powers": GW, proclamation, January 24, 1791.

102 "the situation and distance of objects": PCL to GW, memorandum, June 22, 1791, in Kite, *L'Enfant and Washington.*

102 "[The work] should be begun at various points": Ibid.

104 "extensive view down the Potomac": Ibid.

104 "From the first settlement of the city": Ibid.

104 "No message to nor from the President": Ibid.

104 "all along side of which may be placed": Ibid.

105 "vast esplanade in the center of which": Ibid.

105 "The whole will acquire new sweetness": Ibid.

106 "I would reprobate the idea of imitating": PCL to TJ, April 4, 1791.

114 "A plan was also laid before them of the city": GW diary, June 29, 1791.

114 "The President having approved the sites of ground": *George-Town Weekly Ledger,* June 30, 1791.

115 "exalted genius, elegance of taste": George Walker, in *Maryland Journal,* September 30, 1791.

CHAPTER 7

My thumbnail portrait of Philadelphia, where L'Enfant was staying during many of the most dramatic moments in this story, is drawn in large degree from Reps, *The Making of Urban America;* Hutchins, ed., *Shaping a National Culture: The Philadelphia Experience, 1750–1800;* Smith, ed., *Life in Early Philadelphia: Documents from the Revolutionary and Early National Periods;* and Warner, *The Private City: Philadelphia in Three Periods of Its Growth.*

117 "The Wheel to Give Motion to the Machine": PCL, memorandum, August 19, 1791, in Kite, *L'Enfant and Washington.*

118 "The President had understood for some time past": TJ to PCL, August 18, 1791, DLM.

121 "the old Babylon": TJ to GW, April 10, 1791.

124 "Be sure to settle the figure of the town": William Penn, September 30, 1681, in Reps, *Making of Urban America.*

124 "all the world was assembled there": Trumbull, *Autobiography.*

126 "there still remains the fulfillment of the wish": PCL, memorandum, August 19, 1791, in Kite, *L'Enfant and Washington.*

126 "engross the most of the sale": Ibid.

127 "Being persuaded that money is the wheel": Ibid.

128 "The making of the public walk": Ibid.

128 "so out of the ordinary for developing a town": Ibid.

129 "the sentiments developed at the conferences": TJ to commissioners, August 28, 1791, in Padover, ed., *Jefferson and the National Capital.*

129 "Will circumstances render a postponement": GW to TJ, August 29, 1791.

129 "We have agreed that the federal district": Commissioners to PCL, September 9, 1791, DLM.

130 "If you have no contrary directions": Ibid.

131 "PROCLAMATION": GW, October 17, 1791.

134 "As far as the sale has gone": PCL to Tobias Lear, October 19, 1791, in Caemmerer, *Life of L'Enfant.*

135 "from several intimations we consider the business": Commissioners to GW, October 21, 1791.

136 "It is much to be regretted": GW to David Stuart, November 20, 1791.

CHAPTER 8

Putting together the story of the destruction of Duddington Manor was, more than anything, a matter of coordinating the sequence of events and letters as presented in DLM; Kite, *L'Enfant and Washington;* and *Papers of George Washington: Presidential Series,* which contains a typically excellent editorial note on the affair. DiGiacomontonio, "All the President's Men: George Washington's Federal City Commissioners," was also an important source.

139 The Whole Leveled and Thrown to the Ground: Paraphrase of PCL to commissioners, November 21, 1791, DLM.

141 "mere fancy work": Commissioners' summary of case, undated, in Tindall, *Standard History of Washington.*

143 "should be deemed an obstruction": Daniel Carroll (commissioner) to James Madison, November 29, 1791, in Tindall, *Standard History of Washington.*

144 "we have been much hurt at insinuations": Commissioners to GW, November 25, 1791.

144 "We are informed that you have been directed": Commissioners to IR and Benjamin Ellicott, November 25, 1791, in National Archives (Records of the Commissioners for the District of Columbia, Letters Sent, 1791–1802).

145 "As a similar case cannot happen again": GW to PCL, November 28, 1791, DLM.

146 "I wished you to be employed": GW to PCL, December 2, 1791, DLM.

147 "Anticipating your feelings on this subject": Commissioners to GW, November 25, 1791.

147 "I have said, and I repeat it to you again": GW to PCL, December 2, 1791.

148 "It was proper": PCL to commissioners, December 6, 1791, DLM.

148 "since I find that [the house] being destroyed": PCL to GW, December 7, 1791.

148 "under impossibility of doing this": Ibid.

150 "And be it further enacted, That the said commissioners": Residence Act, 1790.

152 "many circumstances to attend to": GW to PCL, December 2, 1791, DLM.

154 "Sales to individuals or partitions": TJ to GW, December 11, 1791.

155 "there was no more necessity for applying": PCL to GW, December 7, 1791.

155 "if Major L'Enfant is right in saying": TJ to GW, December 11, 1791.

155 "gratify private resentment against Mr. Carroll": Ibid.

155 "The style in which he writes": Ibid.

155 "I do not accurately recollect the tenor of the deed": Ibid.

156 "As we are likely to get every thing happily adjusted": Commissioners to TJ, December 8, 1791, in Padover, ed., *Jefferson and the National Capital.*

156 "I am very glad to find that matters": GW to TJ, December 14, 1791.

157 "Understanding that Daniel Carroll Esquire of Duddington": Proprietors to commissioners, December 21, 1791, in National Archives (Records of the Commissioners for the District of Columbia, Proceedings, 1791–1802).

158 "a more progressive state": GW to TJ, December 14, 1791.

159 "in the execution of this order": PCL to IR, December 16, 1791, DLM.

159 "One of the streets lately to be run": PCL to commissioners, December 22, 1791, DLM.

CHAPTER 9

Isaac Roberdeau was a remarkably thorough correspondent, and his letters in DLM give us a useful picture of what was happening on the site during the first weeks of 1792 while L'Enfant was in Philadelphia, toiling away on his January memorandum to George Washington and oblivious to the rapid approach of his professional doom.

161 "Measures of the Most Immediate Moment": PCL to GW, January 17, 1792.

161 "from whose station all distances": PCL, "Observations Explanatory of the Plan," manuscript plan, 1791.

162 "great circular room and dome": Trumbull, *Autobiography.*

165 "The exporting of stone must be begun": PCL to IR, December 16, 1791, DLM.

165 "not to employ people at the public expense": Commissioners to IR, January 7, 1792 (as transcribed in IR to PCL, January 11, 1792), DLM.

165 "of the propriety and necessity of incurring that expense": Ibid.

166 "The commissioners had discharged": IR to PCL, January 9, 1792, DLM.

166 "The agitation I was thrown into": Ibid.

167 "late resolutions put aside"; "be answerable for the consequences": Ibid.

167 "The country already rings with the idea": Ibid.

168 "If all the hands are discharged": IR to commissioners, January 9, 1792 (as transcribed in IR to PCL, January 11, 1792), DLM.

168 "date your new connection with us": Commissioners to IR, January 10, 1792 (as transcribed in IR to PCL, January 11, 1792), DLM.

168 "I [received] your favor of this day": IR to commissioners, January 10, 1792 (as transcribed in IR to PCL, January 11, 1792), DLM.

169 "When the commissioners were compelled to discharge": Daniel Carroll (commissioner) to TJ, February 3, 1792, in Padover, ed., *Jefferson and the National Capital.*

169 "I much fear some of my letters to you have miscarried": IR to PCL, January 27, 1792, DLM.

169 "in the hands of the sheriff": Ibid.

170 "The approaching season for renewing the work": PCL to GW, January 17, 1792.

170 "Knowing you wished never to be applied to": Ibid.

171 "Wishing then that matters should be determined": Ibid.

171 "The season already far advanced": Ibid.

172 "Their inattention to this doubtless proceeded": Ibid.

172 "put the whole machine in motion": Ibid.

172 "It will be necessary to comprehend the magnitude": Ibid.

173 "the state of turnpike roads"; "good stone bridges": Ibid.

175 "It is necessary to place under the authority": Ibid.

CHAPTER 10

The end of L'Enfant's tenure as designer of Washington, D.C., is well documented in the primary and secondary sources. It does take some effort to tease out the truth that he resigned before he was fired, but I am not the first to notice it. It was Ken Bowling who first warned me to stay away from the conventional wisdom that L'Enfant was "summarily dismissed" from the project.

177 "An Implicit Conformity to His Will": PCL to TJ, February 26, 1792, DLM.

178 "The directions I gave to him": PCL to GW, February 6, 1792, DLM.

178 "Feeling myself doubly interested in the success": Ibid.

184 "This draft to my great surprise I found in the state": PCL to Tobias Lear, February 17, 1792, in Kite, *L'Enfant and Washington.*

185 "Whether this inclination to originate": Ibid.

187 "most advantageously and reciprocally seen": PCL, "Observations Explanatory of the Plan," manuscript plan, 1791.

187 "ill-judged stand": PCL to Tobias Lear, February 17, 1792, in Kite, *L'Enfant and Washington.*

188 "I fear more from the election": Tobias Lear, undated, in Smith, *Patriarch.*

189 "Joy and satisfaction were strongly marked": *Federal Gazette and Philadelphia Daily Advertiser,* February 24, 1792.

189 "the memory of those illustrious heroes": Ibid.

189 "Yesterday was celebrated": *National Gazette,* February 23, 1792.

190 "The plan I think ought to appear": GW to TJ, February 22, 1792.

191 "The advance of the season begins to require": TJ to PCL, February 22, 1792, in Padover, ed., *Jefferson and the National Capital.*

192 "an implicit conformity to his will": PCL to TJ, February 26, 1792, DLM.

192 "that pride of office": Ibid.

192 "allurement of parties": Ibid.

192 "the determination I have taken": Ibid.

192 "If therefore the law absolutely requires": Ibid.

193 "A final decision thereupon must be had": GW to TJ, February 26, 1792.

194 "I have heard enough of this matter": Kite, *L'Enfant and Washington.*

194 "I am instructed by the President to inform you": TJ to PCL, February 27, 1792, in Padover, ed., *Jefferson and the National Capital.*

194 "a man of capacity"; "disinterested views"; "should this business fall into the hands": PCL to GW, February 27, 1792, DLM.

195 "The continuance of your services": GW to PCL, February 28, 1792, DLM.

196 "Should Mr. Ellicott be asked": GW to TJ, February 28, 1792.

196 "the current in this city": GW to TJ, March 4, 1792.

196 "Without enquiring of the principle": PCL to commissioners, March 18, 1792, DLM.

197 "You hardly can imagine the vexations": IR to PCL, March 28, 1792, DLM.

197 "a gentleman who I once considered": Samuel Davidson to commissioners, undated (as transcribed in IR to PCL, March 28, 1792), DLM.

197 "We find by communications from Philadelphia": Proprietors to PCL, March 9, 1792, DLM.

CHAPTER 11

The fitful and sometimes disastrous first decade of Washington's growth is well described in several sources, especially Arnebeck, *Through a Fiery Trial;* Scott, "Moving to the Seat of Government: 'Temporary Inconveniences and Privations' "; and Tindall, *Standard History of the City of Washington.* Chernow, *Alexander Hamilton,* provided me with an outline for my short description of L'Enfant's involvement with the SEUM. Ken Bowling (once again) was the first to explore at length the strange and sad connection between L'Enfant and Richard Soderstrom, despite the evidence sitting there for anyone to find in the very first item in DLM.

201 "The Disappointment of Absolute Dues": PCL, memorial to Congress, December 7, 1800, in Caemmerer, *Life of L'Enfant.*

202 "laid upon a bed of sickness": Abigail Adams to Mary (Adams) Cranch, November 10, 1800, in Mitchell, ed., *New Letters of Abigail Adams.*

202 "As I expected to find it a new country": Abigail Adams to Mary (Adams) Cranch, November 21, 1800, in Mitchell, ed., *New Letters of Abigail Adams.*

203 "to secure us from daily agues": Abigail Adams to Abigail (Adams) Smith, November 21, 1800, in Leish, *The White House: A History of the Presidents.*

203 "keep all this to yourself": Ibid.

203 "If the twelve years": Ibid.

204 "seven or eight boarding houses": Albert Gallatin to Mrs. Gallatin, January 15, 1801, in Reps, *Washington on View.*

205 "No stranger can be here a day": Oliver Wolcott, Jr., to Mrs. Wolcott, June 1800, in Reps, *Washington on View.*

208 "the public interest and my reputation": AH to William Duer, May 23, 1792.

209 "My whole labor": PCL to AH, March 26, 1793.

209 "I had like to have stopped work": Robert Morris to PCL, May 9, 1793, DLM.

212 "I cannot hesitate nor do I delay": PCL to AH, July 1, 1798.

212 "I could not wish to wound you": AH to PCL, July 3, 1798.

213 "By the obstructions continually thrown in its way": GW to William Thornton, December 8, 1799.

213 "friend and principal dependency": PCL, memorial to Congress, December 7, 1800, in Caemmerer, *Life of L'Enfant.*

214 "I lent him money the day we met": PCL, Accounts, Richard Soderstrom, DLM.

214 "two unfurnished rooms": Ibid.

215 "study room"; "old broken table": Ibid.

215 "masters of trading vessels": Ibid.

215 "so auspicious a juncture": PCL, memorial to Congress, December 7, 1800, in Caemmerer, *Life of L'Enfant.*

216 "the high authority by whom I acted": Ibid.

216 "The enemies of enterprise": Ibid.

216 "an inimical envious genius": PCL, memorial to commissioners, August 30, 1800, in Caemmerer, *Life of L'Enfant.*

216 "The dearest interest of the City of Washington": Ibid.

217 "the design of which had been a primary condition": PCL, memorial to Congress, December 7, 1800, in Caemmerer, *Life of L'Enfant.*

217 "The cases offered here for consideration": Ibid.

218 "the work of a century": PCL, appendix to memorial to commissioners, May 30, 1800, in Caemmerer, *Life of L'Enfant.*

218 "as the capital of a great nation": John Adams to Congress, November 22, 1800.

219 "I consider the erection of the Representative's chamber": TJ to commissioners, August 29, 1801, in Padover, ed., *Jefferson and the National Capital.*

220 "Under the apprehension of impropriety": PCL to TJ, March 12, 1802, in Padover, ed., *Jefferson and the National Capital.*

221 "Your letter of the 12th is at hand": TJ to PCL, March 14, 1802, DLM.

CHAPTER 12

The correspondence and editorial apparatus found in Elias and Finch, eds., *Letters of Thomas Attwood Digges (1742–1821),* is the key source for tracking L'Enfant's long end-of-life decline. Morgan, "Historic Fort Washington on the Potomac," provides important context for L'Enfant's work in the wake of the War of 1812.

223 "Getting the Go By": TAD to James Monroe, October 26, 1816, in Elias and Finch, eds., *Letters of Thomas Attwood Digges.*

224 "A political romance": Elias, "First American Novel."

225 "The old major is still an inmate with me": TAD to James Monroe, October 26, 1816, in Elias and Finch, eds., *Letters of Thomas Attwood Digges.*

226 "Upon what principle": PCL, Accounts, Richard Soderstrom, DLM.

226 "With respect to his charge for the wages": Ibid.

226 "I was merely a lodger": Ibid.

227 "Daily through the city stalks the picture of famine": Benjamin Henry Latrobe, journal, August 12, 1806, in Carter, ed., *Papers of Benjamin Henry Latrobe.*

227 "the Art of Engineering": William Eustis to PCL, July 7, 1812, DLM.

227 "unaccepted but not rejected": PCL to James Monroe, July 7, 1812, DLM.

228 "I have not the rigidity of manner": Ibid.

228 "would have to encounter the difficulties": Ibid.

228 "The appointment offered to you": James Monroe to PCL, July 28, 1812, DLM.

229 "a French engineer officer": TAD to TJ, July 29, 1807.

229 "What the devil will they do here?": John Armstrong, quoted in Lossing, *Pictorial Field-Book of the War of 1812.*

230 "The engineer major, as usual": TAD to James Monroe, September 25, 1814, in Elias and Finch, eds., *Letters of Thomas Attwood Digges.*

230 "the evil genius who seems bent": PCL to James Monroe, June 1815, DLM.

230 "caused no doubt by the perplexity": Ibid.

231 "The retrospect review of the cause of my misery": Ibid.

231 "I call it a hotel": TAD to George Graham, December 22, 1815, in Elias and Finch, eds., *Letters of Thomas Attwood Digges.*

232 "a harmless honorable minded man": TAD to James Monroe, July 17, 1818, in Elias and Finch, eds., *Letters of Thomas Attwood Digges.*

232 "Never facing toward the fort": TAD to James Monroe, October 26, 1816, in Elias and Finch, eds., *Letters of Thomas Attwood Digges.*

232 "The snowstorm of the day before": PCL to TAD, March 29, 1821, DLM.

233 "an undeviating republican and patriot": *National Intelligencer,* December 11, 1821.

233 "such is the gloom of my situation": PCL, January 30, 1824, National Archives (Committee Papers, 1816–1946).

233 "I have to inform you": William Dudley Digges to PCL, March 15, 1824, DLM.

236 "In the execution of the plan of the city": Andrew Ellicott to commissioners, January 4, 1793, in Tindall, *Standard History of Washington.*

236 "I do require an examination": Andrew Ellicott to GW, March 16, 1793.

237 "It has been said that the idea of creating": Benjamin Henry Latrobe to Philip Mazzei, May 29, 1806, in Carter, ed., *Papers of Benjamin Henry Latrobe.*

237 "this singular man": Benjamin Henry Latrobe, journal, August 12, 1806, in Carter, ed., *Papers of Benjamin Henry Latrobe.*

237 "gigantic abortion": Benjamin Henry Latrobe to Philip Mazzei, May 29, 1806, in Carter, ed., *Papers of Benjamin Henry Latrobe.*

239 "given up newspapers in exchange for Tacitus and Thucydides": TJ to John Adams, January 21, 1812.

240 "1. That the creation was, not to be a single grand edifice": TJ, 1817, in Lambeth and Manning, *Jefferson as Architect and Designer.*

243 "On the 14th inst. at Green Hill": *National Intelligencer,* June 25, 1825.

244 "An inventory of the personal good and chattels": DLM.

CHAPTER 13

My emphasis on the Olmsteds as prime movers of the redemption of L'Enfant grew out of my repeated readings of Olmsted Jr., "Landscape in Connection with Public Buildings in Washington"; conversations with J. L. Sibley Jennings, Jr.; and my perusal of several sources, including Klaus, " 'Intelligent and Comprehensive Planning of a Common Sense Kind': Frederick Law Olmsted, Junior, and the Emergence of Comprehensive Planning in America"; Roper, *FLO: A Biography of Frederick Law Olmsted;* Rybczynski, *A Clearing in the Distance: Frederick Law Olmsted and America in the Nineteenth Century;* and Streatfield, "The Olmsteds and the Landscape of the Mall."

247 "A Share in the Undertaking": PCL to GW, September 11, 1789.

247 "THE CAPITAL IN 1800": *Washington Post,* December 12, 1900.

248 "One hundred years ago President Adams": *Washington Post,* December 13, 1900.

250 "wiggling roads": Brown, ed., *Papers Relating to the Improvement of the City of Washington, District of Columbia.*

251 "It is sometimes called the City of Magnificent Distances": Dickens, *American Notes.*

252 "It has the aspect of a factory chimney": Twain, *Gilded Age.*

255 "disunion": Roper, *FLO: Biography of Olmsted.*

256 "most important active work": Olmsted and Kimball, eds., *Frederick Law Olmsted.*

256 "distant effects": FLO to RO, September 5, 1890, FLO Papers.

256 "leader of the van": Ibid.

256 "It is too late to turn back": FLO to RO, undated, FLO Papers.

257 "You must make . . . good my failings": FLO to RO, December 23, 1894, FLO Papers.

259 "a discussion of the location of public buildings": RO, "Landscape in Connection with Public Buildings in Washington."

259 "The Mall was not laid out on the main axis": Ibid.

260 "In any great plan time must develop features": Ibid.

CHAPTER 14

The vision of the Senate Park Commission was first and best described in its own words, in *Report of the Senate Committee on the District of Columbia on the Improvement of the Park System of the District of Columbia (Plan of 1901),* ed. Charles Moore. Invaluable interpretation and historical context can be found in Reps, *Monumental Washington* and *Washington on View.*

263 "The Assurance of Things Hoped For": PCL.

267 "THRONGS AT ART GALLERY": *Washington Post,* January 20, 1902.

269 "Make no little plans": Town Planning Conference, London, 1910, various sources.

270 "The Palace of the Tuileries as the Capitol": Moore, *Life and Times of McKim.*

270 "reprobate the idea of imitating": PCL to TJ, April 11, 1791, in Padover, ed., *Jefferson and the National Capital.*

270 "The only way in which we can hope": Theodore Roosevelt, in Moore, *Promise of American Architecture.*

271 "It had no legal standing": Brown, *1860–1930, Memories.*

272 "one man in our history": *Report of the Senate Committee on the District of Columbia on the Improvement of the Park System of the District of Columbia,* 1902.

272 "AN OLD-TIME ARCHITECT": *New-York Tribune,* June 22, 1881.

273 "one of the most obscure characters": Ibid.

273 "clearly a young officer": Ibid.

274 "He has taken the oath as Secretary of State": Jusserand, *What Me Befell.*

274 "to remove and render accessible": *Records of the Columbia Historical Society* 8 (1910).

274 "a layer of discolored mold": *Washington Post,* April 23, 1909.

275 "For Major L'Enfant": Ibid.

277 "There are not many who have to wait": *Washington Post,* May 23, 1911.

277 "I would not for a moment detract": Ibid.

277 "All of those who visit the Federal City": Ibid.

EPILOGUE

279 "particularize"; "grievances": PCL, memorial to commissioners, August 30, 1800, in Caemmerer, *Life of L'Enfant.*

279 "distinguished personage": Ibid.

279 "the forcible seizure of particular drafts and manuscripts": Ibid.

280 "laid open and the contents were then scattered": PCL to Samuel Davidson, January 13, 1802, DLM.

280 "As to the number and magnitude of Major L'Enfant's package": Samuel Davidson to PCL, January 16, 1802, DLM.

Bibliography

Abbot, W. W., ed. *The Papers of George Washington: Retirement Series.* 4 vols. Charlottesville: University Press of Virginia, 1998–99.

Abbot, W. W., and Dorothy Twohig, eds. *The Papers of George Washington: Presidential
Series.* 11 vols. Charlottesville: University Press of Virginia, 1987–.

———. *The Papers of George Washington: Confederation Series.* 6 vols. Charlottesville: University Press of Virginia, 1992–97.

Abbot, W. W., Dorothy Twohig, and Philander D. Chase, eds. *The Papers of George Washington: Colonial Series.* 10 vols. Charlottesville: University Press of Virginia, 1983–95.

———. *The Papers of George Washington: Revolutionary War Series.* 12 vols. Charlottesville:
University Press of Virginia, 1985–.

Achenbach, Joel. *The Grand Idea: George Washington's Potomac and the Race to the West.*
New York: Simon and Schuster, 2004.

Adams, William Howard. *The Eye of Thomas Jefferson.* Charlottesville: National Gallery of
Art, Thomas Jefferson Memorial Foundation, and University of Missouri Press, 1992.

Arnebeck, Bob. *Through a Fiery Trial: Building Washington, 1790–1800.* Lanham, Md.:
Madison Books, 1991.

————. "Tracking the Speculators: Greenleaf and Nicholson in the Federal City." *Washington History* 3, no. 1 (1991).

Auchincloss, Louis. *La Gloire: The Roman Empire of Corneille and Racine.* Columbia: University of South Carolina Press, 1996.

Bacon, Edmund N. *Design of Cities.* New York: Penguin Books, 1976.

Bedini, Silvio A. *The Life of Benjamin Banneker.* New York: Scribner, 1971.

————. "The Survey of the Federal Territory: Andrew Ellicott and Benjamin Banneker." *Washington History* 3, no. 1 (1991).

Bernier, Olivier. *Louis the Beloved: The Life of Louis XV.* Garden City, N.Y.: Doubleday, 1984.

Bill, Alfred Hoyt. *Valley Forge: The Making of an Army.* New York: Harper, 1952.

Bobrick, Benson. *Angel in the Whirlwind: The Triumph of the American Revolution.* New York: Simon and Schuster, 1997.

Bodle, Wayne K. *The Valley Forge Winter: Civilians and Soldiers in War.* University Park: Pennsylvania State University Press, 2002.

Borick, Carl P. *A Gallant Defense: The Siege of Charleston, 1780.* Columbia: University of South Carolina Press, 2003.

Bowling, Kenneth R. *Creating the Federal City, 1774–1800: Potomac Fever.* Octagon Research Series. Washington, D.C.: American Institute of Architects Press, 1988.

————. *The Creation of Washington, D.C.: The Idea and Location of the American Capital.* Fairfax, Va.: George Mason University Press, 1991.

————. "The Other G.W.: George Walker and the Creation of the American Capital." *Washington History* 3, no. 2 (1991).

————. "A Foreboding Shadow: Newspaper Celebration of the Federal Government's Arrival." *Washington History* 12, no. 1 (2000).

————. "From 'Federal Town' to 'National Capital': Ulysses S. Grant and the Reconstruction of Washington, D.C." *Washington History* 14, no. 1 (2002).

————. *Peter Charles L'Enfant: Vision, Honor, and Male Friendship in the Early American Republic.* Washington, D.C.: George Washington University, 2002.

Boyd, Julian P., et al., eds. *The Papers of Thomas Jefferson.* 27+ vols. Princeton, N.J.: Princeton University Press, 1950–.

Brighton, Ray. *The Checkered Career of Tobias Lear.* Portsmouth, N.H.: Portsmouth Marine Society, 1985.

Brown, Glenn, ed. *Papers Relating to the Improvement of the City of Washington, District of Columbia.* Washington, D.C.: Government Printing Office, 1901.

————. *1860–1930, Memories.* Washington, D.C.: W. F. Roberts, 1931.

Browning, Reed. *The War of the Austrian Succession.* New York: St. Martin's Press, 1993.

Bryan, Wilhelmus Bogart. *A History of the National Capital: From Its Foundation Through the Period of the Adoption of the Organic Act.* Vol. 1. New York: Macmillan, 1914.

Burrows, Edwin G., and Mike Wallace. *Gotham: A History of New York City to 1898.* New York: Oxford University Press, 1999.

Bibliography

Caemmerer, H. Paul. *The Life of Pierre Charles L'Enfant, Planner of the City Beautiful, the City of Washington.* Washington, D.C.: National Republic, 1950.

Carter, Edward C., II, ed. *The Papers of Benjamin Henry Latrobe: Correspondence and Miscellaneous Papers.* 3 vols. New Haven, Conn.: Yale University Press, 1984–88.

Chadych, Danielle, Dominique Leborgne, and Jacques Lebar. *Atlas de Paris: Évolution d'un paysage urbain.* Paris: Parigramme, 1999.

Chernow, Ron. *Alexander Hamilton.* New York: Penguin Press, 2004.

Chinard, Gilbert. *George Washington as the French Knew Him: A Collection of Texts.* New York: Greenwood Press, 1969.

Clark, Ellen McCallister. "The Diploma of the Society of the Cincinnati." *Cincinnati Fourteen* 37, no. 1 (2000).

Couperie, Pierre. *Paris Through the Ages: An Illustrated Historical Atlas of Urbanism and Architecture.* New York: George Braziller, 1971.

Coural, Jean. *Les Gobelins.* Paris: Nouvelles Éditions Latines, 1989.

Dalzell, Robert F., Jr., and Lee Baldwin Dalzell. *George Washington's Mount Vernon: At Home in Revolutionary America.* New York: Oxford University Press, 1998.

Dickens, Charles. *American Notes and Pictures from Italy.* 1842. The New Oxford Illustrated Dickens. New York: Oxford University Press, 1957.

Diderot, Denis. *Salons.* Edited by Jean Seznec and Jean Adhemar. 2nd ed. Oxford: Clarendon Press, 1975.

Digges, Thomas Attwood. *Adventures of Alonso.* 1775. 2 vols. New York: United States Catholic Historical Society, 1943.

DiGiacomontonio, William C. "All the President's Men: George Washington's Federal City Commissioners." *Washington History* 3, no. 1 (1991).

Dorwart, Jeffery M. *Fort Mifflin of Philadelphia: An Illustrated History.* Philadelphia: University of Pennsylvania Press, 1998.

Dougherty, J. P. "Baroque and Picturesque Motifs in L'Enfant's Design for the Federal Capital." *American Quarterly* 26, no. 1 (1974).

Driskel, Michael Paul. "L'Enfant's Suitcase: The Imprint of Paris on the Plan of Washington." Presentation for Paris on the Potomac: French Inspired Art and Architecture in the Nation's Capital. Washington, D.C., March 30, 2005.

Duer, William Alexander. *Reminiscences of an Old Yorker.* New York: Printed for W. L. Andrews, 1867.

Duponceau, Peter Stephen. "Autobiographical Letters of Peter S. Duponceau." Edited by James L. Whitehead. *Pennsylvania Magazine of History and Biography* 63, no. 2 (1939).

Echeverria, Durand. *Mirage in the West: A History of the French Image of American Society to 1815.* Princeton, N.J.: Princeton University Press, 1957.

Ehrenberg, Ralph E. "Mapping the Nation's Capital: The Surveyor's Office, 1791–1818." *Quarterly Journal of the Library of Congress* 36, no. 3 (1979).

Elias, Robert H. "The First American Novel." *American Literature* 12, no. 4 (1942).

Elias, Robert H., and Eugene D. Finch, eds. *Letters of Thomas Attwood Digges (1742–1821)*. Columbia: University of South Carolina Press, 1982.

Elkins, Stanley M., and Eric L. McKitrick. *The Age of Federalism*. New York: Oxford University Press, 1993.

Ellis, Joseph J. *American Sphinx: The Character of Thomas Jefferson*. New York: Vintage Books, 1998.

———. *Founding Brothers: The Revolutionary Generation*. New York: Alfred A. Knopf, 2000.

———. *His Excellency: George Washington*. New York: Alfred A. Knopf, 2004.

Ferguson, E. James, ed. *The Papers of Robert Morris, 1781–1784*. 9 vols. Pittsburgh: University of Pittsburgh Press, 1973–95.

Fitzpatrick, John C., ed. *The Diaries of George Washington, 1748–1799*. 4 vols. Boston: Houghton Mifflin, 1925.

Flexner, James Thomas. *George Washington*. 4 vols. Boston: Little, Brown, 1965–72.

Furgurson, Ernest B. *Freedom Rising: Washington in the Civil War*. New York: Alfred A. Knopf, 2004.

Garrioch, David. *Neighbourhood and Community in Paris, 1740–1790*. New York: Cambridge University Press, 1986.

———. *The Making of Revolutionary Paris*. Berkeley: University of California Press, 2002.

Gordon, John W. *South Carolina and the American Revolution: A Battlefield History*. Columbia: University of South Carolina Press, 2003.

Green, Constance McLaughlin. *Washington: Village and Capital, 1800–1878*. Princeton, N.J.: Princeton University Press, 1962.

Greenberg, Allan C. *George Washington, Architect*. London: Andreas Papadakis Publisher, 1999.

Gutheim, Frederick Albert. *The Potomac*. New York: Grosset and Dunlap, 1968.

———. *Worthy of the Nation: The History of Planning for the National Capital*. Washington, D.C.: Smithsonian Institution Press, 1977.

Hardman, John. *Louis XVI*. New Haven, Conn.: Yale University Press, 1993.

———. *French Politics, 1774–1789: From the Accession of Louis XVI to the Fall of the Bastille*. New York: Longman, 1995.

Harris, C. M. "Washington's Gamble, L'Enfant's Dream: Politics, Design, and the Founding of the National Capital." *William and Mary Quarterly* 56, no. 3 (1999).

———. "Washington's 'Federal City,' Jefferson's 'Federal Town,' " *Washington History* 12, no. 1 (2000).

Hawkins, Don Alexander. "The Landscape of the Federal City: A 1792 Walking Tour." *Washington History* 3, no. 1 (1991).

———. "The City of Washington in 1800: A New Map." *Washington History* 12, no. 1 (2000).

Hines, Thomas S. "The Imperial Mall: The City Beautiful Movement and the Washington Plan of 1901–1902." In *The Mall in Washington, 1791–1991*, edited by Richard W. Longstreth. 2nd ed. Washington, D.C.: National Gallery of Art, 2002.

Bibliography

Hoffman, Ronald, and Peter J. Albert, eds. *Diplomacy and Revolution: The Franco-American Alliance of 1778*. Charlottesville: University Press of Virginia, 1981.

Holmes, Oliver W. "Suter's Tavern: Birthplace of the Federal City." *Records of the Columbia Historical Society* 49 (1973–74).

Hutchins, Catherine E., ed. *Shaping a National Culture: The Philadelphia Experience, 1750–1800*. Winterthur, Del.: Henry Francis du Pont Winterthur Museum, 1994.

Jackson, Donald, and Dorothy Twohig, eds. *The Diaries of George Washington*. 6 vols. Charlottesville: University Press of Virginia, 1976–79.

Jacob, Kathryn Allamong. " 'To Gather and Preserve . . .': The Columbia Historical Society Is Founded, 1894." *Washington History* 6, no. 2 (1995).

Jefferson, Thomas. *Notes on the State of Virginia*. 1787. New York: Penguin Books, 1999.

Jennings, J. L. Sibley, Jr. "Artistry as Design: L'Enfant's Extraordinary City." *Quarterly Journal of the Library of Congress* 36, no. 3 (1979).

Jusserand, J. J. *With Americans of Past and Present Days*. New York: Charles Scribner, 1916.

———. *What Me Befell*. Boston: Houghton Mifflin, 1933.

Kennedy, Roger G. *Orders from France: The Americans and the French in a Revolutionary World, 1780–1820*. New York: Alfred A. Knopf, 1989.

Kite, Elizabeth Sarah. *L'Enfant and Washington*. Baltimore: Johns Hopkins Press, 1929.

———. *Brigadier-General Louis Lebègue Duportail, Commandant of Engineers in the Continental Army, 1777–1783*. Baltimore: Johns Hopkins University Press, 1933.

Klaus, Susan. " 'Intelligent and Comprehensive Planning of a Common Sense Kind': Frederick Law Olmsted, Junior, and the Emergence of Comprehensive Planning in America." Master's thesis, George Washington University, 1988.

Kostof, Spiro. *The City Shaped: Urban Patterns and Meanings Through History*. Boston: Little, Brown, 1991.

———. *The City Assembled: The Elements of Urban Form Through History*. Boston: Little, Brown, 1992.

Lambeth, William Alexander, and Warren H. Manning. *Thomas Jefferson as an Architect and a Designer of Landscapes*. Boston: Houghton Mifflin, 1913.

Lawrence, Alexander A. *Storm over Savannah: The Story of Count d'Estaing and the Siege of the Town in 1779*. Athens: University of Georgia Press, 1951.

Leish, Kenneth W. *The White House: A History of the Presidents*. New York: Newsweek, 1972.

Longstreth, Richard W., ed. *The Mall in Washington, 1791–1991*. 2nd ed. Washington, D.C.: National Gallery of Art, 2002.

Lossing, Benson J. *The Pictorial Field-Book of the Revolution*. New York: Harper, 1860.

———. *Pictorial Field-Book of the War of 1812*. New York: Harper and Brothers, 1869.

Louis XIV. *Mémoires for the Instruction of the Dauphin*. Translated by Paul Sonnino. New York: Free Press, 1970.

Luria, Sarah. *Capital Speculations: Writing and Building Washington, D.C.* Durham: University of New Hampshire Press, 2006.

Malone, Dumas. *Jefferson and His Time*. 6 vols. Boston: Little, Brown, 1948–81.

Massey, Gregory D. *John Laurens and the American Revolution.* Columbia: University of South Carolina Press, 2000.

Mathews, Catharine Van Cortlandt. *Andrew Ellicott: His Life and Letters.* Alexander, N.C.: WorldComm, 1997.

McCullough, David G. *John Adams.* New York: Simon and Schuster, 2002.

McNeil, Priscilla W. "Rock Creek Hundred: Land Conveyed for the Federal City." *Washington History* 3, no. 1 (1991).

Miller, Iris. *Washington in Maps: 1606–2000.* New York: Rizzoli, 2002.

Mitchell, Stewart, ed. *New Letters of Abigail Adams.* Boston: Houghton Mifflin, 1947.

Moore, Charles. *The Promise of American Architecture.* Washington, D.C.: American Institute of Architects, 1905.

———. *The Life and Times of Charles Follen McKim.* Boston: Houghton Mifflin, 1929.

Moore, Charles, ed. *Report of the Senate Committee on the District of Columbia on the Improvement of the Park System of the District of Columbia (Plan of 1901).* Washington, D.C.: Government Printing Office, 1902.

Morales-Vazquez, Rubil. "George Washington, the President's House, and the Projection of Executive Power." *Washington History* 16, no. 1 (2004).

Morgan, James Dudley. "Historic Fort Washington on the Potomac." *Records of the Columbia Historical Society* 7 (1903).

Morgan, James Dudley, et al. James Dudley Morgan Collection of Digges-L'Enfant-Morgan Papers, 1674–1923 (bulk 1778–1828). Library of Congress, Manuscript Division.

Morrill, Dan L. *Southern Campaigns of the American Revolution.* Baltimore: Nautical and Aviation Publishing, 1993.

Morris, A. E. J. *History of Urban Form: Before the Industrial Revolutions.* 2nd ed. New York: Longman Scientific and Technical, 1988.

Morton, Brian N., and Donald C. Spinelli. *Beaumarchais and the American Revolution.* Lanham, Md.: Lexington Books, 2003.

Mumford, Lewis. *The City in History: Its Origins, Its Transformations, and Its Prospects.* New York: Harcourt, 1961.

Myers, Minor, Jr. *Liberty Without Anarchy: A History of the Society of the Cincinnati.* Charlottesville: University Press of Virginia, 1983.

———. *The Insignia of the Society of the Cincinnati.* Washington, D.C.: Society of the Cincinnati, 1998.

Newton, Norman T. *Design on the Land: The Development of Landscape Architecture.* Cambridge, Mass.: Belknap Press of Harvard University Press, 1971.

Nichols, Frederick Doveton, and Ralph E. Griswold. *Thomas Jefferson, Landscape Architect.* Charlottesville: University Press of Virginia, 1978.

Oberholtzer, Ellis Paxson. *Robert Morris: Patriot and Financier.* New York: B. Franklin, 1968.

Olmsted, Frederick Law, Jr. "Landscape in Connection with Public Buildings in Washington." Presentation at the American Institute of Architects Convention, Washington, D.C., 1900.

Bibliography

Olmsted, Frederick Law, Jr., and Theodora Kimball, eds. *Frederick Law Olmsted: Landscape Architect, 1822–1903.* New York: G. P. Putnam's Sons, 1928.

Olmsted, Frederick Law, Sr. Papers of Frederick Law Olmsted, 1777–1952 (bulk 1838–1903). Library of Congress, Manuscript Division.

Orsenna, Erik. *André le Nôtre: Gardener to the Sun King.* Translated by Moishe Black. New York: George Braziller, 2000.

Padover, Saul Kussiel, ed. *Thomas Jefferson and the National Capital: Containing Notes and Correspondence Exchanged Between Jefferson, Washington, L'Enfant, Ellicott, Hallet, Thornton, Latrobe, the Commissioners, and Others, Relating to the Founding, Surveying, Planning, Designing, Constructing, and Administering of the City of Washington, 1783–1818.* Washington, D.C.: Government Printing Office, 1946.

Pailhès, Bernard. *L'Architecte de Washington.* Paris: Maisonneuve et Larose, 2002.

Palmer, John McAuley. *General von Steuben.* New Haven, Conn.: Yale University Press, 1937.

Papers of the Continental Congress, 1774–1789. Library of Congress, Manuscript Division.

Partridge, William T. *L'Enfant's Methods and Features of His Plan for the Federal City.* Washington, D.C.: National Capital Planning Commission, 1930.

Peets, Elbert. *On the Art of Designing Cities: Selected Essays of Elbert Peets.* Cambridge, Mass.: MIT Press, 1968.

Perry, Gill, and Colin Cunningham, eds. *Academies, Museums and Canons of Art.* New Haven, Conn.: Yale University Press, 1999.

Peterson, Jon A. "The Mall, the McMillan Plan, and the Origins of American City Planning." In *The Mall in Washington, 1791–1991,* edited by Richard W. Longstreth. 2nd ed. Washington, D.C.: National Gallery of Art, 2002.

Peterson, Merrill D. *Thomas Jefferson and the New Nation: A Biography.* New York: Oxford University Press, 1970.

Pevsner, Nikolaus. *Academies of Art, Past and Present.* New York: Da Capo Press, 1973.

Pomerantz, Sidney Irving. *New York, an American City, 1783–1803: A Study of Urban Life.* New York: Columbia University Press, 1938.

Preston, Daniel, ed. *A Comprehensive Catalogue of the Correspondence and Papers of James Monroe.* 2 vols. Westport, Conn.: Greenwood Press, 2001.

Reps, John William. *The Making of Urban America: A History of City Planning in the United States.* Princeton, N.J.: Princeton University Press, 1965.

———. *Monumental Washington: The Planning and Development of the Capital Center.* Princeton, N.J.: Princeton University Press, 1967.

———. *Washington on View: The Nation's Capital Since 1790.* Chapel Hill: University of North Carolina Press, 1991.

Roche, Daniel. *France in the Enlightenment.* Cambridge, Mass.: Harvard University Press, 1998.

Roper, Laura Wood. *FLO: A Biography of Frederick Law Olmsted.* Baltimore: Johns Hopkins University Press, 1973.

Royster, Charles. *A Revolutionary People at War: The Continental Army and American Character, 1775–1783.* Chapel Hill: University of North Carolina Press, 1979.

Rybczynski, Witold. *A Clearing in the Distance: Frederick Law Olmsted and America in the Nineteenth Century*. New York: Scribner, 1999.

Schama, Simon. *Citizens: A Chronicle of the French Revolution*. New York: Vintage Books, 1990.

Scott, Pamela. "L'Enfant's Washington Described: The City in the Public Press, 1791–1795." *Washington History* 3, no. 1 (1991).

———. *Temple of Liberty: Building the Capitol for a New Nation*. New York: Oxford University Press, 1995.

———. "Moving to the Seat of Government: 'Temporary Inconveniences and Privations.'" *Washington History* 12, no. 1 (2000).

———. " 'This Vast Empire': The Iconography of the Mall, 1791–1848." In *The Mall in Washington, 1791–1991,* edited by Richard W. Longstreth. 2nd ed. Washington, D.C.: National Gallery of Art, 2002.

Smith, Billy G., ed. *Life in Early Philadelphia: Documents from the Revolutionary and Early National Periods*. University Park: Pennsylvania State University Press, 1995.

Smith, Richard Norton. *Patriarch: George Washington and the New American Nation*. Boston: Houghton Mifflin, 1993.

Smith, Thomas E. V. *The City of New York in the Year of Washington's Inauguration, 1789*. Riverside, Conn.: Chatham Press, 1973.

Stegeman, John F., and Janet A. Stegeman. *Caty: A Biography of Catharine Littlefield Greene*. Athens: University of Georgia Press, 1977.

Stephenson, Richard W. "The Delineation of a Grand Plan." *Quarterly Journal of the Library of Congress* 36, no. 3 (1979).

———. *A Plan Whol[l]y New: Pierre Charles L'Enfant's Plan of the City of Washington*. Washington, D.C.: Library of Congress, 1993.

Stinchcombe, William C. *The American Revolution and the French Alliance*. Syracuse, N.Y.: Syracuse University Press, 1969.

———. "Americans Celebrate the Birth of the Dauphin." In *Diplomacy and Revolution: The Franco-American Alliance of 1778,* edited by Ronald Hoffman and Peter J. Albert. Charlottesville: University Press of Virginia, 1981.

Stoudt, John Joseph. *Ordeal at Valley Forge: A Day-by-Day Chronicle from December 17, 1777, to June 18, 1778*. Philadelphia: University of Pennsylvania Press, 1963.

Streatfield, David C. "The Olmsteds and the Landscape of the Mall." In *The Mall in Washington, 1791–1991,* edited by Richard W. Longstreth. 2nd ed. Washington, D.C.: National Gallery of Art, 2002.

Syrett, Harold C., et al., eds. *The Papers of Alexander Hamilton*. 27 vols. New York: Columbia University Press, 1961–87.

Tindall, William. *Standard History of the City of Washington from a Study of the Original Sources*. Knoxville, Tenn.: H. W. Crew, 1914.

Torres, Louis. "Federal Hall Revisited." *Journal of the Society of Architectural Historians* 29, no. 4 (1970).

Bibliography

Trumbull, John. *The Autobiography of Colonel John Trumbull, Patriot-Artist, 1756–1843.* Edited by Theodore Sizer. New Haven, Conn.: Yale University Press, 1953.

Twain, Mark. *The Gilded Age.* 1873. New York: Oxford University Press, 1996.

Unger, Harlow G. *Lafayette.* New York: John Wiley and Sons, 2002.

Walker, Paul K. *Engineers of Independence: A Documentary History of the Army Engineers in the American Revolution, 1775–1783.* Washington, D.C.: Historical Division, Office of Administrative Services, 1981.

Warner, Sam Bass, Jr. *The Private City: Philadelphia in Three Periods of Its Growth.* Philadelphia: University of Pennsylvania Press, 1968.

Weigert, Roger-Armand. *French Tapestry.* Newton, Mass.: C. T. Branford, 1962.

Wills, Garry. *Cincinnatus: George Washington and the Enlightenment.* Garden City, N.Y.: Doubleday, 1984.

——. *Mr. Jefferson's University.* Washington, D.C.: National Geographic Society, 2002.

Zucker, A. E. *General de Kalb, Lafayette's Mentor.* Chapel Hill: University of North Carolina Press, 1966.

Acknowledgments

Peter Charles L'Enfant and his design for Washington, D.C., have inspired many fierce loyalists over the past two centuries—people like Isaac Roberdeau, Rick Olmsted, and Jules Jusserand, to name just a few. I'm very happy to be able to single out two of that club's most important modern-day members in order to thank them for their considerable assistance in the making of *Grand Avenues*. Kenneth Bowling, coeditor of the First Federal Congress Project at George Washington University, has served as writer or editor of dozens of books and articles concerning L'Enfant and the origins of the federal city and possesses an unparalleled breadth and depth of knowledge of the subject. His close reading of two entire drafts of this manuscript was essential to its well-being, as was his willingness to share much of the research and insight he'd collected while doing his own writing. Donald Hawkins, a Washington architect and architectural historian, has for decades applied his seasoned professional eye to the unique urban environment of the American capital; his interpretation of L'Enfant's methods and intents served as my North Star, while his maps and drawings of the eighteenth- and early nineteenth-century landscape of the Potomac site, by far the best available, were crucial in allowing me to cast my mind back to a federal district as yet unacquainted with a National Mall or a Capitol Hill. Hawkins currently serves as chairman of the

Committee of 100 on the Federal City, an organization advocating responsible planning and land use in the capital according to the vision of the L'Enfant and McMillan Commission plans. It is a trust for which he is uniquely qualified.

I also thank J. L. Sibley Jennings, former chair of the Olmsted Foundation, who in 2002 spoke to me for a total of nine hours to provide four quotes for the 2,500-word article in the *Washington Post* that became the seed of *Grand Avenues*. Jennings's opinions about L'Enfant's plan got me thinking about the city as a painstakingly crafted thing as well as a grand idea, and he was also instrumental in illuminating the unique role played by Rick Olmsted. Others whose writing and work proved especially valuable along the way include Bob Arnebeck, Michael Paul Driskel, Richard Longstreth, Priscilla McNeil, Iris Miller, Phil Ogilvie, John W. Reps, Pamela Scott, and Richard Stephenson. Scholars don't always—or even often—agree on what is important about L'Enfant's story, but without their commitment and expertise I would not have known where to begin.

The writing and editorial eye of David Garrioch of Monash University in Melbourne, Australia, helped me make my way through the maze that was and is eighteenth-century Paris. I have plenty of people to thank at the Library of Congress, particularly Mark Dimunation, John Hebert, Maria Nugent, and Heather Wanser. Others who made time to aid me include William Troppman at Valley Forge National Historical Park; William DiGiacomontonio at the First Federal Congress Project; Ellen McCallister Clark and Rebecca Cooper of the Society of the Cincinnati Library; Constance J. Cooper of the Historical Society of Delaware Research Library; and Jennifer Kittlaus, Dennis Pogue, and Mary Thompson at Mount Vernon. Paul Gormont patiently worked with me through multiple drafts to put together his clarifying maps of the federal district and city site as they existed in 1791.

I am grateful for the support of many talented colleagues in the English department at George Mason University, as well as the graduate and undergraduate students of writing there who cheered me along and did the kind of precocious work that teaches the rest of us never to become complacent. Among my fellow faculty, Stephen Goodwin, a writer of fiction and nonfiction and former president of PEN/Faulkner, has been instrumental in bolstering the book and my career, while Terry Myers Zawacki, a scholar of composition and rhetoric, proved herself a good and supportive friend. Peter R. Henriques, for many years the university's resident George Washington scholar, offered comments and made important corrections regarding my presentation of the first president, while the biographer Meryle Secrest provided help in the writing of my original book proposal. I also thank Devon Ward-Thommes for assisting in a series of translations and Scott Weaver for sharing his Internet expertise.

Kevin Simons, formerly of the George Mason University libraries, helped in numerous ways, introducing me to resources and bibliographic methods that saved me a considerable amount of trouble. More than half the items in my bibliography were acquired through the Washington Research Library Consortium (WRLC), which binds George Mason, Georgetown, George Washington, and five other Washington-area universities into a single powerhouse whole. The WRLC is a fantastic use of taxpayer and tuition money for students and scholars alike.

Acknowledgments

It is a pleasure to acknowledge Joyce Jones and Nicole Arthur of *The Washington Post,* along with Jack Shafer of Slate.com, for their friendship and their professional support not only of my writing but of this particular project. I was thrilled that Mark Finkenstaedt, the best and hardest-working freelance photographer in Washington—no lie—was able to take time out to take a few shots of me. And I tip my *chapeau* to Jennifer Poirier and her husband, Philippe, proprietors of the Résidence les Gobelins, who made me feel welcome in the grandest city in the world as I followed in the elusive footprints of the young Pierre Charles L'Enfant.

For nine years now I've been fortunate enough to meet each month (Augusts excepted) with a group of wonderful writers and even better friends made up of Corrine Zappia Gormont, Dallas Hudgens, Robyn Kirby Wright, and Wendi Kaufman (aka the Happy Booker). Their pointed advice during my earliest phase of work was vital in turning the writing in the direction it needed to go. I also thank Todd Hartman, old friend and aficionado of the early Constitutional era, for taking a look at an early draft and, more important, for encouragement throughout my career. Four hugely influential and supportive teachers also deserve special mention: Barton Sutter at the University of Minnesota, Steven Bauer and Eric Goodman at Miami University, and Susan Richards Shreve at George Mason.

I heartily thank Suzanne Gluck of the William Morris Agency for treating my first book with such care and enthusiasm, and my editor at Pantheon, Edward Kastenmeier, for guiding me so assuredly in the direction of my better instincts. Also at Pantheon, Timothy O'Connell earned my gratitude for tirelessly shining a light into so many corners of the publishing process, while the talents of Ellen Feldman, Archie Ferguson, Stephanie Wilson, Charlotte Strick, and Julia Baxter have made the more recent stages of my journey as gratifying as its beginning. Janet Biehl's copyediting, as well, was extraordinarily skillful and reassuring.

I owe an incalculable debt to my brother David and my parents, Margaret and Roger, for never deviating for a moment from their belief that having a working writer in the family was a fine idea. Most of all, and lastly, I thank my wife, Corynne Hill. She alone will ever know just how much ground was covered in the writing of this book. The memory I will treasure most from the creation of *Grand Avenues* is that of Cory beside me sleeping off the fatigue of the pregnancy that eventually gave us our second son, while I sat up late by the light of my laptop computer and did what I could to keep my delivery date ahead of hers.

Index

Pages on which illustrations and maps appear are *italicized.*

Index

Index

ILLUSTRATION CREDITS

Illustration Credits